Tax Goddess Guides

Starting Your Own Business

Do It Right from the Start, Lower Your Taxes, Protect Your Income, and Enjoy Your Life

Tax Goddess Guides

Starting Your Own Business

Do It Right from the Start, Lower Your Taxes, Protect Your Income, and Enjoy Your Life

Shauna A. Wekherlien, CPA,
Master of Taxation,
Tax Goddess

Editorial services by Brenda Hadenfeldt Freelance Editorial, Lafayette, CO
Cover and Interior Design by The Printed Page, Phoenix, AZ

Editorial, design, and production services provided by Tax Goddess Publishing, LLC, Scottsdale, Arizona, www.TaxGoddessPublishing.com.

ISBN: 978-0-9960329-0-2
Printed in the United States of America
2014 printing

Thank You to Those Who Support Me!

This book goes out to my loved ones—family, friends, and puppies.
Thank you to all who contributed and helped make this book a reality!

This book is the accumulation of years of knowledge, lots of mistakes,
and lots of "aha" experiences. If you are about to take this journey, remember:

Being an entrepreneur is a tough path, but it's totally worth it!

I wouldn't have it any other way.

~ Shauna, Tax Goddess ~

How to Connect with Me, Your Tax Goddess

You can connect with me in multiple ways, so I thought I should give those to you right up front:

✔ E-mail: Shauna@TaxGoddess.com

This is the *fastest* way to reach me, always!

✔ Telephone: 602-357-3275

Make sure you leave a message! I only return my calls from 2 to 3 p.m. (Arizona time) each day, so leave details, including how I can reach you.

✔ Websites:
— www.TaxGoddess.com – Business owners and entrepreneurs
— www.TaxGoddessExpress.com – If you are an individual without a business

✔ Make an appointment to meet in person or via Skype:

You can schedule an appointment to come see me if you want—or even set up Skype appointments if you are outside of Arizona.
— www.taxgoddess.com/make-an-appointment/

✔ Facebook:
— www.facebook.com/thetaxgoddess
— www.facebook.com/TaxGoddessExpress

✔ Twitter:
— @TaxGoddess
— @TGXpress

✔ Newsletter:

You can subscribe to our free newsletter for monthly tips, tricks, and ways to be a better business owner!
— www.taxgoddess.com/get-our-newsletter/

✔ YouTube:

Just search for me: Shauna Wekherlien.

Contents

List of Figures

INTRODUCTION

This book is primarily focused on one major audience—new and prospective small business owners.[1] If you're reading this, you're probably an entrepreneur for the first time. Maybe you bought a franchise; maybe you are bringing your own dream to life. It's likely that you don't have a master of business administration (MBA), and you probably have worked for someone else for many years at what I call a "W-2 job." The current struggling economy, and perhaps even a job layoff, may have spurred your entry into a small business of your own.

Many of my clients have been laid off as a result of everything happening in the economy (2009–2013—let's work to get it going strong in 2014 and beyond!). They've come to the conclusion that relying on somebody else to assure their livelihood is not a sound idea. They've decided they'd rather put in blood, sweat, cash, and tears to build their own income, live their own dreams and their own passions, and support their families. Helping people live their passions is what I like best about guiding small business owners.

Most people who start their own businesses choose the industry and business type that they are passionate about, which is not only a lot more fun for them, but also often where their business skills are the strongest.

If you think about how you've learned the business skills, or any skills, you've acquired over the years, you'll probably have to admit that the lessons that stick with you the most are the ones learned by trial and error. How often have you said, "I learned the hard way not to do that again"? This book is committed to teaching you by this time-honored trial-and-error method—but not the hard way. The trial and error will be that of others who have gone before you on this entrepreneurial path. I'll tell you stories of other first-time entrepreneurs—the mistakes they made, the lessons they learned. You'll learn what to do as you build, grow, and manage your business—and perhaps most importantly, what *not* to do.

The questions I'll address here are the ones I've been asked most often, such as:

---

1. This book has multiple references to similar material throughout, as this guide is definitely *not* meant to be read cover to cover but is more of a "hunt and find" resource for what you need to know. Many business owners may already have knowledge in some areas but not all, so this approach is meant to be helpful for whatever you are looking for at the time.

✔ If you're going to partner with somebody else for your new business, what do you need to watch out for when creating that relationship?

✔ What kind of agreements do you need?

✔ How do you talk about and handle the money?

✔ How do you make sure that nobody is getting the short end of the stick at tax time?

✔ How do you find the right employees when it's time to hire? How do you find the right banker for your new firm?

✔ How do you find and choose an attorney or a certified public accountant (CPA)?

✔ What other professionals are you going to need to work with to make your business a great success?

Every field and each profession has its swindlers, unfortunately. How do you tell, especially in professions and trades where you don't have expertise, if people are good at what they do, if they really know what they're talking about, and if they're really going to help you? How do you know they're not just going to take your money and run? In today's economic downturn the "snake oil" sales people are more prevalent than ever, but how do you tell the professional wheat from the chaff?

This book, while it offers the expertise and experience of my sixteen years as a small-business CPA and the experience of my small-business clients, is not meant to be a one-size-fits-all guide for building and succeeding at your small business. I'll go through the must-do tasks for your business success and the generally efficient practices of entrepreneurs, all the while keeping in mind that for most situations there are exceptions. Industry practices differ, trade obstacles vary. Virtually every business is different. You could own a sandwich shop, and I could own a sandwich shop, and we could have completely different needs. You might have plenty of start-up capital but be in a geographic area with low unemployment and a shortage of job candidates. I might have plenty of candidates but not enough funding. I'll talk about that.

Many business owners turn to other people in the industry for help, and while that's natural and might be helpful, sometimes it's disastrous. Remember, other people in your or a similar industry or field who solicit the same geographic market are more than likely your competition. You can't assume that they really want you to succeed. They could deliberately give you the wrong guidance. Of course, some will help, but you shouldn't assume so.

You should read, re-read, and keep handy this book, for several reasons:

- ✔ You'll get a better understanding of the small business basics—the do's and don'ts of how to start and how to manage your small business.

- ✔ You'll learn the meaning of your "set of books," what taxing structure to choose, what legal structure is best for your business, how to work with business partners, and how to hire and manage employees.

- ✔ Business management topics you'll learn about include bookkeeping, outsourcing, billing and invoicing, operating agreements, business stocks and shares, partner agreements, and splits of profit or loss and capital.

- ✔ You'll learn about loans, banks, and real estate.

- ✔ You'll also learn about the experiences of other business owners—probably one of the most valuable reasons to buy this book!

This book is also an excellent resource for your new business strategies. Once you know the basic tax rules, for example, you'll need to make some decisions on how and why to apply them. Do you have partners? Do you have children who work for you? What other circumstances might affect the tax choices you would make? I'll explain why becoming an S-Corporation might be a good or bad idea for your company and when outsourcing particular business tasks could be preferable to hiring full- or part-time employees.

Reading this book will help you come up with new business strategies. On the topic of tax, for example, you will have help determining how you should be taxed. Your decision will rest on whether you have partners or are a sole owner, and perhaps whether or not you have children or other family members working for you. There are many factors to consider, and this book will guide you through the strategies and reasons behind your choice of one method or another.

You'll get guidance in these pages about the professionals who can help you succeed. I'll provide tips on how to determine who you can trust, what questions to ask professional prospects you interview, which fields and trades offer or require certifications or licensing, and where you can turn for ratings and reviews of those you are considering.

After telling you how important it is to ferret out the credentials and trustworthiness of the professionals you seek for help, I'd be remiss if I didn't tell you about myself—my commitment to my clients' ongoing business success, my many resources, my background, my expertise, and my ethics. I've been a CPA for sixteen years and have a master's degree in taxation from Arizona State University (ranked third in the country for taxation) as well as undergraduate degrees in accounting and finance from the University of Arizona. I absolutely love helping small business owners, especially in my field of tax. It's like playing a giant chess game with the IRS; they've set up the rules and we can play within them to get our winning outcome!

When I first started my accounting practice, I had just finished reading *Raving Fans* by Ken Blanchard—a book and author that I highly recommend. Blanchard talked about the importance of creating "Raving Fans." I realized that's what I wanted to do. Then, somewhere in my early CPA years, a client nicknamed me the Tax Goddess, and the name stuck. My other clients picked it up, and I started getting all sorts of e-mails saying, "Hey, Tax Goddess, can you tell me . . .?" What this has taught me is that my clients are happy and satisfied. In fact, to be very sure that was the case, I asked them. Here are a few comments:

Thank you for taking me as a client. As a small business owner, I sincerely appreciate your passion as the "Tax Goddess" that is only surpassed by your knowledge. Not only am I totally satisfied with your abilities and services, every person I have referred to you feels the same way. I wouldn't let anyone else handle my precious business.

Sue Shipman

Where do you get good business advice about your taxes and financial matters? It is a challenge in today's market because of the different voices and different advice which is easy to absorb from the Internet, magazines, television, and other sources. To establish our LLC, we turned to Shauna and her associates at Tax Goddess Business Services and found excellent advice and timely service. With complete confidence, I can recommend Tax Goddess Business Services for your business and tax needs.

W. Terry Whalin

My wife and I are both realtors and have a PLC for our business. We had previously been with another CPA who did not do the job properly. Since Shauna bailed us out and repaired the mess we were in, she has been our primary accounting source and tax planner. We will never go anywhere else. She is an expert in her field and completely honest. Her fees are competitive and her range of business services is impressive. I recommend her wholeheartedly to anyone or any business in need of superior CPA services.

Michael McCall

> *I have worked with Shauna for several years now. As a consultant, my clients rely on me to know the best resources in town. Not only do I go to Tax Goddess Business Services for my own taxes, I refer my clients there as well. I have saved money on my taxes and my returns are accurate and professional. My clients think I'm a genius because I know such great tax people. I can recommend Tax Goddess Business Services without reservation.*
>
> Deb Morgaina
> Avalon Office Organization & Management

Figure 1: Testimonials for the Tax Goddess and Her Team

This book is down-to-earth—no jargon or legalese, no assumption that you know anything more than that you think you probably want to start your own business. This book does not assume you have business acumen, an MBA, or a dictionary at your side as you read it. It merely assumes that you have an interest in building and managing your own business and that you need guidance doing so. I'm going to give you the basics without trying to sell you my next great anything.[2] What I am saying is there is no catch, no flimflam, and no hype. This book offers basic guidance for your small business success. If you're interested in taking charge of your life—if you want to make your own dream come true, live your own passion, and make money doing it—you'll find much value in this book.

The most popular, and usually most fitting, answer to just about anything in the tax world is "It depends." It's fitting because the tax world, just like the legal world, banking world, and almost any industry's world, changes on nearly a daily basis. New strategies aren't new for long. A book, by the time it's published, might well be quoting tax or other law that's out of date, amended or about to be replaced by new legislation. So, rather than reading legislation with the assumption that it's going to be around for a long time, you should read it as a guide to the way the Internal Revenue Service (IRS) thinks. Let me explain.

In 2006 the IRS raised the limit on something called the Section 179 deduction, what most people know as the "Hummer Law." The U.S. government, trying to boost spending, enacted a law that said that any business could buy $125,000 worth of any equipment and take a 100 percent write-off against the income the first year. This legislation, completely outside the federal norm, was telling business people to go buy a car or something else and they could write it all off

---

2. More books are coming out, but each is an independent guide meant to be used for any reader's individual purposes.

the first year. The result was that a lot of business owners decided to get themselves a $120,000 Hummer courtesy of Uncle Sam. Since this result clearly had not been the intent of the federal government, the Hummer Law was changed the following year, to what is currently the vehicle purchase limit: $25,000. The Hummer Law is an example of a clear U.S. tax strategy misunderstood and misused.

One piece of legislation that's been around a long time is the U.S. tax deduction allowance for mortgage interest. The clear intent of the federal government is to encourage home ownership. In fact, in the current recession, with people losing their jobs and then their homes, the federal government has put limited-time tax credits in place to further encourage home ownership. Strategizing around what the government clearly wants you to do might also mean buying rental property to take advantage of the tax gains of writing off depreciation. The strategy idea here is broad-based: realize what the government wants you to do, and then use that direction to your maximum advantage.

So, let's get down to the basics of your new small business.[3]

---

3. Please note that this book is meant to cover the most common situations, rules, and regulations as they apply to *most* businesses, with a few tasty tax treats for all businesses interspersed. This book is not meant to be the "be all, end all" of all tax knowledge; for that, you will want to contact the Tax Goddess herself. ☺

CHAPTER 1

Starting a Business

This chapter reviews the overall issues and points related to starting a new business. It will give you some ideas to ponder before opening your business or buying that franchise. You may even decide, after reading this chapter, that a business is not for you. But wouldn't you want to know that ahead of time, before you really get into it? Now, don't let me start you on the train of thought that I do not encourage new business owners; I believe that business owners are the backbone of this country, what makes America strong. I just believe that you really need to know what you are getting into *before* you get into it!

Know Thyself

One of my favorite books is Michael Gerber's *The E-Myth*. In this book, Gerber describes three main types of personalities in the world: the Technician, the Manager, and the Entrepreneur.

Now, in my own recap, Technicians are the people who really enjoy doing the work. They love the nitty-gritty of it all and just love to be facedown in what they "do."

The Entrepreneurial Fit, per Gerber, is when people who have W-2 jobs, employees working for others, decide they can do this better than their bosses and open up their own businesses doing those same jobs. Typically, per Gerber, this is done by the Technician personality, the people who actually do the work.

The Manager is the type of person who loves people. Managers enjoy handling the human resources (HR) issues, managing the people, directing, and organizing. These people are fabulous at running the organizations that they have created.

The Entrepreneur is the type of person with vision and drive. Not that the other types don't have these, but the Entrepreneur is the one who can lead crowds of people—can get people excited and motivate them toward whatever vision the Entrepreneur has created.

Typically a new business owner is one, maybe two, of these categories of people. However, one must realize, per Gerber, that a good business will have all three of these types of people. So, in the rare case that you are all three, you are off to a pretty good start right off the bat. However, for those of us who are one or two at most, we will need help!

I realized about three months into my business that I am a great Technician and a great Entrepreneur, but not a very good Manager. That is when I hired my very first administrative assistant. She was a great Manager. ☺

So, the real question is: How do you know what type you are? Only you can determine that, but I can give you a few clues:

✔ If you are a Technician, you will
  o Enjoy working all day on your project

  o Find yourself nose down, forgetting about all else—such as calling back customers or eating lunch

  o Feel truly accomplished when your widget, or your service guide, or whatever your product or service, is perfect and you cannot envision any issues with it

✔ If you are a Manager, you will
  o Like working with your customers and your employees

  o Enjoy organizing the shop and creating methods, processes, and maps of the way we work and how the work should get done

  o Feel really accomplished when either your managers or your staff compliments how smoothly everything is working and how organized and easy the systems make the work itself

✔ If you are an Entrepreneur, you will
  o Be excited by thinking, creating, envisioning the future—planning for and achieving your goals

  o Enjoy leading people, describing your vision, and having the company move toward the final outcome

Note: Entrepreneurs do not necessarily care about the people them-selves and can seem standoffish, but typically it is because they are so driven towards the goals and the vision that they do not see the human side. Often this is why the Entrepreneur needs a Manager, someone with good people skills.

○ Feel most accomplished when your goal is achieved or when the company has reached its potential (or is moving toward it)

From my own personal, and favorite, business coach—Fred Kroin of Goal Partners—here are some insights on what it means to be an entrepreneur:

For me an entrepreneur is someone who has, for a variety of reasons, decided that a corporate work environment is not for them. Though visions and memories of childhood lemonade stands may, for some, be early warning signs of needing to live one's professional life as an entrepreneur, I can think of many reasons people choose that path as adults. Here are just a few:
○ You have a unique idea you're certain can be developed into a business (which might have a profit motive or even a philanthropic goal).

○ You have an idea that isn't readily implementable from within a traditional corporate environment or has been rejected by "short-sighted" corporate superiors.

○ You just *must* be the master of your own destiny, making key decisions without needing to follow the directions or dictates of others.

On the other side of the coin, you might reconsider being an entrepreneur if:
○ You're not prepared to work very hard and invest lots of personal time and perhaps money into the pursuit of your dream.

○ You're used to and aren't prepared to give up having lots of other people around to take care of the details and "administrivia" involved in building and managing a business.

RESOURCE
Fred Kroin, owner of Goal Partners (www.goalptrs.com), is one of my favorite business coaches. He is great at "pulling stuff" out of you, even when you don't really want him to (i.e., you would rather stay in your issue/problem—don't worry, we all do this sometimes!). He is a key resource for helping to get you to your goals.

- o You don't have a committed supporting cast to complement your skills and personality in the venture, as well as a solid foundation of support at home.

- o You don't have a well-thought-out, written business plan with considerations not only for growing pains but also Plans B, C, and even D for when things don't go as you hoped (and trust me, they never do).

I hope that after reading this very brief recap of the "E-Myth" ideas you may have a thought as to which of the three categories you must belong to. The question becomes: What do you do next?[4]

Deep Thoughts About Really Starting This Thing

Now, as you think about having your own business, you must ask yourself these questions:

- ✔ How much time do I have in a day?
  - o What other business responsibilities do I need to cover?
    - — Financially?
    - — Socially?
  - o For my family?

- ✔ How much of my own money do I have in savings?

- ✔ How much of that money can I use to start my own business?

- ✔ Am I good with employees?

- ✔ What are my skills and strengths? Make a list.

- ✔ In what areas am I weak or untrained? Make this list as well; this is what you'll be delegating or outsourcing.

- ✔ What is my passion?

- ✔ What is my plan? Is it written?

- ✔ How am I going to get clients?

---

4. Please understand that I am not saying, and I don't think that Gerber is either, that if you are only one of the above you should not start a business. This review of *The E-Myth* is only to help you realize that, if you are one type of personality, you should consider either strengthening yourself in the other areas or outsourcing (get a partner, hire staff that fit the other areas, etc.). A business is *much* easier to create, run, and own if you have all three areas covered.

✔ How am I going to get paid (i.e., will I accept credit cards, checks)? What about paying on credit, and if so, on what terms? How will I resolve collections issues?

✔ With whom do I want to work?

This short list is but the beginning of what you'll need to consider before you start your business. You, the head honcho of your new business, will have to make all the big decisions. Getting all these items down on "paper" before you make the decision to start your business is crucial. Starting a business is tough enough without your handicapping yourself with no preparation. Mind mapping software products such as SmartDraw, MindGenius, and other flowcharting programs can be quite helpful. Any of these software programs will allow you to sort and reorganize the material at any time without your having to reinvent your planning wheel, as you would with manual paper and pencil documentations.

If you have not completed a business plan—five or fifty pages, it doesn't matter, as long as it reflects honest, reflective business planning, forethought, and a set of pro forma financial statements that give you some idea of the resources for your new business—and if you haven't mulled over your business idea for at least three and perhaps as much as seven months, I'm convinced you shouldn't be going into business, even as a partner. While a partnership may seem less taxing on your time, energy, and financial resources, that isn't necessarily the case. There are legal and financial concerns unique to a partnership that can be a headache or even a disaster if you haven't thought it through early on.

I recall one of my clients, a W-2 employee with a $300,000 annual salary, who decided when the market was crashing in 2012 that he didn't want his job anymore.

"I'm going to quit and become a real estate agent," he told me.

I tend to be pretty hands-on with my clients, and fairly frank, and I'd known him for six years—so I was blunt with him: "What do you mean you're going to quit your job?" I asked incredulously, putting my head in my hands, as he told me he really should have quit the job already.

"My wife's been selling real estate for a couple of years now and she's making $40,000 a year," he added.

The man was going to go from $300,000 a year to $40,000 (with luck)—and he thought that was pretty good. Well, I understood that his current job kept him quite stressed out, with little family time, but this was going to be a huge lifestyle change for him and his family. I hoped, as I listened to him, that he had thought it through. At the end of his mini-rant about quitting his job, I asked him, "So, you can live on $40K a year until you start making money, right?"

He looked at me blankly. "What?"

"Well, you just told me you are giving up $300K a year, to start a new business that at its best is going to make $40K a year, right? So, can your family live on $40K?"

He thought for a minute and then said, "Okay, I see your point. Maybe I need to ponder this first. . . ."

Well, at least I helped him take a breather! He may not like his boss, but that kind of income change could be devastating to his family. I could understand his desire to change his lifestyle. In fact, that's why I left the big firms and started my own practice. But, unlike me, he had two daughters about to head to college, and no savings to speak of.

This story turned out to have a happy ending. He and his wife are now making $200,000 each year in their real estate business. Yet, there are plenty of others who don't have the same happy tale to tell—people who just up and leave their W-2 jobs with no planning and no thought except, "Nope, I'm not working for this boss anymore." This lack of planning and preparation can lead to, and unfortunately in many cases has lead to, nightmares for your business. Small Business Administration (SBA) statistics indicate that 95 percent of small businesses fail in the first five years and only 10 percent of the others make it to ten years. Nor is it just businesses that fail to plan that can't make a go of it. Some businesses, seemingly well organized at the start, fail to do their market research and thus begin with inaccurate assumptions that are their downfall.

Have I Scared You Off Yet?

So then the question remains: Are you prepared for the big plunge? If you are ready to read on, let's take a look at next steps.

CHAPTER 2

Market Research

Before making or even considering the legal and tax entity choices for your new business, you must do some market research to determine if your business idea is sound. Some of the questions you must answer:

✔ Are there other companies in your exact niche in your designated market area (DMA)—which, in this technologically advanced world could be as large as the globe or as small as your neighborhood—that are doing exactly what you propose to do and can do it better or less expensively than you can?

✔ Will the profit margin be sufficient for your needs?

✔ Are you passionate about what you propose to do for a living? While this isn't crucial, it surely helps when your initial days will be long and hard. Passion does not replace competitive advantage, profitability, training, or skill set in importance, as you determine what business you'll enter. The term "starving artist" exemplifies this point.

If you are considering buying someone else's business, you might think about enlisting the services of a business broker. The broker can help you decide if a specific business is right for you and how it might impact your finances, your time, and your social life. It's important to keep in mind, however, that the typical business broker has skin in the game, too, and might be committed to selling a particular business. His or her conflict might not provide you the best or unbiased advice.

Part of determining that your business is going to do what you need it to do is creating a personal plan. You should consider what you want in life and the timelines for those goals. You should think about what kind of social life meets your needs. For example, are you okay with working every weekend for the first year or two of your business start-up? If you have children, do you have, or can you make, adequate plans for their care while you're working on your business? Who will be walking your dog while you're working?

Your realization of the blood, sweat, cash, and perhaps even tears that will go into starting and growing your business is vital. That business will be your life for the first year or two. It will affect your life, your time, your family obligations, and all your relationships. Thinking about all these things is a crucial part of determining if you even want to be self-employed. Not thinking it through could be disastrous for you, your relationships, and your business success.

While a business plan is often used as a presentation to potential business lenders, I also value it as a method that makes business owners answer the tough questions. It makes them think through how they're actually going to create and grow their business: What kinds of people with what skill sets and experience are they going to need? What financing will be required? How long might it take to be profitable? And so forth. A lot of business owners start their business with a simple desire to be their own boss and no planning. They make an emotional rather than a logical choice, and all too often it leads to business failure and perhaps even financial ruin.

I can't tell you how many times I've heard about—or from—people who began their businesses with no thought except to leave their W-2 jobs behind. They're at work, and then something happens—the last straw. "You know what, I'm tired of this. I'm leaving this job," they say. With no planning they're left with no income and no business start-up preparation. I've had clients tell me this is how they began their entrepreneurship. I'm not about to jump over the desk and throttle them when they tell me about their emotional business start, but I am going to give them a talking-to.

If you haven't truly and deeply thought through starting or buying a business—if you haven't determined whether you can afford it, what your financial resources will be and when, what type of business you'll start, who your target market will be, and how you will actually make the business profitable—don't quit your day job!

I am sure that you have heard that a new business must start with a business plan. Not everyone, however, takes the time and introspection they must to determine what their product or service will be and what their chosen market will bear in their chosen industry. Both of these are important. Choosing a business type is not just about choosing what you'd like to do. It's also about choosing what is needed, and what the market will welcome—in other words, what people want and what is not being adequately provided by the companies now offering it or similar products or services. You could be an expert at designing and manufacturing a terrific Product A, but if four other firms in the same market provide similar (and, worse yet, less costly) Products B, C, and D, your business might fail. You could also come out with a terrific Product A that no one ever thought of before, but if the public doesn't want it, your business might well fail. These are the things you must research ahead of your business launch and, in fact, these marketing tasks should be part of your business plan.

Your plans for a product or service must be detailed. Let's assume, as an example, that you plan to open a hair salon. This might seem like an excellent idea. Perhaps not all people get their hair styled, colored, or permed, but most everyone needs a haircut on a regular basis.

But, before you decide to proceed with a new hair salon, here are the things you need to study and provide your answers to:

- ✔ Will the market bear your product?
    - o   How many salons exist already for how many people who need haircuts?

    - o   Can you price your service competitively and still make a profit? In order to answer this you must know the cost of each product and piece of equipment involved in providing your hair services. You have to know how much it's going to cost to lease space in an area that has good foot and vehicle traffic and does not already have too many hair salons; how much it will cost to buy the shampoo bowls, shelves, hair products, and so forth to get started; how much telephone and other utilities will cost you; and how much you'll have to pay stylists to lure good ones to your salon.

- ✔ How will you differentiate yourself? In what will you specialize—what products and what target market?
    - o   It's not enough to simply say that everyone needs a haircut and therefore everyone will be your target market. Technically, not *everyone* needs a haircut. There are bald people and people who are growing their hair long and haven't had it cut in over a year. But there are also people who can't afford a high-end salon, as well as those who wouldn't be caught dead walking into a discount shop. While specializing may cut back on the number of prospective customers, it will also let you differentiate yourself and give you more appeal to your target group. In southwest Phoenix, for example, where easily 50 percent of the population is Hispanic and some stores have Spanish names and signage, being the only hair salon within five miles that specializes in Latino and Latina cuts and styles is a smart move.

15

✔ You'll need to decide if you're going to accept walk-ins or require appointments. Also, will you cater to the lower income local population and offer discount services and daily specials, or are you going to move into a high-income area and include pricier add-on services such as nail treatments and massages? The former will get you more customers—if you choose the location well. The latter will earn you more money per customer—again, if you are in the right neighborhood, where the residents can afford your pricier products and services.

Quick recap: I believe that your market research must contain the 5Ws and an H.

✔ Who?

✔ What?

✔ Where?

✔ When?

✔ Why?

✔ How?

If you don't know the answers to these important questions before you begin your business, you're going to face a very messy path trying to reach an outcome that you are happy with and enjoy.

CHAPTER 3

Business Start-Up Options

To start a business, you have two choices: buy someone else's company or start from the ground up. If you buy, you might acquire an independent firm in an industry in which you have interests and skills, or you could purchase a franchise.

Buying a Franchise

Many franchises, such as McDonald's, Subway, and several carpet cleaning firms, are in industries that hire unskilled labor and/or need only a couple of key people to manage them. As you may or may not know, McDonald's has one of the most highly organized systems available to a franchise buyer. When you buy your way into such a franchise, you pay a hefty fee but you also get a fully documented, fully tested business process and plenty of face-to-face training at Hamburger University. Cold Stone Creamery has its own franchise university in Scottsdale, Arizona. Many other large franchisors provide similar training programs and written guidance. Generally, the franchisor will pick your store or office location, provide your signage, and deliver the first of your leads. These well-established franchises are turnkey operations. You read the manual, hire some staff, and start making money. It's not nearly the work, or the risk, of building your own independent company; and it provides you with far more experienced guidance than you can generally find on your own.

The disadvantages can be the cost of entry, the ongoing franchise fee, and the mandate to "do as you're told." Most franchises don't leave a lot of room for franchisee creativity in marketing or business practices.

When I started in business, I knew a franchise was a poor choice for my own entrepreneurship. I like learning things the hard way. I like figuring out my own systems and goals. I dislike the idea of paying a fee to someone else throughout the life of my business. Of course, those first couple of years, while I may not have been paying any franchise fee, I surely wasn't making a profit as I built up my brand, my good reputation, and my client base from scratch.

It takes a while to find the franchise that is going to be right for you. Each business model has a different outcome. Someone who wants flexibility in her daily schedule might choose a Subway franchise, for example, knowing that she could hire staff and would seldom need to be there. Another entrepreneur might want to know that big profits are a sure thing and won't care if it takes long work hours, day in and day out, to make that happen. Such a go-getter might well choose McDonald's.

Time-Honored Ways to Start a Business from Scratch

Two time-honored ways of starting a small business from scratch are (1) growing it part-time while keeping your "day job," and (2) doing as I did and quitting your W-2 job to devote all your time to your new company. Either way you begin, you must be prepared to give it a great deal of time, probably considerably more than you assume before you start out. When I started my business, I was working at it 75–80 hours each week, and only a portion of that was completing client work.

Most new business owners think only of the technical tasks—the work required to complete client services. That's not all you'll be doing for your new business, however.

You will recall that there are three types of business ownership tasks—technical, managerial, and entrepreneurial. At the very beginning you may be taking on all three of those task categories. You may start your firm with one or two large clients that financially enable your self-employment. The technical tasks of your new business are the duties you perform for those clients: writing their marketing materials, repairing their cars, balancing their books, or providing whatever services your company specializes in.

Don't fail to add in hours for managerial and entrepreneurial tasks, unless you're able to hand those off to a contractor or employee, or you're going to keep your business as a part-time avocation, with just the one or two clients. Even in the case of a part-time business, however, you still have to bill your client and balance your books, which probably adds another 10 percent to your anticipated total work hours.

If, however, you intend to run a full-time business, be sure and allow for hours taken up by ordering and keeping track of office supplies, arranging equipment purchases and repair, maintaining your computerized database, keeping the books, prospecting for clients, preparing marketing materials and scheduling advertising, hiring and overseeing staff, maintaining a website and blog, preparing payroll, and perhaps even cleaning the office. A good ballpark estimate is to allow one-third of your time for each of the technical, managerial, and entrepreneurial categories. So, if you've just determined that it will take you 25 hours a week to complete the work your clients hired you for, you now have a 75-hour workweek.

The same breakdown is a good guide for how you divide up your company profits if you're in a service industry. A profit of $90,000, for example, should be divvied up equally among operations, managerial, and entrepreneurial costs. So $30,000 of your profit would be set aside for operations such as paying staff salaries (yours included), office supplies, and other cost of goods sold (COGS) line items. Another $30,000 would pay the managerial costs of overhead such as utilities, office mortgage or lease, and equipment repair and purchases. The final $30,000 would be spent on entrepreneurial tasks such as marketing, advertising, business networking club memberships, and so forth.

Other industries will have other ratios, but for service this one-third-to-each-category approach is the ideal. It may be that you find yourself starting out with 40 percent dedicated to each operations and managerial and only 20 percent allotted to helping you get new business in the door. That's not the end of the world, but should you suddenly find, for example, that 80 percent of what you're making is going back into operations and managerial and you have little left over to help your business grow, you should take a long, hard look at what you're spending. Maybe you are overstaffed or your cell phone bills are too high. Perhaps you're not aggressive enough with your collection of past-due accounts or your office cleaning service is too costly. In this case you need to step back, review what is happening from an outsider's perspective (not someone who has been grinding the days working *in*side the business) and give yourself your own good advice on how to get out of a bad situation. Remember, this is where a great business coach can also help!

These expectations don't hold true for the first two years of your new business, however. During these start-up years, it's rare for an owner to make any money, as the earnings go back into the company or are spent on operations and the purchase of assets.

It's in the third year, approximately, that you'll start to see some of the profits coming to you; and if by the end of your fifth year in business you're not earning what you want as an entrepreneur, something's not right with your company or your management. Perhaps you've tried, unwisely, to reinvent the wheel, or you've chosen an industry that can't support another competitor or is no longer marketable.

Trying to reinvent the wheel is costly. Too often, fledgling entrepreneurs think, "I have the best idea. I'm going to start this new business based on my hot idea. It's going to rock and make me so much money!" Then reality sets in. The cost of manufacturing requires a retail price that consumers won't pay, perhaps; or the business owners choose the wrong market or the wrong location, or market poorly, and buyers are few. This happens because they don't do their market research, and they don't seek the help (often free) of organizations such as the Small Business Administration (SBA) or the Service Corps of Retired Executives (SCORE), who could have helped them see that their product wasn't marketable.

TIP

One trick I learned was to set up an appointment with the competition. This can tell you a lot, not only about the competition, but also about how or how not to do business and what the market is for your type of product or service.

When I first started my CPA business, I had my tax returns done for a couple of years by an outside firm that I respected. I admired their business practices and wanted to learn how their staff interacted with clients and with the owners. I got to peruse their internal forms as well.

While the company knew I was an accountant, they weren't aware I was a tax CPA. I was paying them to do a legitimate service for me and was under no obligation to disclose that. I've had clients who say they've done—or tried to do—the same thing in their industry. Sometimes the competitor rejects them as a customer; sometimes they get lucky and get to observe their competition at work. For many industries, especially retail, it's very easy to be your competitor's customer and observe the way they work.

An auto repair shop is a good example. If your car breaks down, you go to an auto repair shop. No one is going to ask you if you are an auto mechanic. You can take your car in for service or repair without announcing your fledgling business; walk around the shop and talk to the employees; and see how the work load is divided up, how the employees interact with customers, and what the shop charges for services.

Before you unwittingly spend countless hours trying to start a business that is a reinvention of something else already available, do some research. You can keyword-search your idea on Google or another major search engine, you can check with a local trade association for your anticipated industry, and you can even solicit the help of the Small Business Development Center, part of SBA.

Your local trade association and SBDC can be useful for reasons other than market research. Either can be a source for contract and agreement templates as well.

Be careful about how forthcoming you are—and with whom—about your idea, as it could be new and you could mistakenly put the idea in the hands of someone who will steal it. But it's crucial that you determine whether or not you're reinventing the wheel. While having one or more competitors already in place doesn't necessarily make your business concept a mistake, especially if you can find their weaknesses and improve on them, you do need to determine if the market is there for both—or all—of you.

The time you designate to entrepreneurial tasks is primarily going to be taken up by prospecting for new clients. If you neglect your entrepreneurial tasks and time, or allot too few hours to them, you neglect your business's chance to grow. You might make cold phone or in-person calls, e-mail or call your current clients for referrals, host or attend industry networking events, sponsor local nonprofit ventures for the recognition, or wine and dine your clients. I host a monthly wine tasting and margarita event to bring my clients together, invite prospects to meet me in a nonthreatening environment, and reward my clients.

CHAPTER 4

Types of Businesses

One of the questions that you will need to answer is: What type of business do you want to be in? There are many different options—a product business, a service business, a business that leaves residual income, an MLM (multi-level marketing) business. Many of these options are already established for you, depending on what you want to do, but it is important to know that you are not stuck. You can create any business in any type of field.

There are three main types of businesses (any of which could be a franchise operation):

- ✔ Inventory businesses
- ✔ Service businesses
- ✔ Residual stream of income businesses

Each of these has strengths and weaknesses. Let's review each one to give you some hints on what you're looking at.

Inventory Business

An inventory business is one that buys or produces a product to sell. It often includes warehousing the product, due to the nature of having a physical item. Physical products can be good or bad for many reasons, and it is important that you know about these.

- ✔ Pros
  - o Once the product has been created, you don't really have to do more work beyond selling it.

o   You may have invented/created something you can patent, and then you can license production to someone else—in one location/company or all over the world.

o   Inventory can be invented/created and produced by someone else; you may only have to sell it rather than produce it as well.

✔ Cons

o   If you create too much product you will have costs associated with the product, such as storage and wasted inventory.

o   The potential for theft is much higher in an inventory business (product can be stolen) than in the other categories of businesses.

o   You always need a body to "watch the store"—to protect the inventory and handle the daily activities relating to sales. Costs can include cash registers, staff, retail warehouse locations, and so on.

Service Business

A service business is a business that typically exchanges money for a service, some sort of intangible action.[5]

✔ Pros

o   You have much greater flexibility, in general, for when the services are to be done. The service happens when the two parties agree.

o   Depending on the type of service, you may be able to perform it from anywhere in the world (for greater flexibility of location).

o   Service businesses are often easier to start, as they require less overhead.

✔ Cons

o   It may be easier for customers to have complaints about a service business, as unless the two parties' perspectives are clear and identical in understanding, issues may arise.

o   Pricing can be a tough job at first; until you really know your business, you are more likely to underbid or overbid a job.

o   Service businesses are often less likely to accept credit cards when they first start, potentially making cash flow a tough issue.

---

5.   Not always does a service business exchange dollars for hours in direct relation; many service businesses have flat charges for the work to be performed.

Residual Stream of Income Business

Some businesses create what are called residual streams of income for their owners. Residual streams mean that even after the owner stops working the business, no longer selling, or creating, (maybe managing or customer relations depending on the business), the owner still receives income from the business.

- ✔ MLM stands for multi-level marketing business. Some very successful MLMs have surfaced and survived over the past ten years or even longer. SendOutCards and Amway are two examples. Both of these businesses involve either having salespeople below you in a chain or selling directly to customers to earn your money. If you do direct sales to customers, you have a business like any other. If you go the route of getting salespeople under you, who then either sell to other salespeople or sell to customers, you get overrides and earn money on those sales down the chain—thus creating a residual income stream in which you may have to only slightly manage the relationships in order to maintain it.

- ✔ There are also many types of businesses where, once you have your base of clients and you take care of them well, you will continue to earn income for the life of the client, which is considered residual income. A few industries where this holds true include:
  - o   Financial planners
  - o   Insurance agents
  - o   CPAs
  - o   Lawyers

- ✔ Rental real estate[6]
  - o   Most real estate people love being in real estate because it provides schedule flexibility, positive cash flow, and tax savings strategies. These same people absolutely abhor being in real estate because at 2 a.m. they get telephone calls about fixing broken air-conditioning units, fixing broken plumbing, and dealing with evicting tenants. Real estate is a dual-sided and very sharp-edged sword.

---

6.   I am writing a book related solely to real estate (working title: *Tax Goddess Tips for Those Interested in Owning, Renting, Flipping, Selling, Holding, Buying, and Anything-Else-You-Can-Think-Of in Real Estate*). There are so many ways to earn income with real estate, but for *Starting Your Own Business*, I just want to give a brief summary. Real estate can provide you with residual income if you buy and hold properties out for rent and you have a good management company to manage the properties and ensure they are always rented.

Note: To really be successful in creating passive, or residual, income from rental real estate, you will want to have *at least* five properties that are rented out at least 80–90 percent of the time. It is important that these properties are *cash flowing* (providing cash after expenses). I highly recommend that the positive cash flow from these entities is put into a separate account until you have at least one year of mortgage payments on *all* properties covered before you consider using any of this money to live on.

A Brief on Franchises

Just a reminder for those unsure after reading about everything in the past few chapters: remember franchises! Franchises have their appeal for many reasons: financial, operational, and staff/owner hours.

Financial Appeal of Franchises

Franchises have financial appeal because many franchisors will finance their franchisees. While you generally have to come up with a down payment for the equipment, other than that, everything you need—from the equipment to the employee manuals—is financed through the franchisor's headquarters. If, for example, you want to own a McDonald's franchise but you don't have the $250,000 needed to get started, McDonald's will lend you the money. Cold Stone Creamery does that as well. This financing can be very helpful, especially when, as we discussed before, new small businesses don't have lending institutions they can rely on for the first couple of years in their ventures.

Operational Appeal of Franchises

Franchises are wonderful ways to start a business for many people because the franchisors will provide an instruction manual for how to run your chosen franchise from top to bottom. For example, the franchise manual for McDonald's tells you exactly how long the fries are deep-fried and at what temperature. You do not need to create any policies, invest time and money on creating the how-to book for the business, or figure out the answers to problems that pop up. These things are all provided to you in a neat handbook format.

Staff/Owner Hours Appeal of Franchises

When picking a franchise, owners can choose one where either they will work the "job(s)" or they will hire staff to do so. Either way, you as an owner get to choose how many hours you will work, what types of work you will perform, and so on. Of course, in all new businesses, the owner has to do *some* work (though wouldn't that be nice—buy a business and sit on the beach and collect a check!). But in many franchises, the work required is a lot less than starting a business from scratch, since most of the work and processes (marketing, building the widget, managing employee issues, processing/collecting money) have already been handled. That is why you pay such a large sum for a franchise.

CHAPTER 5

Atmosphere and Image

No matter what type of business you start, keep in mind that when you choose your target market and atmosphere, and you start branding your firm accordingly, it will be very difficult to change. For that reason, I advise you work with a business coach to help you make these crucial choices before you even open your business doors.[7]

I recently talked with a brand designer—a coach hired by a new business owner—whose recommendations weren't heeded. She was hired by the owner of what was to be a new, high-end, customizable makeup service. A customer at this store could, for example, walk in and say, "I'm allergic to coconut oil, blue is my favorite color, and I love the scent of lavender," and leave with makeup custom-made to her liking. For this new business, the designer's job was to recommend the colors, theme, and layout for the store.

Since the store was to sell all organic items, the designer recommended a wood and fabric decor. Once the store owner received her recommendations, however, he rejected them because of the cost involved. Against the advice of the coach, the owner painted the store's interior black and put up shelves made of metal and glass. While the bottles of the customized products were adorned with hand-painted labels, they were made of plastic. As a result, the store's branding turned out to be the complete opposite of what the owner intended. The new store failed.

---

7. I was very happy when the moniker of the "Tax Goddess" was first picked up and used by my clients. I am a redhead with a big, friendly, loving, and boisterous personality. Being a three-piece-suited, green-eyeshade-wearing CPA just didn't suit me. Tax Goddess most definitely does, and it makes my day so much brighter every morning when I can come to my business and enjoy my clients, my staff, and my life by being who I am.

If you want to pursue some do-it-yourself design budgeting, take a tour of local shops whose decor you admire. Ask the owners or managers how they accomplished the look and feel of the place. If your new business is not to be their competitor, they're quite likely to be very forthcoming, though keep in mind that these are very busy people. You might have a more productive conversation by inviting him to step next door for a cup of coffee on you, or perhaps invite her to lunch the next day—also on you, of course.

People love to talk about themselves, and if you start by telling them you admire what they created on their own, you're just about assured of getting some good tips. You'll want to find out if they had a coach, and if so, whom? While asking how much it all cost is somewhat delicate, you can ease into it by saying something like "I'm thinking I could get my interior design done for $15,000. Is that reasonable?" If the owner recommends the coach, ask her to pave the way for you. Being a friend of a client might put you at the head of the client-prospect line for a busy coach. It might also get you a discount.

Don't forget, however, to let your new entrepreneurial friend know you'll pass along anything noteworthy you learn once your doors open. In fact, a gift certificate for your new product or service would be a nice way to say thank you and lure an early customer to your new shop.

Don't forget to look at the local shops of major chains. Companies like Shoe Carnival and Barnes & Noble have exemplary services for which they're well known. Learning how these came about and the results of the ideas could help you come up with some distinction for your own service. For those of you who don't know, Shoe Carnival is known for its fun atmosphere: lively '60s music and nearly nonstop games and contests. Barnes & Noble offers cozy easy chairs, the opportunity to sit and read a book or magazine without pressure to buy, and an in-store café. Both businesses bring customers back time and again because it's just so nice to be there.

You must also study the websites of other businesses—not only those in a similar or the same industry, but those who just "wow" you, no matter what they're touting. As I write this, we're in the process of redoing my own company's website. While I like what we currently have, I found another site whose look, navigation, and features impressed me very much. I found out who had designed the site, asked him to redesign mine, and in two days he presented me with a mock-up. If only I had met him when I had started my business, that would have saved me a second development fee with the website guys!

While I assume your new company isn't going to have the budget of Barnes & Noble or Shoe Carnival, you can certainly implement some less costly design ideas for your brick-and-mortar location and your website. As an example, had that customized makeup store I talked about earlier followed the designer's guidance on just the interior paint—blue and orange with bubble designs—instead of the stark and bleak black walls, its owner wouldn't have spent much more on paint. The atmosphere, however, would have undergone a dramatic and quite positive change.

A new coat of paint is one of the cheap things you can do to spruce up your new office or retail space. Another positive step that won't cost you a pretty penny is to lay out your retail space with plenty of roomy aisles. When I go into stores that force me to maneuver through tiny spaces that barely allow me to pass by other shoppers and their carts, I am reminded of a Zen garden. A Zen garden is made up of both small and large stones. As visitors navigate the garden, they jump quickly from one small stone to another: no one wants to remain in any of these tiny spaces. A Zen garden designer places large stepping-stones in the areas where he or she would like visitors to stop and look around.

> *A Zen garden is made up of both small and large stones. As visitors navigate the garden, they jump quickly from one small stone to another: no one wants to remain in any of these tiny spaces.*

Your furnishings, your aisle layouts, and even your furniture should all be designed around this Zen garden concept. Give your store's visitors a roomy, pleasant space in which to wander and they'll stay longer, look more, and probably buy more too. Nor do you have to spend a lot of money on shelving and other store furnishings. Stores such as IKEA offer attractive furnishings at low cost. You can also pick up some real bargains at going-out-of-business sales and secondhand furniture and supply stores.

Improvements in the layout of your existing office can cost little or perhaps nothing at all. My own office experienced a very positive makeover that was free of charge when one of my staff observed that I had overcrowded the space with too much furniture. She moved out several items, did a little rearranging, and created a much more pleasant environment for visitors. We almost immediately noticed that clients and prospects tended to spend more time when they came to see us.

Realize that atmosphere is not related to only a retail space, either. Atmosphere and image also relate to your website, your brochures, your business cards, how you dress when you see clients, what types of artwork you like, and what events you attend. As a business owner, you may find it hard to have a closed social life, as your business and your life tend to intertwine! I am not saying it cannot be done, but wouldn't you rather draw to you customers, vendors, and a business life that tie closely to your own likes and passions? It certainly makes doing business more fun. So remember both what you are trying to accomplish and what type of clients you are trying to draw; but also remember to get a bit of yourself in there, as that is what can make the day-to-day grind more play than work.

A Note About Customer Service

You will have to decide how you want your company to run—what level of service it will provide to your potential customers. There are major differences in how you create your company when you want to have a customer service level of an Oberoi hotel or an Abercrombie & Kent safari versus a Denny's or a McDonald's.

CHAPTER 6

Determining the End of the Business: Your Exit Strategy

The Business Is a Product

New business owners may or may not realize that, whichever type of business they choose to create, they are creating an asset that will be sold in the future. Many owners look at their business as their nest egg, on which they are going to retire and travel the world or spend time with the grandkids. I want you to be aware of a few ideas that you will want to ponder on starting your business to get it ready for sale. Remember, the profit you make on the sale of an asset is in the buying (or creation), not the final sales price!

Now, what do I mean by, the business is a product? If I were a buyer, what would I prefer to buy from you thirty years from now: A business that has methods, systems, staff, a good customer list, and a good set of books reflecting the historical profits and costs over time, or one that has none of these things?

Piyush Parikh, one of our favorite systems guys, gives us the background on why having systems and methods for a business is so important:

If you create a business, you are really creating a product you will have to sell in the end.

Piyush Parikh: Why are systems and methods for a business so important?

Can you imagine a building being built without the foundation, plans, and drawing for it? You'll probably get a few pieces of the building to stand, but very soon the structure will collapse if it wasn't built with a solid foundation and plans. Businesses are very similar, in that they can be run for some finite amount of time without systems and plans but sooner or later the owner and employees run out of steam to keep things going. And this results in the business imploding on itself.

It sometimes amazes me to see companies that have been in business for years without any basic systems in place. Now, don't get me wrong, every company has systems—the question is whether the system is random or deliberate. The owner's energy level and luck can play a big part in keeping these random systems working. However, this business will probably not last through any major swings in, say, the economy, or changing times. Furthermore, these companies will probably only grow to a certain level—typically up to the level of the owner's own capacity and ceiling.

Having deliberate systems can help create the foundation for the business.

Here are five reasons why you may want to create systems and written procedures for the business:

1. To enable business growth

2. To keep the business owner and employees from getting burned out. Without systems, the business depends on the owner's and employees' capacity to multitask, handle complex situations, and keep things straight. Systems enable ordinary people to achieve extraordinary results—and they ultimately allow the business owner to sleep at night.

3. To enable consistency in the business—whether it is getting a consistent stream of leads and clients or providing a consistent level of service and product quality to each and every client

4. To train employees—what a great way to let all new employees know what they are supposed to do right from the start.

5. To allow the business owner to step away from the business—in other words, have a business that is not solely dependent on the owner

RESOURCE

Piyush Parikh is one of our favorite systems guys! If you need help with this part of your business, contact Piyush!

To create deliberate focused systems, I generally suggest prioritizing the systems to implement in some order. It is easy to get overwhelmed by creating hundreds of systems and processes for a company. Start with the ones that either are closest to the money or may be causing the most amount of pain.

By closest to the money, I mean processes that either directly get you a sale or are related to an expense. You can quickly scan through the income statement to identify these processes. The sales process is an obvious one that is closest to the revenue line item on the income statement.

Processes that cause the most pain would be the areas in the business that you know have gaps that need to be fixed. For instance, you may know that there is a large turnover for your store manager that results in significant time spent on hiring and retraining. In this case, the hiring and training process would be on top of the list to develop. Quite often the processes that cause pain and are closest to the money could be the same, which makes prioritizing easier.

Once you have the prioritized list, follow the steps below to set up a system:

o   Remember that a system is a way of doing things that brings about a result. Start by setting a result/target you want to achieve after implementing the system.

o   Next, document the base process by using flowcharts and descriptive text for the process steps. Use "swim lanes" on the process map to indicate who is responsible for what step in the process.

o   Next, identify the metric you will use to track the result once you implement the system.

o   Implement the system and monitor the metrics for a month or two.

Finally, review the results and update the process until you achieve the target. It is always a good idea to involve all those responsible for the process to provide input about what needs to be updated.

When you are creating and implementing systems, it could help to get input from third-party professionals during the creation and implementation process. Not only can they provide a fresh perspective, but they can often bring in ideas for systems based on their experience from implementing similar systems in other industries.

One of the biggest challenges in documenting procedures and measuring results is time—the owner and employees barely have enough time to keep things moving in the business, so sitting down to create, implement, and measure systems can be a big challenge. Bringing in someone from the outside to work on these systems can significantly speed up the entire process—down from months to weeks to get things in place.

Finally, a good systems professional will ask "dumb" questions about certain practices in the business that business owners and employees may take for granted—some of these may be legacy processes that have always been done that way in the business. Slight modifications to these legacy ways can sometimes provide significant results.

Before bringing in systems professionals, make sure you find out the following:
- Specific examples of systems they have implemented in the recent past with data results

- What systems have they implemented in their own business?

- What process do they have to ensure you get the results for systems implemented?

- How do they audit these systems over time?

- Are they business-oriented in mindset or simply systems-oriented? If all they talk about are systems and some cool new technologies and not about how this ultimately meets the goals of the business owner and business, then move on.

If you are interested in some templates and examples, feel free to email me at parikh@engineeryourbusiness.com; and if you haven't read the book yet, I highly recommend reading *The E-Myth* by Michael Gerber. He talks about systems in more detail and explains why you should build your business as if you are going to franchise it.

If there were two businesses to buy today, which one would you want to buy based on the below?

- ✔ A business that is based off of you, the owner, with not really any written systems and staff who would be lost without you, the owner who never takes a vacation because everything would collapse if you weren't there? A nonexistent set of books and your promise that you make money every year, but you can't really prove it?

✔ A business with a long history of solid profits, no major fluctuations, great staff that love working there, and a good solid set of policies and procedures for everything that the business does—and one where the owner gets to take a month off every year?

I am sure that I would prefer to buy the second business, wouldn't you? So, if that's what you prefer, aren't you pretty confident that is what any rational, reasonable buyer would want as well? So, what does that tell you? You need to create the business as a product, something that will answer all of the buyer's needs (just like buying a toothbrush helps you with your needs of keeping your teeth clean!).

Top 6 Items That Increase the Value of the Business for a Potential Buyer[8]

1. **Show high earnings/net profits.**
   Many business owners try their darnedest to show the lowest amount of profit possible in their business because that lowers their tax burden. However, to a potential buyer, all this shows is low profits! Not so good for a high sales price.

2. **Avoid concentration in a specific market area.**
   Concentration in any one area can be very bad for a potential buyer (also for you!). Imagine that you only have four large clients that you service and one of them goes belly-up! You've just lost 25 percent of your income! Not so good. Concentration can also hurt you when it comes to vendors, staff members, options to handle your outsourcing, and so on. Having all your eggs in one basket makes it very difficult to recover if there is a major issue.

3. **Take vacations.**
   You need to make sure that you are unimportant in the business. This is hard to do in some service industries, where the business is really the owner, but what you really want (even in those businesses) is to make sure that you can take a vacation—a month is a good time, perhaps longer—and that everything is okay, nothing falls apart, no one quits, no clients drop your service, and the vendors are getting paid.

---

8. Please note that these are just a few examples of many that can increase the value of your business for a potential buyer. Each buyer has his or her own preferences, figures, and details to look for. When you are preparing a business for sale, you really need to determine what is the best fit for what you are looking for and then try to find a buyer that matches up to your best-fit wants and needs.

These all lead to the point that you have systems in your business that your people can rely on to handle the business while you are gone.[9]

4. **Have job descriptions.**
   Each position in your business should be replaceable by the lowest common denominator. What you do *not* want is to have to rely on the people and their specific sets of skills and excellence to run your business. What happens when your head manager leaves or gets sick? Do you have the manager's job description and duties written out? Can you find a replacement and be back up and running in a week or less? If not, a potential buyer is going to be very worried about who else leaves when you do.

5. **Have systems for everything in the business, including the job you do.**
   Besides having job descriptions, do you know how the phone systems work? Who to contact when the Internet goes down? What to do when a vendor doesn't show up? Do you know where to make bank deposits or how to batch the credit card terminal? You should have written instruction manuals for *everything* in your business. This is *much* easier to do when you are first starting than after you've been in business for while; and then, as you modify your systems, you can just modify the manuals. Also, it makes your business extremely attractive to a potential buyer because *anything* they would or could need to know is all written out.[10, 11]

6. **Have an increasing trend line of sales.**
   For at least two years before your sale, make sure that you are getting your gross sales figures up in any way you can. You may be telling your prospective buyer that you could have raised sales by doing X, but you didn't because Y (I don't like managing extra people; I didn't want to work more hours, etc.). If you want the highest possible sales price, show the highest possible sales!

What this really comes down to saying is: You need to think about the "product" of your business that you are going to sell years from now, so that you can start

---

9. PS: It's amazing to realize that you *can* leave and the world doesn't end. For some people that is nice, for others it can be depressing—so make sure you are mentally ready for either outcome and that you have another hobby to work on so you don't go nuts worrying!

10. You see this in franchise purchases all the time! This is why so many people opt for franchises. They don't need to know the business at all; they have a manual to tell them everything they could need to know.

11. Think for a moment on this quote from *The E-Myth Revisited*: "Systems run the business, and people run the systems." Without systems in place, a business can falter, be crippled, or—even worse—go under. Systems are one of the first things that you want to get into place in any business.

your business the right way from the beginning! I know that this can be a *lot* of work; however, please know from my experience of doing it the hard way (getting all these items in place *after* I began) that doing it in the first place will be so much easier and a lot less time consuming. A few solid days of thinking, planning, and then on to creating will save you *months* of headaches and worry down the road (trust me).

One Last Time: Are You Ready to Jump Down the Rabbit Hole?

All of these arenas must/should be considered *before* you start your business, or as soon after starting as possible, so that you have the best starting foot forward to grow into your dream business! Are you sure you are ready? If yes, keep reading!

CHAPTER 7

Legal Types / Legal Issues

Now that you are ready to start down the path of creating or buying your business, you will need to consider some of the legal aspects of your new adventure. Please note that *tax* issues and *tax* types will come up later in this book; legal and tax issues are different! Also note, I am *not* an attorney, and this should *not* be construed as legal advice—please seek the help of a competent professional in this area. The below is my understanding of this area from my perspective as a CPA.

Entity Types

You'll have different sides of your business to consider as you get started. You'll have the legal side, the tax side, its cash flow, banking issues, real estate aspects such as the purchase or lease of your shop/office, and so forth.

The first step in starting a business, of course, is deciding what type of business you're going to start (see Chapter 4). Once you've decided on your business type, you'll need to tackle basic legal issues before anything else.

Legal entity types vary by state, but generally, a business can choose from these different types: a limited liability company (commonly referred to as LLC), a partnership, a corporation, or nothing at all, which would make your firm a sole proprietorship. All of the first three—LLC, partnership, and corporation—offer that important personal/business world separation. Sole proprietorship does not.

This chapter goes over each of these types of entities from their legal perspectives—pros and cons—to help you determine which may be best for what you need.

Sole Proprietorships

An individual who goes into business without setting up a particular entity for it is, by default, running a sole proprietorship. If you've started a multi-level marketing (MLM) firm, for example, but you haven't formally set up your LLC, partnership, or Inc. (corporation), you're a sole proprietor. One of the biggest concerns with having a sole proprietorship is that you have absolutely no legal protection whatsoever. While the business's assets are your assets, its liabilities are yours as well. As an example, let's say that your MLM is vitamin sales. Should you sell the vitamins to someone who chokes on one and decides to hold your firm responsible, she or he could come after you, your IRA, your house, and your personal money. There would be no restrictions or boundaries on what of yours could be theirs if you lose in court.

The only company that should be a sole proprietorship is one that is liability free, and since there is no such company, I always advise clients to set up their LLC, partnership, or Inc. before they start doing business. There are those who think that if they set up a "doing business as" (DBA) name, they have a business. That is not the case. That is a marketing name, not a business entity, unless it is followed by a PC, an LLC, or an Inc. to indicate you've set up a business entity.

If you're a sole proprietor reading this and you haven't had a legal issue yet, that doesn't mean you won't. Liabilities for something from your past business dealings can follow your company for quite some time. My recommendation is to set up an LLC *now*. In most states, an LLC is the most flexible, the least costly, and the easiest to run—and doesn't require more than one person to exist.

LLCs

In Arizona, where I am based, the LLC is the most flexible and the cheapest of all entities to set up and maintain. One of the benefits of an LLC is that you can have as many members and managers as you wish. You can change those people and positions with great ease. Nor does an LLC require minutes or annual reports. The LLC setup fee is $400–600, and the entity is perpetual. Many people set up several LLCs and put them on the shelf until they need to separate liability between businesses or people. Although LLCs have been around for about twenty years, in Arizona there has been a recent spurt of interest.

An LLC manager, in Arizona, is someone selected to manage the business. An LLC member actually owns the business. Many business owners set themselves up as single owner as both member and manager. Let's take a look at how Joe, manager and member (sole owner) of Joe's Auto Body Shop, would protect himself from personal liability by making a smart entity choice.

In this scenario, Joe, driving customer Ron's car out of the shop, backs over customer Sue's dog. Sue is very upset and now says she'll sue Joe. If Sue were to win her case, she might possibly win Joe's membership interest in Joe's Auto Body LLC. She would not, however, negate his management interest. As manager he would still control the assets, including the bank accounts. He would retain the right to move all the assets into another one of the LLCs he has created to use at just the right moment. Should he make this financial change before Sue completes her lawsuit, there would be no Joe's Auto Body money for her to win.

You see, then, the wonderful flexibility you can have by creating an LLC. You can move assets lickety-split—if you wanted to buy and sell a business, you could keep all the assets, sell a portion of the business or just one line of the business, or sell the whole thing. You might sell or keep the client list as well. This sale might include the goodwill of the business. Say, for instance, before Joe decided to sell his auto body business, his neighbor Sally had been a long-time loyal customer of the body shop; in fact, she used to bring cookies over to the mechanics, she liked them so much. Chances are good that even if Joe were to sell, the new owner would keep Sally as a loyal customer—and all her friends to whom she had been recommending Joe's work.

Partnerships

A partnership, in contrast to an LLC, is complicated, though not as complicated as a corporation. Partnerships include more than one person and, while extremely flexible for tax purposes, are legally complicated. A partnership is flexible, though not as flexible as the LLC.

Partnership tax law was derived from shipping law way back when the newly formed, post–Revolutionary War United States began extensive trade with the British. Then, from partnership tax law, the LLC evolved.

One of the more positive aspects of a partnership is that you can make changes to the entity as long as all the partners agree. If, for example, Mary and Sue decide to open up a doctor's office together, with Mary putting in all the money and Sue doing all the work, it would be permissible for them to be 50/50 owners. Or, as long as they both agree, they could divide equally the monetary investment as well as the office work and still divide the profits equally. Whichever way these partners choose to do business together in a partnership would be honored in court and in tax law. There is no limit on the number of partners the law allows in a partnership.

Taking again the example of doctors, let's say three hundred doctors work at the same large hospital and wish to share their earnings. They could form a partnership that says that any income any of the three hundred partners earned would go into one big "profit pot" from which each member would be paid equally. All it takes is the agreement of all involved. Not that this is easy, however. It can actually be a nightmare. One of the documents you see frequently, and one I insist that my partner clients create at the start of their business, is an operating agreement, sometimes known as a partnership agreement. The best way to think of this document is as a prenuptial agreement for business partners. It is written with all the worst-case scenarios in mind. Decisions to be written into an operating agreement include the following:

- ✔ If one partner dies, who gets the deceased's interest in the business: the spouse, the children, the other partners, or the business?

- ✔ What price/value would be put on the deceased partner's portion of the firm? How would that be calculated?

- ✔ If partners' votes on a particular business issue result in a tie, how would you break the tie to come to a business decision?

- ✔ If the business is sold, will you be selling assets or the entity itself?

Many major international service firms are set up as partnerships, as are numerous accounting and legal firms. The designation LLP (limited liability partnership) or LP (limited partnership) generally indicates that the company is organized as a partnership.

Let's revisit Mary and Sue and their new partnership. In this scenario Mary is single; Sue is married to Ron, whom Mary dislikes. Sue then passes away. Hopefully Mary and Sue have an operating agreement in place that speaks to this scenario. If not, does Mary get Sue's 50 percent of the business, and at what price? Or might Ron now become Mary's partner—or might Ron and Sue's eighteen-year-old son, Steve, inherit half the business? What if Sue had initially committed herself to doing half the work for the company but had been slacking off for the last twelve months, with Mary keeping the profits rolling in the past year—would that alter Sue's business worth (i.e., might her portion of the business drop below 50 percent)? Imagine the wrangling these questions might cause in a family already suffering from grief and the negative impact it might well have on the business, if no operating agreement has already addressed these issues in writing.

I am convinced that the best partnerships are those of two or more entities (businesses) as opposed to two or more individuals. What I've seen happen so often when individuals partner is that some emotional, financial, or work issue comes up that so frustrates one or more partner that he, she, or they don't want to be in partnership anymore. This can have, and has had, dire consequences for the business—when there is no operating agreement in place or when the divisive issue is not addressed in the operating agreement.

Business partnerships, just like personal partnerships, go through a honeymoon stage. They're in love with the concept of doing business together. The partners' rose-colored glasses are firmly in place. "Oh, it is okay that you didn't put in the $10,000 you promised," Partner Mary says to Partner Sue. "Now I'll just put in my $10,000 until you get the time or the money to do so yourself." From experience, I can promise that this or similar situations will result in a serious squabble between Mary and Sue if all is not remedied within about a month.

Legally, partnerships are quite flexible, much like LLCs. A partnership is a little more costly than an LLC and has a few more regulations to worry about. You'll need to keep minutes of meetings; and, while you are not legally required to do so, starting with a sound operating agreement to which all partners agree may make or break your partnership success. Partnerships can take many forms, a few of which are listed below. Because partnerships are so flexible, many iterations of the below are possible.

GP – General Partnership

In a general partnership (GP), partners share equal rights and responsibilities in connection with management of the business, and any individual partner can bind the entire group to a legal obligation. Each individual partner assumes full responsibility for all of the business's debts and obligations.

LP – Limited Partnership

A limited partnership (LP) allows each partner to restrict his or her personal liability to the amount of his or her business investment. Not every partner can benefit from this limitation; at least one participant must accept general partnership status, exposing him- or herself to full personal liability for the business's debts and obligations. The general partner retains the right to control the business, while any limited partner does not participate in management decisions. Both general and limited partners benefit from business profits.

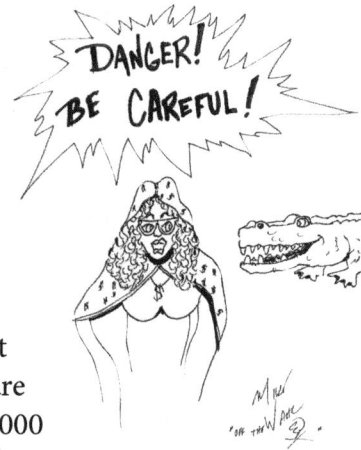

LLP – Limited Liability Partnership

Limited liability partnerships (LLP) offer some personal liability protection to the participants. Individual partners in an LLP are not personally responsible for the wrongful acts of other partners or for the debts or obligations of the business.

FLP – Family Limited Partnership

A family limited partnership (FLP) is a legal partnership agreement between members of a family for the management and control of property for the benefit of family members. It is a limited partnership in which family members control the entity for purposes of the special valuation rules under the gift and estate tax law. Although one or more non-tax business purposes are required, this entity is frequently used to own family assets.

Corporations

For purposes of brevity, I'm going to refer throughout the book to a corporation as an "Inc." or a "corp" (short for incorporated). Or, when explaining the difference between corporation types, I might say "S corp" or "C corp," which we'll get to later.

An Inc. is the oldest of all U.S. entity types. It has the most case law written about it, and it's the strictest business type. The government can dictate to an Inc. owner, for example, whether she or he can even have an Inc., depending on where she is, and how many shareholders he's allowed to have (which differs depending on his choice of a C or S corp). She might even be told that there are limits on types of shareholders. Some Inc. entities can't have foreign shareholders, for instance. Generally, international companies and very large firms are Inc. entities. We'll discuss this more when we cover taxes.

If your company is formed as an Inc., you'll be required to prepare annual reports and to take and keep minutes for any kind of major business decision, from simple things like opening a bank account to buying a large piece of business equipment. An Inc. requires much documentation and can be formed in states other than the one in which you reside or even do your day-to-day business. For instance, a lot of businesses are formed in Delaware or Nevada, where an Inc. is assured more privacy. The disadvantage of choosing these out-of-state arrangements is, generally, higher taxes. The IRS tends to offset the protection with rates that can be double or triple the norm of forming the Inc. in your own state.

Before you decide that an Inc. is much too restrictive for you, look at the bright side. So much case law has been written about Inc. entities that were you to ever have someone try to reach into your own pocket in court because of something that happened with regard to your business, you can be confident that the issue has been addressed in some court somewhere in the United States, and you'll have the guidance and the precedent you need to protect yourself. Additionally, as you'll see when we get to the tax chapter, many deductions are available for an Inc. that cannot be taken by a partnership, an LLC, or a sole proprietorship.

The type of business you're starting will be a big determinant of whether an Inc. is your best business entity. How much liability you'll have, how much money you'll spend and earn, and how large your company will be are primary factors in this entity decision.

Here are some of the pros and cons of each entity type, recapped:

Type	Pros	Cons
Sole Proprietorships	Nothing to set up, very easy—you just start!	No legal protection at all
LLCs	Flexibility of the entity Cheap and easy to form on your own*	Not a lot of case law on these entities yet—they are too new
Partnerships	Very flexible Great for multiple people	Need to make sure you have all the right legal documents in place for all partner agreements
Corporations	Most court cases, lots of history and precedence	Expensive to maintain Must have books and records, and many fail to keep them properly Expensive to form
*Although as I've mentioned, I don't recommend doing it on your own—always seek professional help to get it done right the first time!		

Figure 2: Basic Pros and Cons of Each Entity Type

As you can see, there are many different legal forms of entities, and each one can be used—and is best used—for different purposes. Please note that this decision, while very important, is rarely your terminal decision. Businesses can be re-created, re-built, re-formed, and even, in some cases, changed completely. It is best, if at all possible, that you pick your entity type correctly the first time, but never feel that you are stuck!

Partners, Shareholders, and Owners

Many types of people are involved in your business: clients, employees, vendors, consultants, and even other owners in your business. This section talks about the various ways in which you may have other owners in your business.

The name used for each type of owner in a business can change depending on the type of entity, but under any name, an owner is an owner. Owners may be called partners (in a partnership), shareholders (in a corporation/Inc.), or spouses (in a sole proprietorship).

Let's review the differences.

Partners in a Partnership

Partners in a partnership have the powers granted to them as a part of their operating agreement or as a part of their ownership in the partnership. Typically each partner has the same level of ownership as other partners, but this is extremely flexible. You can have multiple types of partners, a few of which are listed below.

Silent Partners

The silent partners are often the partners who contribute money, but really do nothing else in the business. Typically they have no votes or authority over business decisions and are only partners in that they receive a portion of the business profits or losses.

Managing Partners

Managing partners do what the title reflects; typically they manage the business and lead the decisions for the business and the direction the business is headed.

Managing partners often will earn their money in both or either of two ways: (1) as a percentage of the profit and or loss; and/or (2) as guaranteed payments—similar to a salary for the work that they do in managing the business.

Passive or Active Partners

Any type of partner can be passive or active. This category speaks more toward how the partner is taxed, so we will go over this more in the taxes section of this book.

General Partners

General partners are the partners that take on the responsibility and liability of the company. For any decisions the company makes or issues it encounters, these are the partners responsible for the outcomes.

Limited Partners

Limited partners are very similar to what the name describes. Typically, they do not engage in making management decisions.

Shareholders in a Corporation/Inc.

There are two types of shareholders in a corporation, voting and nonvoting. Usually, voting shareholders hold a stock type called *preferred* (this can change if you are an S-Corporation, as we will see later). Nonvoting stock is typically *common* stock.

Spouses in a Sole Proprietorship

When going into business, don't fail to recognize that your spouse, children, and other family members may have a deep interest in your business—and not only for your success. For example, in Arizona (because we are a community property state), unless you have a specific document describing otherwise (like a prenuptial agreement), anything you create is 50 percent owned by your spouse!

It is important that you are aware of how your state treats your small business and that you appropriately structure it to your needs and best fit.

LLC Owners?

The reason I use a question mark after LLC owners is because, on their own, LLC owners are called either members or managers. But, typically, once the LLC has chosen a taxing structure, the name of the manager/member will change to whatever is most appropriate for that entity type.

In Arizona, for example, a member and a manager play two very different roles in the business.

Member

The member is the owner of the actual business. This person (or persons) is the controlling entity of the business and can close the business, sell the business, merge the business, or anything else she or he so desires. This member is similar to the person who owns the stock of the company.

Manager

The manager of the business is the one who manages the day-to-day activity. In small companies, the member and the manager are often the same person, but not always. The manager could be likened to the manager of the store for the person who owns the store.

The idea of manager and member is a great way to introduce the schizophrenic idea that if you own your own business you wear many hats. You get to play the owner, then the manager, and then the employee (remember our discussion of entrepreneur vs. manager vs. technician). This is an idea that I think is very important for business owners to get into their minds early, as sometimes you need to make tough decisions as an owner—that the business isn't working, that it is time to sell your baby (the business) to someone else, and so on—that the technician or day-to-day operations manager in you will not want to do. And this is a part of the reason why it is so important that you work *on* the business sometimes (as the owner, the entrepreneur, the visionary) and not always *in* your business (as the manager/technician).

Documents That You Need to Have

There are a few very important documents that, as a business owner, you must have in place *before* you start any business. This section explains what each document is, how it pertains to your business, and why I believe each one is so important.

Operating Agreements

Whether you are a partnership, or a sole proprietorship, or really any other type of entity, an operating agreement **is the single most important document you will create for your business**.

Why Is an Operating Agreement the Most Important Legal Document for a Business?

The operating agreement is your map for how you will deal with issues down the road. Without this document, especially if you have partners, it is as if you are getting married without ever knowing your bride (or groom) or the bad habits she (or he) may have. An operating agreement describes exactly how your business will be run, who gets to make decisions, who can open bank accounts, who can sign contracts, and how the business will be broken up when it is time to dissolve it. A good operating agreement will be approximately fifty pages and should be reviewed and approved by the lawyer of every person who is expected to sign it.

What Should an Operating Agreement Include?

The following is a list of the areas that you will want your operating agreement to cover at a *minimum*. Many more considerations will apply to your industry, you and your partners, and so on.

- ✔ Ownership:
    - ○ What are the ownership splits?
    - ○ Is there first right of refusal on the purchase of shares if someone dies or wants to sell?
    - ○ What happens if someone dies? Does that person's spouse get the shares of stock? What if the other partners do not like the spouse?
    - ○ Are there rules about to whom shares can be sold?
    - ○ Are there legal or industry restrictions on who can own stock?
    - ○ Who has voting powers?
- ✔ Management:
    - ○ Who has what responsibility?
    - ○ Who can open bank accounts? Sign contracts? Buy major equipment?
    - ○ Who can hire or fire?
    - ○ What are the rules for a manager?
    - ○ When you do decide you need a new manager?
    - ○ Will a partner be the manager, or will you hire outside the partners/members?
- ✔ Tax liabilities:
    - ○ Who is responsible for preparing the tax returns?
    - ○ If there are penalties, how will those be handled?
    - ○ If the business has to pay tax, where will that money come from?
    - ○ Is it the job of the partnership to lower taxable income? At what cost?
- ✔ Profits/loss/capital:
    - ○ What is the split of the profits/loss/capital? Who gets what and in what percentages?

o   Note that in a partnership, partners can change the allocation of these three categories any way they desire, and this can change from year to year. One year a loss can be allocated to one partner, then the next year to a different partner. Capital typically only matters either when there is a capital call (more $ must be contributed to the business to cover some expense or project or asset) or at the point of the sale of the business or of that partner's share of the business.

o   Here is an example of one of the two partners in a potential partnership; see how there are options to be had:

	Profits	Loss	Capital
Option 1	50	50	50
Option 2	30	50	100
Option 3 (Etc.)	25	25	100

See how, in Option 2, if the company sells, this partner gets all of the profit from the sale of the business? Normally this means that this partner put up all the money to start the business in the first place.

✔ Compensation:
   o   For staff?
   o   For owners?
   o   Raises? Demotions?
   o   Part-time? Full time?
   o   Benefits?

✔ Sales:
   o   Who is responsible for sales?

   o   Are goals set for sales? Minimum gross sales needed to keep the business open?

✔ Budget:
   o   Is there a budget?

   o   There are multiple types of budgets—cash flow budgets, profit and loss budgets, and balance sheet budgets. Which types are you looking at?

   o   What is acceptable over and under on a budget?

✔ Spending during operation:
   o   How much can be spent on categories XYZ?

- What types of expenses are agreed upon by all members/shareholders? Is everyone willing to have the company pay for the cars and meals and entertainment for all of the members/shareholders? How about
  — Health insurance?
  — Medical costs?
  — Day care?
  — Gym memberships?

✔ Bookkeeping:
- Who will handle the books? Will you do it internally? Or hire an external firm?
- If you hire an external firm, to whom will this firm report?

✔ Purpose(s) of the business:
- What is the purpose? Is there more than one?
- Can the business change its purpose(s)?
- If the business changes it purpose(s), can partners leave or be added at that time?

As you can see, you and your other owner(s) have many issues to discuss and agree to before you even begin your business. Some of these questions will be very difficult to answer, because you won't be sure what you'll want to do until a situation happens; but I can tell you from experience that if you can agree to your ground rules ahead of time, you will save yourself many fights down the road!

I have to tell you a brief story about one of the partnerships-to-be that I saw break up at my very desk. Two business partners came in to set up a restaurant. One of the owners was the financial backer and the other was the head chef. We had begun discussing who was going to do what in the business (the chef was to handle the operations and the money partner was to handle the bank accounts). The money partner then asked me what types of things they should consider as write-offs and deductions in their joint business. I spoke about cars, cell phones, some meals and entertainment—all of which I thought were pretty basic.

Well, after about ten minutes, the fighting began. The chef said that if the business could pay for his car, then it should also cover his insurance, the gasoline, the repairs and maintenance, and car washes. The money partner said that wasn't what he was thinking; rather, he thought that the business would reimburse the chef for the number of miles he drove for the business

and that the chef would have to track his miles. Can you see the blooming of the argument? The two partners had discussed in general what they wanted to do but not the details. What were they missing? They had *no* operating agreement! How could they have missed this most important document?

I felt rather upset at having brought this to their attention and starting a fight. After the meeting was over, the two partners decided to go home and truly think about how each saw the business. Then they would get together again later to discuss it before they started anything. About three weeks later, I heard back from the money partner, who told me that the chef wasn't really ready for a business and the sacrifices that a business owner must make to get started. The chef was ready to get a salary and his car covered, while the money partner wasn't going to see any return or profit for four or five years. They jointly decided to call it off.

I am now happy, looking back on it, that I helped bring to light these points they had not yet discussed. Imagine them being two or three years into a business, now hating each other for what they both perceived as wrongdoings on the other partner's part when it was all just miscommunication!

This is why I believe it is *so* important to have the operating agreement *first*. It is a document that lays out how the business will be run, as well as the understanding by each owner of the roles that she or he needs to know within the business. This is the document that controls the actions of each owner and the business itself as a company.

Should I Have an Operating Agreement If I Am a Single-Member LLC?

I absolutely believe that you should have a basic operating agreement if you are a single-member LLC. Not only does it help you show that your business is a business and not just a hobby, but also it gives you a logical place to go back to if major issues come up in your business. Instead of thinking in the moment, you can refer to your operating agreement for what you thought you should do (when you were thinking logically).

Process Map for Your Business

The process map is the second most important document. This document describes what you do and how you do it, including the details of exactly when, with what tools or checklists, and so on. Basically, anyone should be able to pick up this document and replicate almost anything in your business by following the instructions. The idea for the process map really came from Ray Croc, the creator of the McDonald's that we all know today. He broke down everything into the smallest jobs—and jobs that can be done by any person with the lowest common denominator of understanding. The process map for McDonald's is what has allowed it to become the massive franchise business it is now. You need to be able to sell your business as a product, right? The easiest way for you to do that is to have an effective operator manual.

What Should Your Process Map Include?

You should cover the various functions in your business. Below are just a few ideas. In no way does this list include everything; think of it more as a starting point.

- ✔ Operations
- ✔ Production
- ✔ Finance
- ✔ Customer service
- ✔ Management
- ✔ Human resources
- ✔ Shipping

As you can imagine, this list can go on and on. Think about what happens in a typical day in your business. These are the areas and functions you are going to want on your map.

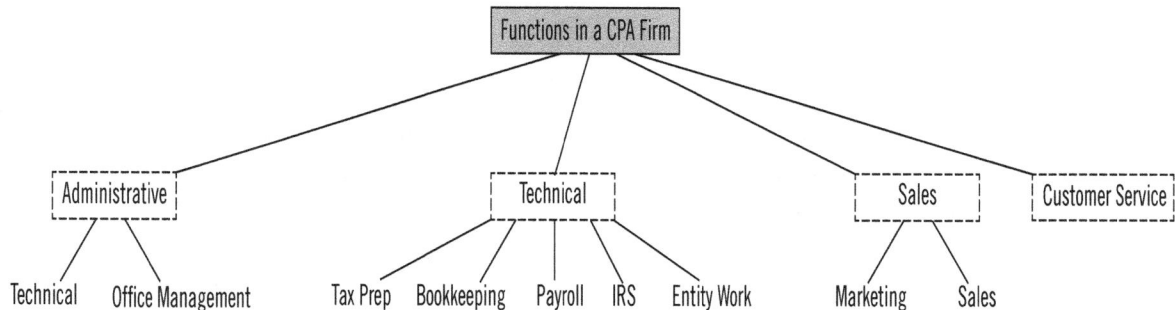

Figure 3: What Are the Major Functions in a Business?

What Do the Functions Do?

Explain in detail what each function does. So, for example, production: *How* is your widget produced? *How* do you consult with a client? Is there a list of questions you ask to come to your conclusions?

Note: If you don't have a basic idea of what your business will look like when it's fully cooked and ready to go, you can get off track pretty easily. Having this diagram will at least help keep your mind and path planning on track!

> *If you don't plan,*
> *you plan to fail!*

How Do the Functions Interact?

Next you should map out how your business functions interact. So, for example, once the product is created, it is then tested; and once tested, then it goes to shipping to be sent to the client. So, *how* does the product go to testing? *How* do the testers know that the product is then ready to ship? *How* does it get to shipping?

Note that some businesses may need to have more highly paid people—for example, in a financial planner's office. The secretary can follow a list of job tasks; however, the financial planner would need a lot of training and education, and not all of the planner's decisions are going to be able to follow a process map. (Or they may, but that would make for one *really large* flowchart for the decision tree, right?)

In Figure 4, you can see an example of our workflow, simplified, so you can get a basic understanding of what your process map may look like.

Can you tell yet that most of your process map is about "*How* do we do things here?" This map is one of the most important things you can have in your business. If you know how things are done, you can explain them to other people.

A List of the "Tools" You May Need to Find or Create to Do Each Function, Job, or Task

- ✔ Do you need any checklists?
- ✔ What about physical tools?
- ✔ Do you need to rent? Borrow? Buy the tools?
- ✔ A list of the people that are needed to complete the various functions
- ✔ Who do you need for these functions?
  - o Production people?
  - o Bookkeepers?
  - o Managers of staff?
  - o HR people?

How Is Our Product/Service Completed?

- ✔ Customer drops off data
  - ○ Admin team asks client basic questions (new children? moved? new address? etc.)
  - ○ Admin team: Scans, updates our tracking sheet, gets to the bookkeeping team by updating tax software
- ✔ Bookkeepers go through the tax documents, answer any questions as needed before data goes to the tax prep team (get data adn make adjusting entries to prepare for tax)
  - ○ Bookeepers, once all answers received from client, pass file to tax prep team by updating tax software
- ✔ Tax prep team begins work on the return
  - ○ Tax prep asks client any final questions
  - ○ Tax team sends return to review
    - — Reviewers either pass file on to CPA for signature or back to preparer with additional questions
  - ○ Once return is done, it goes to final review with CPA
- ✔ Final review with CPA
  - ○ CPA calls/e-mails client with results and to go over return
  - ○ CPA prints return for assembly and gives back to admin team
- ✔ Admin team assembles returns and signs with clients so they can E-file

Figure 4: Process Map of the Tax Return Process

How Detailed Should Your Map Be?

As I mentioned before, the more detailed you can be here, the better off you will be in the long run. So, for example, if you put down "sell to a customer," you are going to have to hire a salesperson who knows how to sell. However, let's say that you put down a list of steps, such as (only the first few are listed here): (1) obtain a list of potential new clients, business owners, from the local Chamber; (2) call at least one hundred potential clients a day; (3) speak with an owner or decision maker, discuss your top five services with each client; and so on. As you can see, there are already holes even here. How do you know what your top five services are? How do you know you are discussing these with a decision maker? You can get *very* detailed with your map, and the more detailed you get, the better it will be, because in the long run you can hire basic cold-caller contractors versus having to hire (and pay) for a much more expensive full-time salesperson.

HR Documents

Each and every business is going to have a different set of business HR (human resources) documents that it will need, but there are a few, in general, that apply to all businesses.

The HR Basics

✔ Payroll forms
✔ Employment contracts
✔ Contractor forms, such as W-9s
✔ Employee handbooks
✔ Various other forms and documents that relate specifically to your business (see below for some options we use in our business)

I always recommend that you speak with a qualified HR professional and an attorney when you first start your business to make sure that you have everything you need to protect you and your employees or contractors!

The following are some other documents that may or may not apply to you.

Confidentiality Statements

A confidentiality statement includes language that restricts an employee or contractor from sharing any information, details, lists, customer registers, trade secrets, or anything else with anyone else. The document typically lists what the remedies and costs will be of sharing any information with anyone.

Non-Competes

A non-compete document typically is set to prevent an individual from performing work in an identical capacity within a certain time limit and distance range of your business. It is often used for key employees or other partners or shareholders so that they do not take your materials and business processes and use them to open up another business in the same model and industry as your business.

Note: Non-competes tend to be very difficult to uphold in court due to the fact that these types of documents can be written to be overly restrictive, to the point where sometimes they are restricting the individual from earning an income in the only field he or she can. *Be careful* to word your document specifically. I highly recommend that you work with a professional on this, and on *any* of these documents, to ensure that they will withstand court, mediation, or other remedies in your favor.

Buy/Sell Agreements

The buy/sell agreement is the fourth most important document in your arsenal. Often you will not be able to prepare this until your business has been around, operating profitably, for at least five or six years. But you should begin to think about how you would like this to happen when you are ready to sell. A buy/sell agreement is typically an agreement with another business owner in your same industry—or your staff members, or a trusted key employee—that talks about what should happen when or if you are forced to sell or choose to sell.

For example, let's say you passed away and were married with two children. Not only would your spouse be dealing with your passing—but also now with running a business? Perhaps in a field that your spouse knows nothing about? Doesn't sound like too great of an idea, right? Well, a buy/sell agreement with your friend Bob, who does what you do—let's say you were an auto mechanic—allows Bob to expand his business, at a set price that you two have determined beforehand based on a formula involving gross sales and net profit. Bob, typically, would buy a life insurance policy on you (and you on Bob) so that when you pass, Bob would get the money to pay your spouse for the newly acquired business. Your spouse would have the cash out of the business, and Bob would have an addition to his business (including all of your great owner's manuals, etc.) that could help him expand and grow even bigger. Everyone is happy!

Now, for a buy/sell to work, you really need to involve some specialty types of insurance, so make sure that you are seeking professional help in preparing for this eventuality!

Generally life insurance is used to fund buy-sell agreements that are triggered by the death of the owner. (Note: Not always is the buy/sell related to the death of an owner. What about incapacitation?) You need to make sure that you involve your spouse in your buy/sell planning so that he or she knows and understands what is happening. You want to make sure that your spouse has consented to such a payout; otherwise, the proceeds will be disputed.

The most common scenario here is when an owner dies, the business collects the life insurance proceeds and pays those monies out to the owner's estate in return for the deceased owner's share of stock.

Make sure that you:

✔ Consider both your personal marital situation and what issues may be involved with any plans you have for your business.

✔ Discuss this with the other owners of your business, or the people who are going to be taking it over. Consider their marital status, as you may end up with a spouse owning the business that you didn't want!

✔ Consult your advisors to determine how to best handle the spousal issues (consent, waiver, agreements, etc.) relative to the buy/sell agreement.

✔ Work with your insurance and financial advisors to assure that you have the proper funding in place, as well as the appropriate ownership and beneficiary designations.

✔ Remember that marital relations can change just as business relations can change. Stay on top of these situations and make changes as needed.

Licensing and Bonding

As you begin your business, it's vital that you learn of, and secure, all appropriate licenses to operate in your chosen industry and locale. It's not something I can provide much information on, as licensing is municipal-, county-, or state-run and varies from one area to the other.

Here in Arizona, for example, business owners who plan on hiring employees must have a withholding license. Those selling a product must have a sales license. And no matter where you are in the United States, your local municipality is going to require that you have a business license—even if you operate out of your home. Contractors must establish themselves with the local contracting board.

I recommend that you contact a local SCORE office or the revenue offices of your city or state; any of these will be able to tell you what licenses you need and where and how to get them. Remember that, depending on where you are

RESOURCE

You can find links to all of the state tax authorities here (a great place to learn about your state's requirements for licensing, sales taxes, income taxes, etc.): www.taxadmin.org/fta/link/default.php.

and what size city you're doing business in, you might have to comply with city, county, and/or state sales taxes. The bigger the city, the more likelihood that there will be a city tax if you're selling items, rather than services, to the public.

Bonding is an important tool you need to understand. It's somewhat similar to licensing your business, and it's not for every industry. Bonding is an offering that will help you stand out against your competitors, in many cases, and something you'll want to offer your customers if you're in a profession or trade that, of necessity, requires you or your staff to have unlimited or unsupervised access to the client's home, business, or informational products in order to complete your contracted service for them. What bonding does is simply guarantee to customers that they're protected should you or your staff be less than ethical in the care of and access to their real or intellectual property.

Some industries in some states are required to be bonded. Even if it's not a requirement, being able to advertise that your company is bonded gives you a leg up on the competition.

As I mentioned, bonding requirements vary by state. In Arizona, for example, cleaning crews don't have to be bonded, nor do plumbers or handy men.

You might think of bonding as another level of insurance for your business. The bonding agency does background and credit checks on you and/or the employees you are having bonded and, assuming those checks don't turn up anything negative, provides the bonding that serves to say, "We believe this person is trustworthy." Consumers who have unresolved problems with your work or work product won't generally turn first to the bonding company for financial recourse, however. If they haven't resolved the issue with you, they generally approach your insurance company; and if that doesn't resolve the issue to their satisfaction, a lawsuit is their next step. It isn't unless and until a lawsuit is not decided in their favor that your unsatisfied customers would seek compensation of your bonding company.

The unfortunate part of having your business bonded is that you fork over the cost of the bonding and you never see it again. That money just sits in trust in case anything untoward happens that requires your customer to be reimbursed. While bonding amounts vary, in Arizona the minimum bond is $500. If your state does not require your type of business to be bonded, and you and your staff are placed in situations where you or they have unsupervised access to the goods or intellectual property of your customers, you might wonder if you want to give up that $500 or more. My suggestion is that you do. Bonding is a marketing tool. A consumer who sees that you are bonded—especially when your competitors are not—is much more likely to consider you trustworthy and hire you. One moderately priced job from a customer and your bond may well be paid for, and you still have that marketing tool in place to lure others to buy your services.

Tax Issues

Entity Types for Tax Purposes

First, a note on tax basics: you'll hear me refer to "full-out" entities throughout the book. A full-out entity is one whose legal structure is the same as its tax structure. The best example of this is an LLC, which can be taxed as a sole proprietorship, a partnership, a C corp, or an S corp. (I'll explain the difference between these last two at a later time.) In fact, an LLC can change its tax structure every five years to any type of taxing entity and not have to change its legal entity from LLC to do so.

Sole Proprietorships

The most basic taxing structure is the sole proprietorship (which I'll be referring to as "sole prop"). If you are a sole prop (a sole prop that's also taxed as a sole prop) or an LLC taxed as a sole prop, your business profit gets charged a self-employment tax and income tax at the tax bracket of your personal income. Most of the time a sole prop will be taxed on IRS form Schedule C, which means the income or loss claimed on Schedule C will flow through and be added to or deducted from your other income on your personal income tax return. Some of this could change, however. On October 30, 2009, the IRS publicly stated that it is considering disallowing Schedule C losses to offset other personal income. More than 40 percent of small Schedule C businesses are not what the IRS considers "real" businesses, and the IRS feels that people are using these business claims to lower their tax bills without really having lost money from their small businesses. Yet, as usual, here we are in 2014 and the IRS still hasn't made a decision on this. Until they lay down the law for sure, I think small businesses that are really trying to make a profit at it should be fine.

Let's assume that John has a W-2 job working for Macy's. He also teaches guitar lessons on the side. If he turns a profit on his guitar business, he's going to pay approximately 20 percent of his profits as self-employment tax, as well as income tax on the guitar lesson earnings at his personal income tax bracket—anywhere from 0 to 38 percent, depending on how much he earns. If, however, his guitar business loses him money—for example, his guitar students paid him $1,000 that year, but he spent $2,500 on business expenses, leaving him with a deficit of $1,500—that $1,500 is deducted from the income of his W-2 job. Additionally, he'll have no self-employment tax to pay because he has no business profit to claim.

Self-employment tax can be hefty and many new small business owners are ill prepared for the amount or the fact that it needs to be estimated and prepaid quarterly, with a filing of IRS Form 1040ES. It's hefty because it's a combination of what an employer pays for his or her employees' FICA (Medicare and social security taxes) and what the employee pays for all these. Currently, the rate is about 20 percent of profit. So, unlike being an employee, as a self-employed person, you not only pay up front instead of waiting for the money to come out of your check, but you also pay a great deal more.

See Appendix B or www.irs.gov/pub/irs-pdf/f1040sc.pdf for a copy of Schedule C 2013 from the IRS.

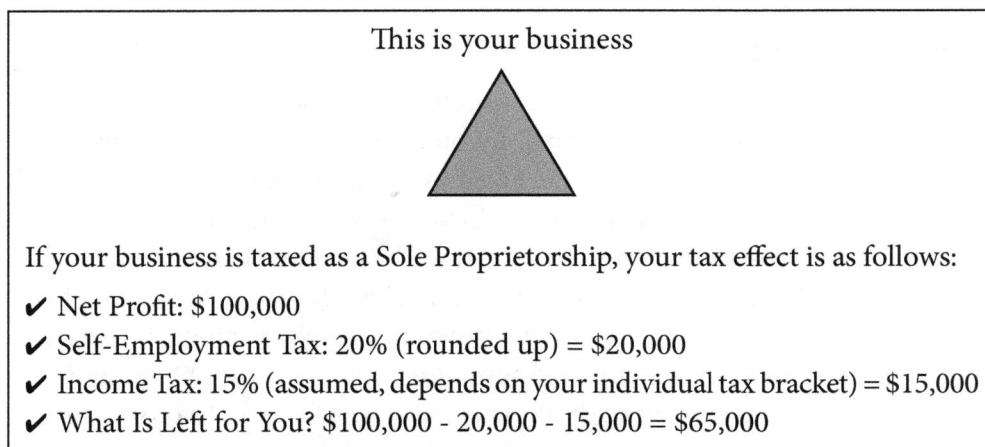

This is your business

If your business is taxed as a Sole Proprietorship, your tax effect is as follows:

✔ Net Profit: $100,000
✔ Self-Employment Tax: 20% (rounded up) = $20,000
✔ Income Tax: 15% (assumed, depends on your individual tax bracket) = $15,000
✔ What Is Left for You? $100,000 - 20,000 - 15,000 = $65,000

Figure 5: Schedule C Taxation – Sole Proprietorship

Partnerships

In partnerships, in contrast to sole props, the entity files a tax return entirely separate from that of the personal tax returns of its partners. Tax returns for partnerships are information returns only. There is no partnership tax at the business level, although each partner's share of the company profit or loss flows through to his or her respective personal account by way of IRS Form K-1.

Let's say, for example, that 50/50 Partnership AB completes its IRS Form 1065, filing notification of $1,000 in profit and $2,000 in expenses and thus a $1,000 loss for the year. The K-1s for partners A and B would claim a $500 business loss on each of their personal tax returns. Because it's a flexible partnership entity, owners A and B can simply agree to split the losses in half whether A and B have each put in half the money, or A put in all the money and B put in all the work, or whatever arrangement they together decided was fair. In fact, they could even decide that in a year with a profit the split is 50/50, but in a year with a loss the split is 90/10, because the partner who put in most of the money wants to be able to get the biggest tax break. As long as they both agree, that's okay. Not all entities are this flexible, but partnerships are.

A partnership tax return has three elements: profit, loss, and capital. How profit and loss are treated with regard to taxes is fairly easy to understand. When you first start a partnership, if you have a loss—and you probably will—the loss will be split up among the partners as agreed to in their operating agreement. These losses are then reported on each partner's IRS Form K-1 to be reported on each individual's personal Form 1040 return. To go back to Mary and Sue's partnership, if their profit and losses are both going to be split 50/50, then each claims half the profit or deducts half the loss. If, however, they've decided that Mary's majority financial contribution entitles her to 90 percent of any loss, while Sue claims 10 percent, then that is how they'll divide it on their K-1s.

Another important consideration, and one that should be addressed in the operating agreement, is how everything gets divided up should the business (i.e., the partnership) be sold. In the example of Mary putting in all the money and Sue never doing so, Mary might feel that she deserves 80 percent of any profit from the sale because her money is what started the business. As long as Sue agrees to take only a 20 percent cut of the profit from the sale, all is fine with the IRS. Partners can change these monetary arrangements as many times as they want, even daily. With most partnerships, the operating agreement spells out the original arrangement, and then the partners meet every six months (or annually or perhaps just every two years) to discuss any need for percentage changes.

Partners can be active or passive (also known as silent). The IRS looks at each individual's participation in a partnership in terms of a certain number of hours. Currently, Uncle Sam considers as active any partner that spends 500 hours in a calendar year on any activity for or within the partnership. Even if the company runs on its own fiscal year, this active/passive figure is determined by calendar year. The code also has a section that talks about active interests and passive interests. If Sue, as primary contributor of the start-up money, doesn't do any work in the partnership, then her K-1 can be considered passive. Being a passive partner has its pros and cons. Pro: Sue would *not* have to pay any of the self-employment income on the K-1 profit that flows through to her. Con: Sue would be able to write off any passive loss only against other passive income streams, such as interest, dividends, or K-1s from any other business in which she was involved.

...the basic questions in a partnership start-up... "Is the partnership making a profit or loss?" and "Do I want to be active or passive?"

When income flows through to a partner from a partnership, for tax purposes it is almost the same as if the partner were a sole proprietor; she or he may or may not have to pay that self-employment tax. If, for example, you are an active partner, any income from that partnership is considered self-employment taxable. So one of your strategies as the owner of a partnership is to try to have at least one active partner (overall, out of the many partners, someone who is putting in 500 hours). All the other partners could be passive partners, with no self-employment tax on their income.

One of the downsides to being a passive partner is that when the business suffers a loss, you can't claim that loss. The loss gets captured until your business shows a profit. Most new businesses show a loss for the first couple of years, of course, so as a passive partner you'd probably have a couple of years when your loss would not be able to offset anything else on your personal income tax. Once the business started showing a profit, however, you'd be able to claim losses to offset the partnership's profit. In contrast, an active partner can take any losses against her or his W-2 income right from the start.

Although it can get complicated, the basic questions in a partnership start-up are "Is the partnership making a profit or loss?" and "Do I want to be active or passive?" If you decide to be passive, your additional question would be "Do I have something else I can offset that passive income against?"

There is a way around this active/passive issue, which starts with giving up the notion of partners as people. Think instead about bringing in other entities as partners—a trust, a C corp, or an S corp, for example. You could make that entity the active partner and all the individuals involved in your business the passive partners. Keeping in mind that an active partner must spend 500 hours involved in the business each year, you make this entity active by putting its employees to work for the necessary 500 hours in your business. As an example, let's say your construction business were to bring in a landscaping company as a partner. The employees of that landscaping firm could work for your construction firm for 500 hours that year, making that landscaping company your company's active partner.

Of course, unforeseen circumstances could alter the reality of your business from what you anticipated. In other words, your business, which you expected to end the year with a profit, could end up with a loss. Let's assume you're a passive partner who unexpectedly has a loss you can't write off. The question that comes up often is can you, after the fact, change from passive to active in order to write off this loss in the year it happens? The answer is that it depends on the timing. I also want to point out that there is the technical way to do this and, in contrast, the way that most of the world works.

If you want to be absolutely technical about it, your beginning decision—in this case, to be passive—runs through the time period until you switch your decision to something else. If on January 1 you decide you're going to start a business and it is going to make a profit that year, but in June you realize that the year is going to end with a loss, you'd be considered a passive partner from January through June, and whatever change you make then would be in effect from July through December. Of course, you'd also have to put in 500 hours on the business at this point. That is the technical way to do it.

What often happens, however—though a CPA would be remiss in advising a client to take this action—is that active/passive partnership status time frames don't get studied by outsiders except during audits or lawsuits. A business owner's or partner's intentions are not on record unless that owner puts them in writing. If a partner were to alter her or his passive or active partnership status prior to year's end and backdate that status, nothing would be on record to show that wasn't the situation from January 1.

Partner A (60%)		Partner B (40%)	
Profit	$60,000	Profit	$40,000
SE Tax	$12,000	SE Tax	$ 8,000
Income Tax (20%)	$12,000	Income Tax (15%)	$ 6,000
Cash Left to Owner	$36,000	Cash Left to Owner	$26,000

Figure 6: Partnership Taxation

Please note that partnerships can take many forms, a few of which are listed below. Because partnerships are so flexible, many iterations of the below are possible (note that you've already read some of this information in the previous legal section). Here we are going to discuss the tax advantages and disadvantages of each.

GP – General Partnership

In a general partnership (GP), partners share equal rights and responsibilities in connection with management of the business, and any individual partner can bind the entire group to a legal obligation. Each individual partner assumes full responsibility for all of the business's debts and obligations.

Although such personal liability is daunting, it comes with a tax advantage: all partners are given additional availability to deduct losses by the amounts of the debts that they are responsible for paying if there is ever an issue. This is extremely helpful in the first few years of a new business when losses, not profits, are typically expected.

LP – Limited Partnership

A limited partnership (LP) allows each partner to restrict his or her personal liability to the amount of his or her business investment. Not every partner can benefit from this limitation; at least one participant must accept general partnership status, exposing him- or herself to full personal liability for the business's debts and obligations. The general partner retains the right to control the business, while the limited partner or partners do not participate in management decisions. Both general and limited partners benefit from business profits. A partner who is a limited partner will not have the additional ability to deduct losses as a general partner would. This may limit how much a limited partner is able to deduct in years in which there are losses on the tax return.

A limited partnership is similar to an LLP because LLPs (see below) offer some personal liability protection to the participants and because individual partners in an LLP are not personally responsible for the wrongful acts of other partners or for the debts or obligations of the business.

LLP – Limited Liability Partnership

Limited liability partnerships (LLP) offer some personal liability protection to the participants. Individual partners in a limited liability partnership are not personally responsible for the wrongful acts of other partners or for the debts or obligations of the business.

FLP – Family Limited Partnership

A family limited partnership (FLP) is a legal partnership agreement between members of a family for the management and control of property for the benefit of family members. It is a limited partnership in which family members control the entity for purposes of the special valuation rules under the gift and estate tax law; although one or more non-tax business purposes are required, this entity is frequently used to own family assets.

Corporations

On the legal side of your business, you can be a full-out Inc. taxed as an S corp or a C corp, or you can be an LLC taxed as an S corp or a C corp.

S-Corporations

As an S corp, your company still files an information tax return, and any shareholder will receive a K-1 that reflects the company income flowing through to her or his personal income. At the moment, the IRS is not imposing any self-employment tax on an S corp. The only thing the IRS requires of an S corp is that each of the shareholders takes a salary. That salary would then flow through to you (and other shareholders) as income, and as such is subject to both income tax and self-employment tax. If your salary is low, however, any of the remaining company profit once your salary is taken out would be subject to self-employment tax but *not* income tax.

To explain, let's assume your company has made a profit of $100,000. You want to follow one of the two rules of thumb from the IRS that would create a safe-haven situation for you—that is, you will be safe if the IRS takes a look at your compensation from your S corp.

Your first option is the IRS 35/65 rule. This basically states that of your company's profits you may take 35 percent, or $35,000, as salary and the other 65 percent ($65,000) in draw or K-1 (interchangeable IRS expressions about an S corp) without the IRS looking askance at your return. The result, then, is that, of the $100,000 profit, only $35,000 would be subject to self-employment tax.

Your other IRS-approved option would be to claim "reasonable compensation" as your salary figure. Using the same $100,000 profit, and assuming you are an auto mechanic, let's also assume you got sick and had to take a less active part in the repair of your customers' vehicles. You'd have to hire somebody to do the work you temporarily couldn't do. The amount you'd have to pay that

person to replace you is what would be considered reasonable compensation for your salary in your firm. Let's look at two different scenarios for compensating your replacement: $40,000 and $70,000. In the $40,000 salary scenario, of your $100,000 profit you'd pay both self-employment tax and income tax on $40,000, and only $60,000 would be claimed on your K-1, which would thus be subject to income tax alone. That's a better split than using the 50/50 formula. If, however, you discover that $70,000 is the reasonable compensation figure for replacing you—which would mean $70,000 of your $100,000 profit is subject to self-employment tax as well as income tax—you'd be better off with that 50/50 split.

I always encourage my clients to have a story prepared so that, if asked by the IRS, they have reasonable documentation and backup about their chosen path for this or any other business transaction and situation. Mileage records are another example of required record keeping. Business owners complain about keeping these records, but if you want the deduction, you must keep the records to prove the deduction. That's the ball game.

For determining reasonable compensation, I recommend Salary.com. On this site you'll find nearly every job at almost every different level, from entry level to senior executive. You can search by zip code, job title, or job function. I recommend that as part of your decision between 50/50 and reasonable compensation you go to the site each December or January to see what the median salary is for your position. Print this information and include it in your tax backup file. Should you find a very low compensation figure, you're in luck. The lower your salary, the more you save in self-employment tax.

The IRS, in setting up entities and determining how they will be taxed, creates a balanced amount of good and bad news for business owners. Every time you get good business tax news, you also get some bad along with it.

In partnerships, for example, the "bad" is that each active partner must pay self-employment tax in addition to personal income tax. The "good" that goes along with that, however, is that partnerships are flexible. As a business partner, you can manipulate your tax requirements by changing between active and passive, and among profit, loss, and capital.

An S corp protects your K-1 income from self-employment taxation, but it is not very flexible about taxation. If we go back to the example of Mary and Sue, when Mary was doing all the work and Sue was putting in all the money, as an S corp they couldn't be 50/50 shareholders. At least one element of what they contribute would have to be identical for a 50/50 division, such as both contributing half of the work, or both half of the money. If, for example, Mary puts in $5,000 to start the business, Sue would need to put in $5,000 as well. The alternative would be for Sue to put in as many working hours for the company as does Mary. This is, however, simplifying what can be rather complicated. In some cases partners have each contributed one half of the investment in the company, but only one of the partners has performed the work. But because the salary structure wasn't within the range of what the IRS required, the IRS removed the S election/S corp filing requirements, thus wiping out the partners' protection from self-employment tax.

That S election filing (currently IRS Form 2553) is required of any Inc. or LLC that wants to file as an S corp. A tricky procedure, the election form must be filed within two months and fifteen days of the day for which the partners want the S election. There are some late-relief elections offered, and they can be found on the IRS website or your tax preparer can help you find and understand them. My best advice is that at the point when you determine you want to be an S corp, file the form right away.

As I mentioned earlier, the terms *K-1* and *draw* can be used interchangeably. That's because you, the shareholder, are allowed to take a portion of your K-1 income out of the company for personal purposes. In fact, each shareholder can have a draw against her or his capital account. In this situation, the S corp is disadvantageous, in that those draws must be in exact percentages of whatever your overall company percentage is. If, for example, Mary is a 50 percent owner of the S corp and decides to take out $10,000 against her draw, Sue must take out a $10,000 draw from her capital account in the same year. If she does not, the company could lose its S election.

In contrast, a partnership is considerably more flexible, allowing partners to withdraw as they see fit, without making demands on what the other partners must do as a result.

Another important point with S corps is that any perks to owners of S corps (and partnerships as well) can be paid for by the company, though they cannot be claimed as deductions on the business tax return. This is in contrast to C corps, which we'll discuss next. The disadvantage is that if the business pays benefits such as the owner's health insurance or life insurance, for example, those items must be separately listed on the K-1s, which means they must be claimed as income on the personal income tax return of the partners or shareholders that received the perks.

Net Profit $100,000

Draw Portion		W-2 Portion	
65% of Profit	$65,000	35% of Profit	$35,000
SE Tax	0%	SE Tax (20%)	$ 7,000
Income Tax (20%)	$13,000	Income Tax (20%)	$ 7,000
Net Cash to Owner	$52,000	Net Cash to Owner	$21,000
Total Net Cash to Owner	$73,000		

Figure 7: S-Corporation Taxation

C-Corporations

Tax advantage is number one on the list of reasons businesses choose to become a C corp. As a C corp, the company can pay for any benefits to its shareholders that it wishes without those shareholders having to claim the benefits as income. The C corp can provide private jets, massages, health or life insurance—just about anything. It's not quite that simple, but we'll hold that thought for later. Most business owners set up a C corp because a primary shareholder has had a major illness, such as cancer, and is either uninsurable or paying a very high premium for health coverage. Paying the insurance and medical expenses as a corporation expense saves the shareholder money, as the payments are now a company deduction.

There are two levels of C corp taxation, however, and here's where its disadvantages come in. In contrast to what I mentioned earlier—that partnerships and S corps are flow-through entities and thus must file IRS information returns—C corps act like separate individuals. As such, a C corp tax return shows company income and expenses, and the company must pay taxes on whatever is left. As a C corp shareholder you would thus have to pay W-2 taxes, which could result in your being double or triple taxed on the same dollar of earnings.

As you think about what type of business entity you want to create, a major part of your decision is the profit you expect to make. Once you pinpoint that figure you can start to look at the entity that will best minimize your taxes.

In the case of a C corp, any profit up to $50,000 is currently taxed at 15 percent. If your individual tax rate is now at 38 percent, and you don't expect your new company to make more than $15,000 profit, that C corp is going to look very attractive as a business entity. It would be far more attractive, for example, than an S corp, which would flow all that income to you to be reported on your personal income tax return at the 38 percent rate.

You must consider your company's profit expectation, your decision to provide benefits such as medical coverage, your designation of which partners are active or passive, the individual tax rate of each partner, the desire and acceptance of responsibilities within the company, and many more factors to decide what type of entity you really want for your business. My recommendation is that you meet with your CPA and your attorney to have them help you determine what is best for you and your situation.

LLCs

LLCs are a special breed of entity. They are much newer than the rest of the entity types (created in the last twenty-five years or so). LLCs are extremely flexible and the top choice for most small or medium businesses. They really have no expenses (no annual reports, no annual meetings, no real requirements), are cheap and easy to form (depending on your state, of course), and already have all their "rules" figured out—they follow the rules for the entity type that they are taxed as. Now, you'll notice that I said "taxed as." LLCs do not have any specific taxation rules for themselves; they are automatically classified depending on how many owners they have (either as a sole prop or a partnership), unless they make a specific election to be taxed as a C or S corp.

Types of Taxes and Fees

Income Taxes

There are multiple levels of income taxes and, depending on which of the taxing entities you are, you may fall into one or more of the categories. The income taxes are broken out below by entity taxing type.

Corporation Ownership Taxes

CORPORATE-LEVEL TAXES

At the corporation level, the business may be taxed in the 15%–39% range of brackets at the federal level. Corporations also pay state taxes, but those will vary with the state, so you will want to check with your tax professional or state government. Corporate-level taxes are based on the ending profit of the business after all the income and deductions have been tallied.

OWNER-LEVEL TAXES

After the taxes have been paid at the corporation level, any remaining funds may be distributed to the owners or kept in the business for future use. If the funds are distributed to the owner, the owner will have to pay a 15% (current rate) dividend tax on the distribution.

If the money is kept in the business, and too much money is accumulated, the business may be subject to an accumulated earnings tax. Unfortunately, when this tax gets applied is somewhat subjective. You, the business owner, will need to prove that you are accumulating funds in the business for a business purpose; otherwise this tax may be applied to your business.

You may also face something called a personal service corporation tax. This tax is applied if your C-Corporation is an entity that, as its principal activity during the year, performs personal services (defined later). The company is a personal service corporation if its employee-owners substantially perform the services and:

- ✔ More than 20% of the corporation's compensation cost for its activities of performing personal services during the testing period is for personal services performed by employee-owners.

- ✔ If the employee-owners own more than 10% of the fair market value of its outstanding stock on the last day of the period.

Personal services include any activity performed in the fields of accounting, actuarial science, architecture, consulting, engineering, health (including veterinary services), law, and the performing arts. In this case, the tax rate is currently a flat 35% no matter how much taxable profit you made.

C-Corporations are also subject to something called the alternative minimum tax. It is more commonly referred to as the AMT. This tax typically applies when there are large differences between types of depreciation allowed and taken, as well as if there are larger dollar amounts of municipal interest income.[12]

Tax Rate Schedule 2012 Form 1120			
If taxable income (line 30, Form 1120) on page 1 is:			
Over—	But Not Over	Tax is	Of the Amount Over
$ —	$50,000	15%	$ —
$50,000	$75,000	$7,500 + 25%	$50,000
$75,000	$100,000	$13,750 + 34%	$75,000
$100,000	$335,000	$22,250 + 39%	$100,000
$335,000	$10,000,000	$113,900 + 34%	$335,000
$10,000,000	$15,000,000	$3,400,000 + 35%	$10,000,000
$15,000,000	$18,333,000	$5,150,000 + 38%	$15,000,000
$18,333,333	—	35%	—

Figure 8: C-Corporation Tax Rate Schedule 2012

Flow-Thru Entities and Individual Taxes

S-Corporations, partnerships, and sole proprietorships are what are known as "flow-thru" entities. These types of entities do not have any taxes at the business level; the taxes due are paid at the individual levels.

Individuals may be taxed, just like C-Corporations, with the AMT. It is very important that you have a tax planning session with your tax professional to determine whether these taxes might apply to you, as they can often add upwards of a 20% additional tax to your current tax bill.

---

12. Always check the IRS website (www.IRS.gov) for the most up-to-date rates for the year and type of filing you are preparing.

Here are the current 2013 individual tax rates for each type of individual filing.

30-Jan-13

**2013 Individual Income Tax Rates, Standard Deductions,
Personal Exemptions, and Filing Thresholds**

If your filing status is Single

Taxable Income		
Over ---	But not over ---	Marginal Rate
$0	$8,925	10%
$8,925	$36,250	15%
$36,250	$87,850	25%
$87,850	$183,250	28%
$183,250	$398,350	33%
$398,350	$400,000	35%
$400,000	and over	39.6%

If your filing status is Married filing jointly

Taxable Income		
Over ---	But not over ---	Marginal Rate
$0	$17,850	10%
$17,850	$72,500	15%
$72,500	$146,400	25%
$146,400	$223,050	28%
$223,050	$398,350	33%
$398,350	$450,000	35%
$450,000	and over	39.6%

If your filing status is Head of Household

Taxable Income		
Over ---	But not over ---	Marginal Rate
$0	$12,750	10%
$12,750	$48,600	15%
$48,600	$125,450	25%
$125,450	$203,150	28%
$203,150	$398,350	33%
$398,350	$425,000	35%
$425,000	and over	39.6%

If your filing status is Married filing separately

Taxable Income		
Over ---	But not over ---	Marginal Rate
$0	$8,925	10%
$8,925	$36,250	15%
$36,250	$73,200	25%
$73,200	$111,525	28%
$111,525	$199,175	33%
$199,175	$225,000	35%
$225,000	and over	39.6%

Standard Deduction

	Standard	Blind/Elderly
Single	$6,100	$1,500
Married filing jointly	$12,200	$1,200
Head of Household	$8,950	$1,500
Married filing separately	$6,100	$1,200

Standard Deduction for Dependents

Greater of $1000 or sum of $350 and individual's earned income

Personal Exemption	$3,900

Threshold for Refundable Child Tax Credit	$3,000

Filing Threshold

	Number of Blind / Elderly Exemptions				
	0	1	2	3	4
Single	10,000	11,500	13,000		
Head of Household	12,850	14,350	15,850		
Married filing jointly	20,000	21,200	22,400	23,600	24,800

Source: Internal Revenue Service, Revenue Procedure 2013-15, downloaded January 30, 2013 from
http://www.irs.gov/irb/2013-05_IRB/ar06.html

Figure 9: Individual Tax Rate Schedule 2013

Payroll Taxes

Payroll taxes come down to two different pieces of the same tax, the employer side and the employee side. If you've ever received a W-2, you know that your employer withholds taxes from your check: federal income tax withholding, state income tax withholding, and a portion of FICA and Medicare. As an employer, you are responsible for paying the other half of the FICA/Medicare as well as FUTA (Federal Unemployment Tax Act) and SUTA (State Unemployment Tax Act) taxes. Often these taxes can be a hefty toll on the business. The best way to think about these payroll taxes is that you've given all your employees at least a 9.65% (current rate) raise over and above their current salaries (you know, the dollar amount you promised to actually pay them!). This is why many business owners realize, after they have employees, just how expensive those employees are.

Note 1: Do not, under any circumstances, fail to remit the payroll taxes you've withheld and thus owe to the government. Since the bulk of this money was not yours in the first place (it was money you withheld from your employees), the government gets pretty nasty about not receiving this money in a timely fashion. I have often seen them levy bank accounts or file liens against personal homes and cars and other assets to make sure they get their money. They are not nice, not in the least, about this issue.

Note 2: Many business owners quickly realize that if they keep or make all their employees contractors (as paid on a Form 1099 instead of a W-2 with the withholdings and taxes taken out), the business owners' costs would drop by at least that 9.65%. Now, although that sounds great, the IRS has specific rules about who is and is not allowed to be treated as a contractor. There is a 20-point test as well as a specific IRS submission form if you cannot determine on your own how someone should be taxed. The 20-point questions are used to determine the control over the individual that the company maintains. See Appendix C of this book for the list of 20-point questions as most recently provided by the IRS.

Self-Employment Taxes

If you are a sole proprietorship, then self-employment taxes are your equivalent of the payroll taxes listed above. Instead of having an employer to pay half of the taxes, you are both the employer and employee and you get to pay all of these taxes. Aren't you lucky! ☺

Sales Taxes

Sales taxes, similar to payroll taxes, are monies that you, the business owner, are collecting on behalf of a government agency. As with payroll taxes, you will always want to submit these taxes in a timely manner and be sure they are calculated properly. If, for example, you accidentally over-collect from a client, you do not get to keep that money—the difference goes to the government agency. If you under-collect? Guess what, you get to make up the difference! So be aware of the different tax rates for your cities, states, and localities.

An important note here is to know when and to whom you need to remit taxes. Most states and cities use a concept called *nexus* to determine whether you do or do not need to collect and remit sales tax. Nexus is made up of three main factors: gross sales in a locale, whether you have a permanent structure in that locale, and whether you have salespeople in that locale. Typically, if you have any of these three, you will need to collect and remit the sales taxes for that area. Take, for example, a plumber in Arizona. The main office is in Tempe, but the business does repairs and construction jobs in Scottsdale, Chandler, Mesa, and Phoenix. The business will be responsible for collecting and remitting tax in *each* of those cities, and it will need to cross-report sales between the cities to the state and pay at a state level as well.[13] Fun, isn't it? This is why you always want a skilled tax professional on your side to help you calculate and remit your taxes each month.

Nexus can also apply to out-of-state sales. Do you have salespeople going into another state—not living there, but traveling there to sell your product? An example: if you are an Arizona business, but you have salespeople traveling to Washington State to train and sell product there, you will be required to collect and remit state sales tax in Washington and most likely in the city and locality as well. Exciting and confusing and lots of moving parts! This is why very large businesses often have departments within their accounting departments just to handle sales tax collection and remission.

Penalties and Interest

I am including information on penalties and interest in this book to give you an idea of other ways the government can get money from you. Hopefully you will never be subject to any of these, but here is a brief overview, just so you have the information in the back of your mind.

---

13. We are in Scottsdale, Arizona—for our city, you would want to check the City of Scottsdale website (www.scottsdaleaz. gov/taxes/salestax) for information on the sales and use tax rates.

Here is a short list of penalties and interest categories you may potentially run into (but hopefully not!):[14]

✔ Failure to File Penalties
✔ Failure to Pay Penalties
✔ Estimated Tax Penalties
✔ Failure to Deposit Penalties
✔ Interest on Underpayments
✔ Overpayment Interest
✔ Interest on Carryback of Net Operating Losses

Licenses, Fees, and Annual Reports

Depending on the state you live in, you may have to pay additional fees for setting up and maintaining your business. For example, California has an $800 per year minimum tax that is really a business license fee (for the great pleasure/honor of doing business in the state). In Arizona, depending on how your legal entity is set up, you could be looking at a $45 per year annual report that charges a $19 per month late fee if you don't remember to file it on time. (And PS—the state doesn't e-mail or mail you anything to let you know when the report is due; you have to remember! Not like, as a business owner, you don't have fifty million other things to remember!). So, what about your business license, your sales tax licenses, your permits? All of these things cost little bits of money, and they do add up. You want to make sure that you check with your lawyer, or other appropriate professional (depending on the nature of the fees), as to which fees will apply to you beyond these common ones that apply to everyone.

Deductions, Expenses, and Credits—Oh, My! Definitions

Deductions, expenses, and credits are three different words that you will hear in relation to your business spending in the way that items will offset your taxes. Of these three, credits are the most valuable when it comes to the final tax bill.

Deductions

A deduction is defined by the IRS as something that is ordinary and necessary to the business that you are then allowed to take against your total taxable income for the year. Note: That's ordinary and necessary—**Ordinary and Necessary**!!! Have I drilled that in enough? If you are spending business money and it does

---

14. For a full list, you can always check the IRS's website at www.irs.gov/irm/part20/.

not fall under *both* of these categories, the IRS will not allow you to write it off for tax purposes. Deductions will protect you from a tax burden at the rate of [1 × (your ordinary tax bracket)]. For most people, the average tax bracket is between 15% and 23%.

Now, it is important to note that Ordinary and Necessary mean different things to different people. For example, for a rock star, it is Ordinary and Necessary to look good (great hair, great body, great nails, and great clothes), to have a great voice or talent, and to be psychologically happy (e.g., must have blue M&Ms in their tour bus). What that means, for rock stars, is that they get to write off the gym memberships, the personal trainers, the tour bus, the blue M&Ms, the hair stylists and makeup artists. Do you think your business makes these items Ordinary and Necessary for you? In most cases, I would say I doubt it. However, it is very important that you consider what items *are* ordinary and necessary for your business. For example, as I am a Tax Goddess, tax books, education, seminars, and lots and lots of paper (for all those IRS forms) are ordinary and necessary for me.

A few types of deductions are often overlooked. These can be particularly small or big, depending on the deduction. A few of my personal favorites are as follows:

✔ **Your Dog(s):** If you are a single female whose line of work takes you to places where you may not feel safe, and your dogs are trained (notice I did *not* say guard trained), and the dog or dogs are taller at the shoulder than your knee height, those dogs can be written off as security *if* you take them with you to appointments where you feel in potential danger.[15]

✔ **Travel to Luxurious Places:** So, have you always wanted to know how to write off that vacation to Hawaii? London? Bangkok? You can, but of course it has to be Ordinary and Necessary, right? So the real question is how do you ensure that?

In order to write off your travel, you need to have an Ordinary and Necessary business purpose for going to that location. That purpose could be meeting a long-time mentor, meeting new people in your industry to learn tips and tricks of the trade, meeting a new client in her or his hometown, or taking educational courses.

---

15. A great example of this is a female mortgage broker, insurance agent, or real estate agent who meets people at their homes to discuss services. It may be wise, especially since the woman does not know these new people, for her to bring her dog(s) with her to these appointments as protection. If this happens with regularity, she would be able to write off the dog food, the pet insurance, the vet visits and shots, the dog toys, and the training as security deductions on her tax return. Please note that I use a *female* for this example. It is very *rare* in the IRS case law that a man can use this deduction; I've only ever seen it work for males working in a junkyard.

Big things that you want to make sure of when you do this type of travel:

o   Your trips should always envelop the weekend. Leave on a Thursday and return on a Monday. Make sure that you have appointments on *any* business day that you are still in town so that you have a reason for why you couldn't go home on a Friday evening.

o   Get business cards, save lunch/dinner receipts, and *have actually met with someone*. You need to have proof of your business reason, not just your saying that you "met with some guy" whose name you cannot even remember.

o   If your family is coming with you, buy their tickets on a separate credit card. Get a second hotel room that your kids are going to stay in and pay for that personally. Note: If your spouse/kids also work for your company (do the books, empty the trash, etc.), then you could use the trip as your corporate retreat and for the meeting of new clients. But make sure it's both. Traveling for a corporate retreat when all the people involved live in the same town (your hometown) doesn't work, as the IRS will ask you what made you go out of town for the meeting.

o   Also note: You could do a "staycation," where you stay in a hotel in your hometown with your family.[16] That could qualify as a retreat (e.g., you needed a space, not your main office, where you could clearly think through the upcoming goals and needs of the business over the next year).

✔ **A Personal Chef:** Big corporations do this one all the time; they have internal cafeterias. So why not a small business? *If* you are trying to help your employees (remember, these could be you and your family) work longer hours and not have to leave to get breakfast/lunch/dinner, then it may be of benefit to the company to have a chef come in and prepare these meals for your staff. Now, I am not sure I can recommend doing this every day (not unless your people are pulling 12- to 14-hour shifts every day!), but for special times of the year, busy seasons, and so on, this may make a lot of sense!

✔ **Production Deduction:** This one is just amazing! The government will give you a special deduction for producing something. This write-off could work for architects, construction companies, manufacturing, piping, and so on. This is a huge deduction that will help you lower your tax bill significantly.

---

16. If you are going to write off the costs for your family to join you, make sure that your family members are members/shareholders/partners in your business or are in some other way connected to your business. Otherwise, why would their costs be ordinary and necessary?

Please note that there are also some deductions known as *noncash deductions*. These items, the most popular examples of which are depreciation and amortization, are deductions that lower the taxable income on your return, but are not actually cash outlays (expenses) of the business.[17]

Expenses

An expense is defined as money that you have spent in relation to a business. Not all expenses are necessarily business deductions. Using one of the examples above, a female business owner who spends money on her dog(s) would have an expense, but, unless she owned a junkyard, she would not have a deduction (something she could write off against her income at year-end).

If you ever want to see where expenses that are not deductions are reported, look at Schedule M-1 of your business return (for partnerships, S-Corporations, and C-Corporations).

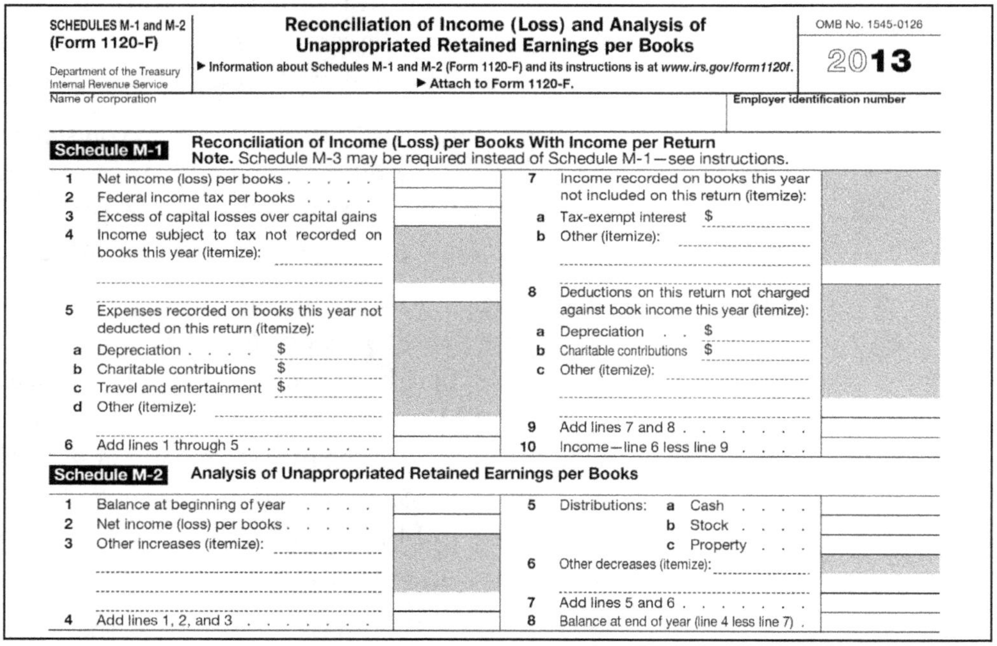
SCHEDULES M-1 and M-2 (Form 1120-F)
Department of the Treasury Internal Revenue Service

Reconciliation of Income (Loss) and Analysis of Unappropriated Retained Earnings per Books

▶ Information about Schedules M-1 and M-2 (Form 1120-F) and its instructions is at www.irs.gov/form1120f.
▶ Attach to Form 1120-F.

OMB No. 1545-0126
2013

Name of corporation | Employer identification number

Schedule M-1 **Reconciliation of Income (Loss) per Books With Income per Return**
Note. Schedule M-3 may be required instead of Schedule M-1—see instructions.

1 Net income (loss) per books
2 Federal income tax per books
3 Excess of capital losses over capital gains
4 Income subject to tax not recorded on books this year (itemize):
5 Expenses recorded on books this year not deducted on this return (itemize):
a Depreciation $
b Charitable contributions $
c Travel and entertainment $
d Other (itemize):
6 Add lines 1 through 5
7 Income recorded on books this year not included on this return (itemize):
a Tax-exempt interest $
b Other (itemize):
8 Deductions on this return not charged against book income this year (itemize):
a Depreciation $
b Charitable contributions $
c Other (itemize):
9 Add lines 7 and 8
10 Income—line 6 less line 9

Schedule M-2 **Analysis of Unappropriated Retained Earnings per Books**

1 Balance at beginning of year
2 Net income (loss) per books
3 Other increases (itemize):
4 Add lines 1, 2, and 3
5 Distributions: a Cash
b Stock
c Property
6 Other decreases (itemize):
7 Add lines 5 and 6
8 Balance at end of year (line 4 less line 7)

Figure 10: M-1 for an S-Corporation Return

Credits

Credits, as I mentioned previously, are the most desirable of all items in the tax law. These are expenses for which the spending of the money is allowed as a

17. You can see a list of common deductions here: taxgoddess.com/wp-content/uploads/2011/09/IRSStandardDeductionsList.pdf.

one-to-one write-off, dollar-for-dollar, against your ending tax bill. These items are incentives provided by the government to guide taxpayers into performing certain actions or making certain purchases.

There have been some amazing credits in the history of the IRS. Some of the more recent ones and their "at-the-time" societal drives are listed below. Make sure that you ask your tax professional about the current credits available to you in your business.

Energy-Efficient Improvements

The government sometimes offers dollar-for-dollar returns if you install any of the following energy efficient items: solar panels, geothermal or wind power generators, specialty windows to prevent heat loss/gain, and so on. Basically, the government wants to lower energy consumption and so has provided credits for people who follow the direction the government wants to move in.

Credits for Money Given to Public Schools, Private Schools, or Charities That Help the Working Poor

The State of Arizona government, for example, gives you dollar-for-dollar credits against your state tax return for monies given to these specific types of organizations. The state government was running out of funds to help support these organizations and so determined that if it could get the public to help, it would give the public a break, dollar for dollar, on their taxes.

Note: This credit actually *made* you money when you got involved. If you gave the maximum for the 2010 tax year ($1,800 among the three credits), you would actually make money because both the state and the federal returns would give you a benefit. In this case, it was [$1,800 × (1 + xx%)], where the xx is your ordinary tax bracket percentage!

Purchasing a Hybrid Vehicle

Here we come back to the energy-efficient items, this time to autos. When hybrid vehicles first started coming out, the government, in an attempt to lower gasoline consumption, gave massive credits (upwards of $7K per car) toward the purchase of certain hybrid vehicles. Often the purchase price of a vehicle in its hybrid model was higher than that of the normal vehicle (non-hybrid) of the same type, but many people still purchased the new hybrid vehicles to get the credits (and, of course, to try and help the environment—and their pockets, with smaller fuel bills).

How Does Your Business Relate to Your Personal Taxes?

When you are a business owner, your business ties to your personal return in many ways. These connections are outlined below by the type of entity to which they relate. Remember to assume that if you are an LLC taxed as one of these entities, your rules will be the same as for that entity type.

C-Corporations

As the owner of a C-Corporation, you will be required to take a reasonable salary. Now, the definition of reasonable is currently somewhat up in the air, but I can give you a few examples. Let's say that a business—a gas station—is making a profit of $100,000 per year. The question to help you determine reasonable salary is: If you, the owner, were out sick for a year, how much would you have to pay someone to run your business for you and keep it in the same running condition as you have it? In this scenario, it might be $50,000. If it were a doctor's office, the cost might be the full $100,000. In a C-Corporation, the only other way—besides salaries and perks—to get money out of the company is to take a dividend. Dividends are currently being taxed at 15%, so this could be a very good deal: Take a salary of $50,000, pay the approximately 20% self-employment tax, and then pay your ordinary income tax bracket on top of that, which could cost you upwards of 50% in taxes. After you pay taxes on the remaining $50,000 (of our scenario's $100,000 in profit) at the corporate level (which currently can range anywhere from 15% to 45%), you would then get to take whatever is left as a dividend at 15%! As you can imagine, with this kind of outcome, most owners would want their salaries to be very high in a C-Corporation, or at least calculated in such a way that the double level of taxation at the corporate and then personal level balances out, to pay the lowest rates across the board.

S-Corporations

In an S-Corporation, you will not be able to file your personal return until you have received your Form K-1 from the business. The Form K-1 describes how items of income and expense should be reported on your personal return. It also provides you with your basis in your interest in the business. Basis is what allows you to deduct any losses in the business, and it records all the history of your interaction with the business in a single account (meaning that if the business makes a profit, your basis will go up, and if you take a draw/distribution, your basis will go down). In an S-Corporation, if you do not have any basis in your stock/membership in the company and the company has a loss, you will not be able to take the deduction for that loss on your personal return.

Also, in an S-Corporation you are required to take a reasonable salary, or a salary that is at least 35% of whatever your net profit is (remember the diagrams from earlier, showing that the W-2 portion was 35%?). However, in an S-Corporation the taxes work very differently (a great benefit of a flow-thru). If you take that same $35,000 salary, and pay the 20% self-employment taxes and then your ordinary income taxes, you can take any remaining money (the rest of the $65,000) out of the business and pay only your ordinary tax bracket rate on it. In some cases, if you have other offsetting expenses on your personal return, you could drop your ordinary rate to a very low percentage and make this a great deal!

You may be required, as the owner of an S-Corporation, to report some of the benefits that you receive from the business on your W-2. Some of these benefits could be: your health insurance, your medical expenses paid for by the company, and even some of your perks (gym memberships, etc.). Make sure you are checking with your tax and payroll professionals as to what else, in your scenario, you may need to report.

You will also need to pay attention to your withholding on your company W-2 versus your estimated payments to cover the income of the business as it flows through to your personal return. Please re-read the example in the previous chapters if you have questions on how to plan for this.

Partnerships

As with an S-Corporation, in a partnership you will not be able to file your personal return until you have received your Form K-1 from the business. The K-1 will provide you with data similar to that on the K-1 for an S-Corporation; however, it will include additional information with relation to your basis for the partnership. Your partnership basis is the same as the S-Corporation basis, in that the basis is what allows you to deduct any losses in the business and records all the history of your interaction with the business in a single account (meaning that if the business makes a profit, your basis will go up, and if you take a draw/distribution, your basis will go down). There is one slight difference. In a partnership, your basis includes the portion of corporate debts that you are held responsible for. These debts can come in three forms: recourse debt, non-recourse debt, and qualified non-recourse debt. Recourse debt means that the person/company to whom the money is owed can come after the owners if the debt is not paid. Non-recourse debt means the opposite; the lender cannot take anything from the owners other than what may be put up as capital for the loan. Some specific debts are considered qualified non-recourse debt to a partnership, including debt that was borrowed by you in connection with holding real property; is secured by real property used in the activity; and is not convertible debt. These debts must be loaned or guaranteed by any federal, state, or local government and borrowed by you. Qualified non-recourse debt and recourse debt increase your basis because you are personally responsible for repaying the debts. As in an S-Corporation, if you do not have any basis in your stock/membership in the company and the company has a loss, you will not be able to take the deduction for that loss on your personal return.

You may also be required or directed to take something called a guaranteed payment from the partnership. A guaranteed payment is similar to a salary, in that you need to pay self-employment taxes and income tax on this money and it represents normal, recurring work that you perform for the partnership. However, you need to be careful to pay in enough in quarterly estimates to cover these additional taxes, as—unlike for the S-Corporation W-2—no withholdings are ever taken on a guaranteed payment.

Sole Proprietorships

In a sole proprietorship, the form Schedule C is included as a part of your Form 1040. It is on Schedule C that you will report your gross income and expenses with relation to the business. You may file your Form 1040 as soon as your Schedule C is complete and accurately reflects your transactions for the year.

Important note: Schedule C sole proprietors do *not*, under any circumstances, take payroll (W-2 or guaranteed payment) for themselves. If the owner of a sole proprietorship wishes to take money for personal use from the business, she or he needs only to transfer the funds from the business to a personal account—preferably by writing her- or himself a check on which the memo section states "owner's draw."

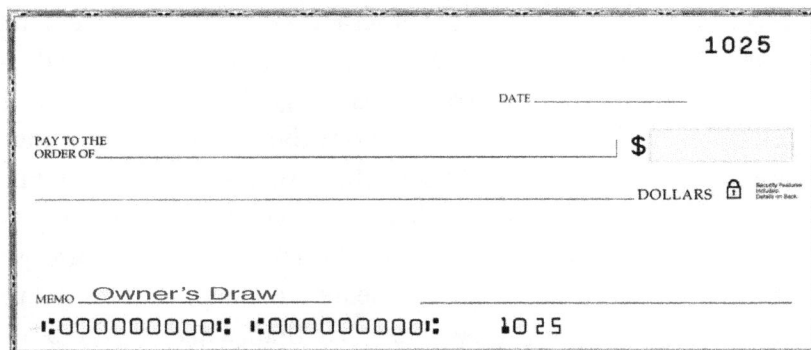

Figure 11: Check with "Owner's Draw" Memo

Deadline Dates

Deadline dates differ for businesses, personal returns, and other types of entities. You will want to check with the IRS for their calendar of events each year, as these dates have been known (rarely, but known) to change.

Business Deadlines

Income Taxes

Normally, for a partnership, S-Corporation, or C-Corporation, or an LLC taxed as any of the above, the tax return is due two months and fifteen days after the end of your tax year. If you are a calendar-year taxpayer, whose year ends on December 31, your deadline is March 15 of the year following your year-end. You also have the opportunity to extend the filing of your return by six months, making your final due date (no additional extensions allowed) September 15.

Note: You will notice that the deadline for businesses is one month ahead of the deadline for individual tax returns (typically April 15 and October 15 with extension) so that individuals have time to receive their Form K-1s from any businesses that they may be related to.

If you are a Schedule C sole proprietorship or an LLC taxed as a sole proprietorship, then your filing deadline is the same as for the individual return (April 15 and October 15 with extension).[18]

Payroll Taxes

Payroll taxes can be somewhat complicated, as their due dates depend on how much in taxes you owe. In most cases, payroll taxes are due on the fifteenth of the month following the month that payroll was run (for example, if you ran a payroll in January, your payroll taxes for that month would be due on February 15). It is very important that you check with your payroll provider (be that your tax professional or a payroll provider firm) as to what your specific due dates are and where you fall in the cutoffs to be moved up to more frequent filing deadlines or down to be a less frequent filer. More frequent filers may have to pay their payroll taxes before three days after the payroll run, and less frequent filers may not have to pay until year-end (January 15 of the following year).

---

18. The best place to see the true deadlines of all items related to tax is www.irs.gov/publications/p509/ar02.html. This is the web page for the IRS calendar of events. Note that sometimes the fifteenth of a month lands on a weekend, which normally pushes the deadline to the following Monday.

Sales Taxes

Sales taxes are charged at state and local levels, so you will want to check with your local tax professional for the due dates in your state and city. In Arizona, as well as in most of the cities in Arizona, the sales taxes are due to be turned into the governments by the fifteenth of the month following the month of the sale. Be sure to recognize that these monies are taxes that you have collected on behalf of the governments; this money is not yours. The state and local authorities do not take it too well if you hold on to their money past their submission deadline dates and will often levy your bank accounts or file liens against your business if you fail to submit the monies.

Estimated Taxes (For the Owners of Businesses)

Depending on how your business entity is taxed and how you plan, you may or may not have to pay in quarterly estimates. Typically quarterly estimates are based on one of a few different formulas, with the two most common formulas being: (1) 90% of the current year tax, paid in across four quarterly estimates, and (2) 110% of last year's tax, paid in across four quarterly estimates. Note that if you did not make any profit in a specific quarter, or you made less than 25% of the total profit, you can change the amount of your quarterly estimates by quarter in order to pay in more when you have more profit and less when you have less. The payment dates for quarterly estimates, for all entities and individuals, are April 15, June 15, September 15, and January 15 of the following year.

Note: A C-Corporation is the only type of entity that has to pay quarterly estimates at the business level. You must pay your quarterly estimates using EFTPS (Electronic Federal Tax Payment System) at the federal level and by sending a check to the state (in most states; some have their own electronic payment programs).

Personal Deadlines

Income Taxes

The personal income taxes for you, as an owner of a business, are due on April 15—or, with extension, October 15—of the year following the end of the year in discussion. Note that the extension to October 15 is an extension of time to file, *not* the time to pay. This area often seems to cause issues for taxpayers. If you owe the government money, you will need to pay that money on or before April 15 to avoid any additional penalties or interest.

Estimated Taxes (For the Owners of Businesses)

Depending on how your business entity is taxed and how you plan, you may or may not have to pay in quarterly estimates. Typically quarterly estimates are based on one of a few different formulas, with the most common two formulas being: (1) 90% of the current year tax, paid in across four quarterly estimates, and (2) 110% of last year's tax, paid in across four quarterly estimates. Note that if you did not make any profit in a specific quarter, or you made less than 25% of the total profit, you can change the amount of your quarterly estimates by quarter in order to pay in more when you have more profit and less when you have less. The payment dates for quarterly estimates, for all entities and individuals, are April 15, June 15, September 15, and January 15 of the following year.

Others (At the Individual Level)

All of the other entities—partnerships, S-Corporations, sole proprietorships, and LLCs taxed as any of the above—do not have quarterly estimated tax payments. These entity types, because they are flow-thrus, pass on their income or losses to their owners, and so it is at the individual owners' level that quarterly estimates need to be determined. Many owners will increase their withholding from their company W-2s or their spouses' W-2s so that they do not need to pay in quarterly estimates. However, these decisions should always be made with the assistance of your tax professional during the creation of your annual tax plan. Below is an excellent example of when you would need to file quarterly estimates and when you would not. This example will also show you the forms needed for when you file this type of return with these types of income sources:

- ✔ Husband owns a small business; its net profit is $25,000. He is taxed as a Schedule C sole proprietorship and has no LLC.

- ✔ Wife has a W-2; her gross box 1 earnings taxable is $50,000. She has federal withholding of $5,000.

Note that we are ignoring the state for this example.

- ✔ The husband and wife do not have a home or other itemized deduction, and they have no other income or expenses that would increase or reduce their taxable income.

- ✔ They do not have any dependents.

- ✔ They are both 40 years old.

See Figures 12 through 16 for the forms that would be required in this example.

Form **1040** | Department of the Treasury — Internal Revenue Service (99)
U.S. Individual Income Tax Return | **2013** | OMB No. 1545-0074 | IRS Use Only — Do not write or staple in this space.

For the year Jan 1 - Dec 31, 2013, or other tax year beginning _____, 2013, ending _____, 20___ | See separate instructions.

Your first name and initial	Last name	Your social security number
JOE	SMITH	111-11-1111

If a joint return, spouse's first name and initial	Last name	Spouse's social security number
MARY	SMITH	222-22-2222

Home address (number and street). If you have a P.O. box, see instructions. | Apartment no.

111 E MAIN ST

▲ Make sure the SSN(s) above and on line 6c are correct.

City, town or post office, state, and ZIP code. If you have a foreign address, also complete spaces below (see instructions).

ANY CITY, AZ 85256

Foreign country name | Foreign province/state/county | Foreign postal code

Presidential Election Campaign
Check here if you, or your spouse if filing jointly, want $3 to go to this fund? Checking a box below will not change your tax or refund. ☐ You ☐ Spouse

Filing Status
Check only one box.

1 ☐ Single
2 ☒ Married filing jointly (even if only one had income)
3 ☐ Married filing separately. Enter spouse's SSN above & full name here... ►
4 ☐ Head of household (with qualifying person). (See instructions.) If the qualifying person is a child but not your dependent, enter this child's name here.. ►
5 ☐ Qualifying widow(er) with dependent child

Exemptions

6a ☒ **Yourself.** If someone can claim you as a dependent, **do not** check box 6a ....
 b ☒ **Spouse** ....

c **Dependents:**	(2) Dependent's social security number	(3) Dependent's relationship to you	(4) ✓ if child under age 17 qualifying for child tax cr (see instrs)
(1) First name Last name			

If more than four dependents, see instructions and check here... ► ☐

Boxes checked on 6a and 6b.. **2**
No. of children on 6c who:
• lived with you
• did not live with you due to divorce or separation (see instrs)...
Dependents on 6c not entered above..
Add numbers on lines above..... ► **2**

d Total number of exemptions claimed ....

Income

Attach Form(s) W-2 here. Also attach Forms W-2G and 1099-R if tax was withheld.

If you did not get a W-2, see instructions.

7	Wages, salaries, tips, etc. Attach Form(s) W-2	7	50,000.
8a	**Taxable** interest. Attach Schedule B if required	8a	
b	**Tax-exempt** interest. **Do not** include on line 8a 8b		
9a	Ordinary dividends. Attach Schedule B if required	9a	
b	Qualified dividends 9b		
10	Taxable refunds, credits, or offsets of state and local income taxes	10	
11	Alimony received	11	
12	Business income or (loss). Attach Schedule C or C-EZ	12	25,000.
13	Capital gain or (loss). Att Sch D if reqd. If not reqd, ck here .... ► ☐	13	
14	Other gains or (losses). Attach Form 4797	14	
15a	IRA distributions 15a	b Taxable amount	15b	
16a	Pensions and annuities 16a	b Taxable amount	16b	
17	Rental real estate, royalties, partnerships, S corporations, trusts, etc. Attach Schedule E.	17	
18	Farm income or (loss). Attach Schedule F	18	
19	Unemployment compensation	19	
20a	Social security benefits 20a	b Taxable amount	20b	
21	Other income _____	21	
22	Combine the amounts in the far right column for lines 7 through 21. This is your **total income** .... ►	22	75,000.

Adjusted Gross Income

23	Educator expenses 23		
24	Certain business expenses of reservists, performing artists, and fee-basis government officials. Attach Form 2106 or 2106-EZ 24		
25	Health savings account deduction. Attach Form 8889 25		
26	Moving expenses. Attach Form 3903 26		
27	Deductible part of self-employment tax. Attach Schedule SE 27	1,766.	
28	Self-employed SEP, SIMPLE, and qualified plans 28		
29	Self-employed health insurance deduction 29		
30	Penalty on early withdrawal of savings 30		
31a	Alimony paid b Recipient's SSN .... ► _____ 31a		
32	IRA deduction 32		
33	Student loan interest deduction 33		
34	Tuition and fees. Attach Form 8917 34		
35	Domestic production activities deduction. Attach Form 8903 35		
36	Add lines 23 through 35	36	1,766.
37	Subtract line 36 from line 22. This is your **adjusted gross income** .... ►	37	73,234.

BAA For Disclosure, Privacy Act, and Paperwork Reduction Act Notice, see separate instructions. FDIA0112L 08/05/13 Form **1040** (2013)

Figure 12: Page 1 of the 1040

Form **1040** (2013)   JOE AND MARY SMITH   111-11-1111   Page **2**

Tax and Credits	38	Amount from line 37 (adjusted gross income)............................	38	73,234.
	39a	Check if: ☐ **You** were born before January 2, 1949, ☐ Blind. **Total boxes** / ☐ **Spouse** was born before January 2, 1949, ☐ Blind. **checked** ▶ 39a		
Standard Deduction for —	b	If your spouse itemizes on a separate return or you were a dual-status alien, check here. ▶ 39b		
• People who check any box on line 39a or 39b **or** who can be claimed as a dependent, see instructions.	40	**Itemized deductions** (from Schedule A) **or** your **standard deduction** (see left margin)............	40	12,200.
	41	Subtract line 40 from line 38..	41	61,034.
	42	Exemptions. If line 38 is $150,000 or less, multiply $3,900 by the number on line 6d. Otherwise, see instrs.....	42	7,800.
	43	**Taxable income.** Subtract line 42 from line 41. If line 42 is more than line 41, enter -0-...............	43	53,234.
• All others:	44	**Tax** (see instrs). Check if any from: a ☐ Form(s) 8814 c ☐ _____ b ☐ Form 4972	44	7,091.
Single or Married filing separately, $6,100	45	**Alternative minimum tax** (see instructions). Attach Form 6251...........	45	0.
Married filing jointly or Qualifying widow(er), $12,200	46	Add lines 44 and 45.. ▶	46	7,091.
	47	Foreign tax credit. Attach Form 1116 if required.......	47		
	48	Credit for child and dependent care expenses. Attach Form 2441......	48		
	49	Education credits from Form 8863, line 19...........	49		
Head of household, $8,950	50	Retirement savings contributions credit. Attach Form 8880...	50		
	51	Child tax credit. Attach Schedule 8812, if required........	51		
	52	Residential energy credits. Attach Form 5695.........	52		
	53	Other crs from Form: a ☐ 3800 b ☐ 8801 c ☐	53		
	54	Add lines 47 through 53. These are your **total credits**...............	54	
	55	Subtract line 54 from line 46. If line 54 is more than line 46, enter -0-........ ▶	55	7,091.
Other Taxes	56	Self-employment tax. Attach Schedule SE..............................	56	3,532.
	57	Unreported social security and Medicare tax from Form: a ☐ 4137 b ☐ 8919.	57	
	58	Additional tax on IRAs, other qualified retirement plans, etc. Attach Form 5329 if required........	58	
	59a	Household employment taxes from Schedule H.....................	59a	
	b	First-time homebuyer credit repayment. Attach Form 5405 if required.	59b	
	60	Taxes from: a ☐ Form 8959 b ☐ Form 8960 c ☐ Instrs; enter code(s) _____	60	
	61	Add lines 55-60. This is your **total tax**................... ▶	61	10,623.
Payments	62	Federal income tax withheld from Forms W-2 and 1099..... 62	5,000.	
If you have a qualifying child, attach Schedule EIC.	63	2013 estimated tax payments and amount applied from 2012 return. 63		
	64a	**Earned income credit (EIC)**.................... 64a		
	b	Nontaxable combat pay election...... ▶ 64b		
	65	Additional child tax credit. Attach Schedule 8812. 65		
	66	American opportunity credit from Form 8863, line 8....... 66		
	67	Reserved.......................... 67		
	68	Amount paid with request for extension to file...... 68		
	69	Excess social security and tier 1 RRTA tax withheld........ 69		
	70	Credit for federal tax on fuels. Attach Form 4136. 70		
	71	Credits from Form: a ☐ 2439 b ☐ Reserved c ☐ 8885 d ☐ 71		
	72	Add lns 62, 63, 64a, & 65-71. These are your **total pmts**........... ▶	72	5,000.
Refund	73	If line 72 is more than line 61, subtract line 61 from line 72. This is the amount you **overpaid**.........	73	
	74a	Amount of line 73 you want **refunded to you.** If Form 8888 is attached, check here. ▶ ☐	74a	
Direct deposit? See instructions.	b	Routing number........ ▶ _____ c Type: ☐ Checking ☐ Savings		
	d	Account number ▶ _____		
	75	Amount of line 73 you want applied to your 2014 estimated tax........ ▶ 75		
Amount You Owe	76	**Amount you owe.** Subtract line 72 from line 61. For details on how to pay see instructions............... ▶	76	5,714.
	77	Estimated tax penalty (see instructions)................. 77	91.	

DO NOT FILE

Third Party Designee	Do you want to allow another person to discuss this return with the IRS (see instructions)?......... ☒ **Yes.** Complete below. ☐ **No**
	Designee's name ▶ _____ Phone no. ▶ (602) 357-3275 Personal identification number (PIN) ▶ _____
Sign Here Joint return? See instructions. Keep a copy for your records.	Under penalties of perjury, I declare that I have examined this return and accompanying schedules and statements, and to the best of my knowledge and belief, they are true, correct, and complete. Declaration of preparer (other than taxpayer) is based on all information of which preparer has any knowledge.
	Your signature ▶ / Date / Your occupation: SELF-EMPLOYED / Daytime phone number
	Spouse's signature. If a joint return, **both** must sign. ▶ / Date / Spouse's occupation: EMPLOYED / If the IRS sent you an Identity Protection PIN, enter it here (see instrs)
Paid Preparer Use Only	Print/Type preparer's name / Preparer's signature / Date / Check ☐ if self-employed / PTIN
	Firm's name ▶ TAX GODDESS BUSINESS SERVICES, PC
	Firm's address ▶ 6728 E AVALON DR / Firm's EIN ▶ 201485000
	SCOTTSDALE, AZ 85251-7100 / Phone no. (602) 357-3275

Form **1040** (2013)

FDIA0112L 08/05/13

Figure 13: Page 2 of the 1040[19]

---

19. Notice on Line 62 that the taxpayers owe more money to the IRS for 2013; they should have paid quarterly estimates throughout the year of 2013 to cover this April 15, 2014, bill due.

SCHEDULE C-EZ (Form 1040) Department of the Treasury Internal Revenue Service (99)	Net Profit From Business (Sole Proprietorship) ► Partnerships, joint ventures, etc., generally must file Form 1065 or 1065-B. ► Attach to Form 1040, 1040NR, or 1041. ► See instructions.	OMB No. 1545-0074 **2013** Attachment Sequence No. **09A**

Name of proprietor JOE SMITH	Social security number (SSN) 111-11-1111

Part I   General Information

You May Use Schedule C-EZ Instead of Schedule C Only If You:	• Had business expenses of $5,000 or less. • Use the cash method of accounting. • Did not have an inventory at any time during the year. • Did not have a net loss from your business. • Had only one business as either a sole proprietor, qualified joint venture, or statutory employee.	**And You:**	• Had no employees during the year. • Are not required to file **Form 4562,** Depreciation and Amortization, for this business. See the instructions for Schedule C, line 13, to find out if you must file. • Do not deduct expenses for business use of your home. • Do not have prior year unallowed passive activity losses from this business.

A Principal business or profession, including product or service PROFESSION	B **Enter business code** ► 999999

C Business name. If no separate business name, leave blank. ANY BUSINESS	D **Enter your EIN (see instructions)**

E Business address (including suite or room number). Address not required if same as on page 1 of your tax return.

City, town or post office, state, and ZIP code

F Did you make any payments in 2013 that would require you to file Form(s) 1099 (see the Schedule C instructions).	☐ Yes	☒ No
G If 'Yes,' did you or will you file required Forms 1099?.	☐ Yes	☐ No

Part II   **Figure Your Net Profit**

1	**Gross receipts. Caution.** If this income was reported to you on Form W-2 and the 'Statutory employee' box on that form was checked, see *Statutory Employees* in the instructions for Schedule C, line 1 and check here. . . . . ► ☐	1	25,000.
2	**Total expenses** (see instructions). If more than $5,000, you **must** use Schedule C.	2	
3	**Net profit.** Subtract line 2 from line 1. If less than zero, you **must** use Schedule C. Enter on both **Form 1040, line 12,** and **Schedule SE, line 2,** or on **Form 1040NR, line 13** and **Schedule SE, line 2** (see instructions). (Statutory employees, **do not** report this amount on Schedule SE, line 2.) Estates and trusts, enter on **Form 1041, line 3.**	3	25,000.

Part III   **Information on Your Vehicle.** Complete this part **only** if you are claiming car or truck expenses on line 2.

4   When did you place your vehicle in service for business purposes? (month, day, year) ►   _ _ _ _ _ _ _ _ _ _ _ .

5   Of the total number of miles you drove your vehicle during 2013, enter the number of miles you used your vehicle for:

   a Business   _ _ _ _ _ _ _ _ _ _   **b** Commuting (see instructions)   _ _ _ _ _ _ _ _ _ _   **c** Other   _ _ _ _ _ _ _ _ _ _

6	Was your vehicle available for personal use during off-duty hours?.	☐ Yes	☐ No
7	Do you (or your spouse) have another vehicle available for personal use?.	☐ Yes	☐ No
8a	Do you have evidence to support your deduction?	☐ Yes	☐ No
b	If 'Yes,' is the evidence written?.	☐ Yes	☐ No

BAA   For Paperwork Reduction Act Notice, see the separate instructions for Schedule C (Form 1040).   Schedule **C-EZ** (Form 1040) 2013
FDIA8301L 10/23/13

Figure 14: Schedule C-EZ[20]

---

20. Note that, normally, if you have more than a few expenses, you will file a Schedule C (which is two pages or more, depending).

Chapter 8 Tax Issues

SCHEDULE SE (Form 1040)	Self-Employment Tax	OMB No. 1545-0074
Department of the Treasury Internal Revenue Service (99)	▶ Information about Schedule SE and its separate instructions is at www.irs.gov/schedulese. ▶ Attach to Form 1040 or Form 1040NR.	2013 Attachment Sequence No. 17

Name of person with self-employment income (as shown on Form 1040): JOE SMITH

Social security number of person with self-employment income ▶ 111-11-1111

Before you begin: To determine if you must file Schedule SE, see the instructions.

May I Use Short Schedule SE or Must I Use Long Schedule SE?

Note. Use this flowchart only if you must file Schedule SE. If unsure, see *Who Must File Schedule SE*, in the instructions.

Did you receive wages or tips in 2013?

No — Are you a minister, member of a religious order, or Christian Science practitioner who received IRS approval **not** to be taxed on earnings from these sources, **but** you owe self-employment tax on other earnings? Yes ▶

No — Are you using one of the optional methods to figure your net earnings (see instructions)? Yes ▶

No — Did you receive church employee income (see instructions) reported on Form W-2 of $108.28 or more? Yes ▶

No — You may use Short Schedule SE below

Yes — Was the total of your wages and tips subject to social security or railroad retirement (tier 1) tax **plus** your net earnings from self-employment more than $113,700? Yes ▶

No — Did you receive tips subject to social security or Medicare tax that you **did not** report to your employer? Yes ▶

No — Did you report any wages on Form 8919, Uncollected Social Security and Medicare Tax on Wages? Yes ▶

You must use Long Schedule SE on page 2

Section A — Short Schedule SE. Caution. Read above to see if you can use Short Schedule SE.

1a	Net farm profit or (loss) from Schedule F, line 34, and farm partnerships, Schedule K-1 (Form 1065), box 14, code A.	1a	
b	If you received social security retirement or disability benefits, enter the amount of Conservation Reserve Program payments included on Schedule F, line 4b, or listed on Schedule K-1 (Form 1065), box 20, code Z	1b	
2	Net profit or (loss) from Schedule C, line 31; Schedule C-EZ, line 3; Schedule K-1 (Form 1065), box 14, code A (other than farming); and Schedule K-1 (Form 1065-B), box 9, code J1. Ministers and members of religious orders, see instructions for types of income to report on this line. See instructions for other income to report.	2	25,000.
3	Combine lines 1a, 1b, and 2	3	25,000.
4	Multiply line 3 by 92.35% (.9235). If less than $400, you do not owe self-employment tax; **do not** file this schedule unless you have an amount on line 1b ▶	4	23,088.
	Note. If line 4 is less than $400 due to Conservation Reserve Program payments on line 1b, see instructions.		
5	Self-employment tax. If the amount on line 4 is: • $113,700 or less, multiply line 4 by 15.3% (.153). Enter the result here and on **Form 1040, line 56,** or **Form 1040NR, line 54** • More than $113,700, multiply line 4 by 2.9% (.029). Then, add $14,098.80 to the result. Enter the total here and on **Form 1040, line 56,** or **Form 1040NR, line 54**	5	3,532.
6	Deduction for one-half of self-employment tax. Multiply line 5 by 50% (.50). Enter the result here and on **Form 1040, line 27** or **Form 1040NR, line 27** ⎸ 6 ⎸ 1,766.		

BAA For Paperwork Reduction Act Notice, see your tax return instructions.

Schedule **SE** (Form 1040) 2013

FDIA1101L 10/24/13

Figure 15: Schedule SE – SE Stands for Self-Employment (Taxes)

93

DO NOT FILE

Mail to:

INTERNAL REVENUE SERVICE
P.O. BOX 510000
SAN FRANCISCO, CA 94151-5100

▼ **Detach Here and Mail With Your Payment** ▼

Department of the Treasury   **Calendar Year —**   **2014 Form 1040-ES Payment Voucher 1**
Internal Revenue Service   **Due 4/15/2014**

File only if you are making a payment of estimated tax by check or money order. Mail this
voucher with your check or money order payable to the **'United States Treasury.'** Write your
social security number and '2014 Form 1040-ES' on your check or money order. Do not send
cash. Enclose, but do not staple or attach, your payment with this voucher.

Amount of estimated tax you are paying by check or money order.......... ▶		1,406.

FDIA1901L 06/24/13   1030

111-11-1111   222-22-2222
JOE SMITH
MARY SMITH
111 E MAIN ST
ANY CITY, AZ 85256

PO Box 510000
San Francisco   CA 94151-5100

111111111 DJ SMIT 30 0 201412 430

Figure 16: The First of Four Total Quarterly Vouchers[21]

---

21. Note that the vouchers are for 2014 so that they can "pre-pay" their tax bill to the IRS. Note also that these quarterly
    estimates are based on their 2013 tax bill. If the husband or wife earns more money in the next tax year, they are
    required to increase their quarterly payments or increase the withholding on the wife's W-2.

As you can see from these forms—1040 pages 1 and 2, Schedule C-EZ, Schedule SE, and 1040-ES Q1 (I did not include all four vouchers for the sake of space)—this family would still owe, come tax time, an additional $5,714 of federal taxes including a $91 penalty.[22] This couple needs to be paying quarterly taxes to not have the penalty, as well as to follow the IRS rules. If they fail to pay quarterly estimates, each year the IRS will become stricter on their account, often leading to issues such as:

TIP

✔ A lack of leniency if any issues arise and the taxpayers need to ask for forgiveness or help from the IRS (setting up payment plans, waiving penalties, etc.) The IRS wants you to be a "good taxpayer" and that means following the rules.

✔ Audits: If the IRS has told you previously that you need to pay quarterly estimates and you fail to do so, you can bet you are more likely to be audited. You'll increase your chances by about 2%–3% above normal!

---

22. What are these forms?
    1040: the basic form that everyone files
    Schedule C: the business for the husband
    Schedule SE: the form that calculates self-employment taxes for the business
    1040-ES: the estimates that would need to be sent in for the next year (not for the current year, as those would have been paid the prior year)—note that they state 2014 and we are showing a 2013 filed return
    Not shown, 2210: the form that calculates the penalties due for underpayment of the estimates—normally this would also be prepared (FYI)

CHAPTER 9

Your Business Team

In a small organization, the operations of the business tend toward teamwork structures. In such a business you might have five or six people, all of whom know how to do almost anything in the office. Some of those people may have specialty skills for focusing on a couple of key tasks, but anyone in the office can and does perform general tasks, such as handling the mail and helping a walk-in client.

It's important to determine your operations structure because it forces you to think about your own skill set and the skill sets of your current partners or shareholders—to know what, if any, business tasks you should be outsourcing. While many hear the word *outsource* and think of a hefty business bill they want to avoid, they should be thinking instead of what it might mean in wasted time and effort and, ultimately, lost profits to have unqualified people doing necessary tasks.

Any business, no matter what industry or structure, has tasks that can be outsourced. My rule of thumb is to focus on what you are good at and outsource what you are not. Before we dive into the different personnel and experts you may need for your business, let's explore further how you can decide when to outsource (or hire someone in-house) and when to handle a task yourself.

Human and Professional Elements: What Do You Need and Why?

First you need to determine your own strengths and weaknesses. This goes back to the idea we discussed in Chapter 1 of business owners being managers, entrepreneurs, technicians, or a combination. Of course, when you initially

97

start your business, you may be required to be all three, because you—and only you—are the business. You do everything for that business from emptying the trash cans to prospecting for and serving the clients.

But calling upon experts will help you before you even start your business, and after you're up and running, the time will come when you need to expand your team. What some small business owners don't understand—or understand but fail to follow through on—is the importance of outsourcing the business tasks at which they don't excel. Everyone has his or her own set of skills, just as each business owner will have his or her stumbling blocks—business tasks which he or she is ill equipped to accomplish solo.

Suppose that you're a trained auto mechanic, and you open an auto repair service. You don't know the first thing about accounting. You also don't have a lot of start-up money, however, so you decide you're just going to have to do the bookkeeping yourself, in between or after a day of fixing cars. You spend many hours trying to learn QuickBooks, get thoroughly frustrated, and don't learn enough to do it well. In the meantime, you've turned away customers because there just aren't enough hours in the day. At some point, the time you spend on doing the bookkeeping yourself may well cost you more in lost profits than you would have spent had you outsourced the bookkeeping to an accounting specialist.

If you're having trouble understanding the concept of manager, technician, or entrepreneur, or you're not convinced you can't be all three, think about your own doctor and how her or his office runs. Have you ever seen your doctor leave in the middle of conducting your exam—perhaps administering a shot—to take a call from another patient who doesn't understand a bill? Or have you seen the nurse who is about to record your vitals leaving the room because someone else called to schedule an appointment? Or perhaps because the deadline is near for the doctor's Yellow Pages ad and she hasn't finished writing that copy?

You can see how poorly this kind of office system would run. The doctor and the nurse are technicians. They aren't trained, and are probably not skilled, to resolve billing questions, handle appointment schedules, or design ads. The billing questions might be handed off to either a staff member or a contractor, the appointment setting to a staff member, and the ad design to a consultant. Doing it any other way would lead to chaos, and a less effective work environment, as people struggle to complete tasks for which they're ill suited and neglect those for which they've been trained. To carry this concept one step further, how would you feel about that billing clerk stepping in to finish your physical exam while the doctor is down the hall resolving a billing conflict?

When you try to do it all—when you fail to delegate or outsource those tasks for which you are less equipped than for your primary skill set—you undermine the efficiency and even the profit-making capability of your firm. If you don't care if your business succeeds and you decide that doing it all by yourself is more important than making money from your own business, then take on all the tasks of technician, manager, and entrepreneur. But if you want a business that thrives and the enjoyment of doing what you love, then determine where you excel and hire out the rest. Don't fall into the trap of trying to do it all!

This is the "team building" part of your business start-up. It is always smarter to surround yourself with people more brilliant than you, no matter what the field—though the caution here is to be sure you put a system of checks and balances in place that lets you know quickly if someone is acting in a way that can hurt your company and/or break the law.

People you definitely want on your team are your business or corporate lawyer and a CPA/accountant or bookkeeper. Or perhaps you'll want a bookkeeper as well as a CPA; the functions of bookkeeping differ from those of a CPA, and you may or may not find everything you need in one person or firm. If you buy a building to house your company, you'll want a commercial (not residential) real estate agent. You'll also need a business banker. The next sections will look at these and other professionals you may need to utilize in your business.

Before You Start Your Business

You may need help in any number of areas. The following is a basic list of those professionals and areas I believe to be most important for a good business start, as well as some hints, tips, and questions that you should be asking potential vendors or other assistance-providing experts.

Mentors

Mentors are one of the most important sources of guidance when you start your business. They are the people you admire, who are successful in the ways you want to be, have what you want, and are who you want to be. I have found that having mentors in your life will help keep you from making major mistakes (because they have already made them). They can help you make important, life-changing decisions—decisions that can make your business great!

I mentioned SCORE (Service Corps of Retired Executives) earlier as a resource for you and your new business. It's a fabulous organization of retired business executives who have been where you are, through the good and bad. Most have valuable connections at financial institutions and in municipal and state governments; many are members of company boards of directors. You can inquire of them regarding any part of your business, either online or in person. The SCORE website is a great place to start, as it allows you to search by location, industry, and topic to find just the right SCORE member to counsel you. You can post your question online and get a number of responses, or you can make an appointment to meet a local SCORE mentor in person. Best of all, all this help is free.

Note: You have to be willing to really *listen* to your mentors. If you find the right mentors, they are there to help you, not hurt you; and even if the advice they are giving doesn't sound nice/helpful/useful, it really is. Keep your ears open and your ego (the one inside you, saying "you don't need them—you know what's best") at bay at least long enough so your logical mind can choose the best path for yourself.

In my life I have two mentors—the people I look up to and respect, and whose judgment I trust above all else: my mother, an amazing woman who came from nothing and who has it all; and my stepfather, a kind and wise man who always has a jump in his step and a thoughtful and insightful response to any question.

Remember, most people are honored when you ask them if they can mentor you. Everyone has something to share, and most of us love to do that! To find your perfect mentor(s), seek the people you look up to the most, whose actions and words resonate with you. Ask them if they would be willing to mentor you—to be sounding boards for your ideas and questions and maybe even share with you some of their life experiences to help you choose your best path. You will find the right people—just keep your eyes open!

Banker

Bankers are important service providers for your business. They assist you in managing cash flow, getting loans and lines of credit, and establishing business credit, and, of course, they handle your cash.

Before you start looking for the right banker, ask yourself some questions:

- ✔ Am I privately funding my business?
- ✔ Am I putting in my own money?

✔ How much money will I need beyond my own personal funds?

✔ How do I think the business is going to run, and what kinds of cash flow do I anticipate? (We'll talk more about this later, in Chapter 13.)

Here a few questions to ask a banker you are considering:

✔ What area do you specialize in for the bank? Business? Personal?

✔ Can you help me with loans?

✔ Can I speak to some referrals (in the same type of work you are looking for—business banking, personal banking, loans) who can give testimony as to your work?

✔ How long have you been with the bank? (The answer should be *at least* three years.)

✔ Have you won any awards as a banker? What were they? What do they represent?

✔ If I am a brand-new business and I want to cash a $10,000 check on day five of our relationship, how many days' hold are you going to put on that check?[23]

Shop around carefully for your business banker. Having the right one can make a big difference in your company's cash flow and even its ability to survive. A banker who doesn't know who you are—or your company's banking history—and who doesn't have your best interests at heart can be detrimental to your cash flow. If you've had a personal account with the bank, that can help, though not as much as you might think. When it comes to banking, a new business is a new business—less so with a sole proprietorship, where your company's financial troubles are yours, than any other type of business entity. The others—partnerships and C or S corps—are brand new persons with brand new EINs (Employer Identification Numbers), and each can be thought of as a brand-new person by that bank. Most banks will not consider your company for a business loan until it has been in business for two years.

---

23. This is a crucial question for a new company that doesn't have a lot of funding resources and needs to convert client payments to cash rather quickly. Some banks take up to ten days to take the hold off of these funds, and when you're a new small business, ten days can seem like a lifetime. You might need to pay a carrier or one of your workers—or buy equipment if you get that big job. Not being able to get your hands on your money for ten days can make or break your business. Many banks have an automatic five-day hold during the first ninety days of your relationship with them, and then they will cut back to a one-day hold. I've seen this issue firsthand. One of my clients was with a small Arizona credit union, depositing $50,000 in his checking account when he opened it and started his business. He wanted the credit union to view his business as stable, with a good amount of cash on hand. Still, the credit union put a five-day hold on the funds he deposited, until the ninety-first day, when the hold changed to one day. He met personally with the head of risk management at the credit union to have the hold removed for any deposit under $5,000. That was the best concession he could get.

While the idea of a small local bank or credit union might appeal to you, this is generally not the best decision. First, in this economy, some smaller banks are being closed or sold out, and as a result they're less likely to have the funds to lend to your business and/or may be stricter about lending. Within just these past few years, for instance, Desert Hill Bank was closed down by federal regulators and Wells Fargo bought Wachovia. My own credit union cannot do small business association (SBA) loans; they don't even communicate with the SBA. In fact, only the larger banks do, such as Bank of America, Chase, and Wells Fargo.

Remember that your banker and your lender do not need to be the same person. Often lenders can be family, friends, an SBA/government loan, or many other options. Don't close your eyes to the possibilities of financing around you.

New business owners all too often fail to prepare for supporting themselves, their family, and their business for approximately two years, the time it generally takes a new business to start turning a profit. The owner launches her new business, all excited about it, assuming life is about to become fabulous, but she fails to consider things like where she'll get the financing for the equipment her new company is going to need.

Lawyer

A key figure, both before you set up your business and throughout the life of your business, will be your lawyer/attorney. There are many different types of attorneys; to start, you will want a corporate attorney. This person can help you draw up your operating agreement, if you have partners or are in a state that requires one for setup. A corporate attorney can help answer questions such as: Who should sign the shares of stock? When should you patent your product? And so on. Note that a good lawyer can cost $300 per hour or more. It is important that you get correct advice when you start, so be prepared to spend at least $5K on getting your business going.[24]

Here are some questions to ask lawyers as potential new consultants:

- ✔ What types of cases do you work on? What is your specialty?

- ✔ What type of referral network do you have? If I have another type of legal need, whom would I turn to?

---

24. I get asked about this a lot. Clients comment that they've been told they can set up their business and be ready to "rock and roll" for only $395 at some website. Realize that you get what you pay for. I have seen way too many cases where a business owner pays $395 now and $30,000-plus later because something is seriously wrong or missing and now the owner has to fix it. ***Do not skimp on this piece***; it is the foundation for your house, here! Buy the best you can afford. In some cases, especially if it has to do with a partner, I often recommend that if you cannot afford to do it right now, don't even bother. Let one partner start the firm and pay the other partner as a contractor/employee until you can afford to do it right.

✔ Are there other lawyers who can provide references for you?

✔ Can you give me the number of the state governance board for lawyers? If I need it, can I have your lawyer registration number?

✔ What are your fees? Can I have an engagement letter in writing?

✔ How long have you been in practice? For whom? Doing what types of work?

CPA / Tax Professional[25] (Make Sure You Read This Footnote!)

One point I've made here—and several places throughout this book—is that your CPA is not just someone you turn to at tax preparation time. A CPA should be helping you plan your business strategies, with an eye to how they will affect your financial statements and your bottom line. Not many business owners *want* to plan, but planning is important. It's the difference between proactively growing your business and reactively letting it grow or fail on its own.

You want a CPA who is in periodic contact with you throughout the year, e-mailing you with reminders and tips, perhaps even offering an e-newsletter, and just in general letting you know that she or he is keeping abreast of new tax legislation and how it might affect your business.

You should have a face-to-face planning meeting with your CPA sometime in May, right after your taxes are filed, and again in October or November. You'll first look at whether or not you met the goals you set in the previous year's planning sessions (if you met in the previous year) and then plan for the coming tax season. You might discuss, for example, if you should set up a retirement account, or buy a new business vehicle, or pay your child a W-2 wage. If you don't plan in this way, all of a sudden it's December 31 and you don't have a lot of options to alter what could be bad news at tax time. From December 31 through April 15, your only options for altering your current tax outcome are Simplified Employee Pension (SEP) accounts and IRAs. For anything else, it's just too late.

A tax return is not about creativity; it's not about altering your company's bottom line. Preparing a tax return is simply the act of putting figures on a form. Nearly everything that would alter those figures for the benefit of the company's profit had to have happened prior to tax deadline.

I always recommend planning sessions every May and October. I've had clients who didn't use my services for planning throughout the year and suffered due

---

25. Because you purchased this book (or it was given to you as a gift by a wise person!), the Tax Goddess wants to give you something in return: *a free thirty-minute telephone consultation on any issue you may have.* Call 602-357-3275 to book your telephone call today! If you don't already have a CPA, this is a great, free, helpful way for you to start talking with a professional.

to that lack of planning. One particular client couple met with me in May, and their business plans were going along well. In October, however, they both had the flu and our meeting had to be postponed. In the meantime, before year-end they had sold their business—without consulting me beforehand. I discovered this only when they showed up in January for help with their annual taxes.

"We got as much as we could claimed as tangible assets," they told me proudly.

"On the contrary," I replied. "The buyer talked you into putting everything into hard assets and you got the worst of the deal. Now you have to pay ordinary tax rates on all those assets. We could have saved you all sorts of money, but you didn't tell me ahead of time."

To reiterate this important point, major events such as buying or selling must be planned ahead with your tax preparer. Talk with your professional as well before buying and selling a company car, deciding whether to pay health insurance premiums out of your business funds, or contributing to a SEP. Some things you just won't know that your CPA will. For instance, paying health insurance premiums on behalf of your company owners is now a big no-no for S corps if those premiums aren't declared on the W-2s. That's only one example of the kinds of bumps in the tax road that can occur if you make decisions without consulting your tax planner. Make it part of your business strategy to meet with your company CPA three times a year: twice for planning, once for taxes. And if you have a CPA who only wants to complete tax returns and doesn't want to help you plan, get another CPA. I take pride in the fact that some of my clients refer to me as their "rented CFO"—someone who can help keep them on financial track throughout the year, not just prepare their taxes. You'll want your own rented CFO as well. After all, your goal in owning a business is to keep the money you make and not give it to the government, right?

Of course, having a trained and objective eye look at your business processes can be helpful with far more than getting a tax break. In comparing the current- and prior-year financial statements of one client's business, I noticed that employee expenses had nearly doubled. Neither sales nor profit had increased as a result, however. I inquired of the client. She said she had hired her brother to do some selling and had been paying him a salary for six months, but he had produced no sales to date. Had she been the only one overseeing those financial statements she might never have given that unproductive sibling of hers the boot. In general, business owners can get so involved in running the business day to day—putting out each day's fires, so to speak—that they fail to step back and take a look at the business as a whole. Having that external eye to take an objective look is almost always helpful, whether it's about taxes or any other part of the workings of your business.

Business Coach

Business coaches, just like mentors, are very important to a new business. Honestly, they are important for a growing and stable and end-stage/wrapping-up business as well. They are just all-around important. Why, you may ask? A good business coach will hold you accountable. Just like a coach in basketball or baseball, the business coach's job is to push you to your limits and beyond, with the training and coaching to get you there. To make sure that you don't pick wimpy goals. To see that you are on track and doing what you said you would do. Everyone needs a coach, though not everyone wants one. Some people are okay with staying in their comfort zones. But if you do what you've always done, you'll get what you've always gotten (per Tony Robbins, and many other great minds, anyway).

I believe that it is the job of a coach to help you determine what your goals in life are and then to help you reach them. Not everyone's goals are the same. While some people are interested in amassing tons of money, others want just enough money to live on and lots of time to spend with their families. Remember, your goals are *your* goals. No one can determine them for you; no one can tell you what you "should" be when you grow up. Only you can do this, and you need to really ponder where you are trying to get to so that you can lay out the proper map with your coach and your mentors.

I have two coaches in my life: my business coach, Fred Kroin, an awesome and inspiring and tough man who always holds my feet to the fire; and my personal coach, Katie, who knows just which buttons to push and when—and then helps me find my own answers. Between the two of them, I feel completely within my own power to be able to handle anything that comes my way. That's a pretty powerful feeling, and I love living in that every day. Do you have people in your life like this? People who push you, in a good way, past your limits? I know, sometimes you don't love it; but it's like taking medicine when you are sick—you know it will make you better even if it does taste like cough syrup.

So let's check in with Fred Kroin, owner and executive business coach at Goal Partners (whom you met in Chapter 1), on the benefits of a business coach:

Why is it important for a small business to have a business coach?

Mostly because we're all human! And it's not just true for small businesses—leaders and executives at larger companies need coaches, too. We all have strengths and weaknesses (okay, call them "opportunities for improvement" if you want to be politically correct), and we're rarely the best qualified to identify which are which and know how to mold them to our best advantage. A professional business coach has the experience and the tools to evaluate skills and, if the subject is motivated to improve, can be a great help in developing a plan for improvement and holding you accountable to your commitments.

When should the business hire one?

Asking [me] "When should a small business hire a business coach?" is somewhat analogous to asking the wolf when it's okay for him to mind the henhouse. But seriously, there are actually many answers that could be given (that is, if you are hiring a top-quality coach):

o Whenever you feel like you're over your head and don't know where to turn

o Whenever you find yourself with too many things to do and not enough time to do them

o Whenever you want someone to give you nonjudgmental advice on achieving your business goals or personal leadership abilities

o Whenever you find yourself unable to comfortably and confidently answer critical questions or make decisions about your business, its employees, or its customers

o Whenever you get serious about (sorry for the cliché) taking your business to the next level and want a professional facilitator to guide you through the creation of a strategic business plan

o Whenever you wake up and realize that you've not set *any* goals (for the business or yourself) or that you have, but no one is holding you accountable to accomplish them

o Whenever you find your managers or employees are not meeting their roles and responsibilities and you're not sure how to remedy the situation

o Whenever you begin to think you already know everything you need to know about business or life!

While this list goes on and on, any one of these alone could be a signal that a small business owner should think about engaging a coach.

Is it important to have one from the get-go?

While many business owners think that having a coach is a luxury only a mature, flourishing business can afford, it doesn't have to be that way. You wouldn't start a business without having a lawyer or a *fabulous CPA* like the Tax Goddess, would you? A business coach need not cost you more than a good lawyer and can be enormously valuable in saving you from making very costly mistakes. That said, don't go out and hire a coach the minute you get an idea for a business in your mind. Think the idea through, and draft an outline for your business plan (if you can't find one on the Internet, contact me and I'll send you one) and its mathematical model (i.e., How is my business going to make money?), even if it's on the back of the proverbial napkin. This process is likely to create lots of questions in your mind and I'd suggest you write them down to use as potential interview questions for your coach candidates. As soon as you have more than three or four questions, start interviewing coaches.

What does a business coach do (what are the top five most important things)?

While this could again develop into a long list with corresponding elements for each of the bullets in the answer above, below are what I would consider the top five most important things a coach does:

o   Encourages you to set S.M.A.R.T. goals (i.e., Specific, Measurable, Achievable, Relevant, and Time-bound)

o   Holds you accountable to those goals, initiating processes to measure and monitor goals to keep you on course

o   Helps you determine key priorities to make sure you focus on the most strategic things you, as the business owner, *must* do

o   Asks the tough questions to challenge your thinking (making you face decisions in a timely way, keeping you from procrastinating and improving your time management)

o   Assists you in impartially evaluating your strengths and opportunities for improvement as a leader and developing a plan for further personal growth

What questions should a business owner ask when interviewing a coach?

o   What should I expect from you as a coach and how is that different from other coaches?

o   How long should we expect to work together? How often?

o   What requirements do you have of me?

o   What questions do you have of me, before you will agree to take me on as a client?

- o Please describe your basic philosophy toward coaching a small business owner. How is that different from how you'd coach an owner of a business ten times my size?

- o What makes one small business more successful than another?

- o Why do you think you can help me specifically?

What should business owners listen for that should make them run away from a potential coach?

Like most relationships, relationships with coaches take time to develop and there is often a get-acquainted learning curve or even a honeymoon period in some relationships. So, assuming the interview process leaves the business owner comfortable that there is some good basic chemistry with the coach they're inclined to select, a certain minimum time period of two to three months should be established with the expectation that it could continue for a longer period of time. However, if a coach insists that a longer term contract is required up front and that the client must agree to work with them for six months or more, I'd certainly need to understand why before making any commitment that long. That said, either party (yes, the coach, too) should have the ability to terminate the relationship with minimal notice.

As every coach-coachee relationship is different, anything that suggests a magic formula or rigidity in approach would be danger signs to me. Furthermore, recognizing that every business owner has a unique personality and style, a coach that dictates solutions or insists that a client follow every piece of advice the coach gives to the letter of the law would scare me.

A good coach will do the opposite—that is, coach their client to come up with possible solutions to problems or make decisions and then encourage the client to examine the pros and cons of each alternative. Clients learn more from the questions the coach asks than from the answers the coach gives.

Insurance Agent

A good insurance agent is not just someone that you pick because the commercial for the company looks good. A good insurance agent is someone who will interview you, yearly. This person will ask all the tough questions and find out about changes in your business. Have you added more people or a new line of business? What new things are you doing that you need protection for, and for which are you paying too much or overprotected? It is important on both sides that you have the *right* coverage, not just any coverage. Your agent should be able to guide you to what is right for you and what you should or should not do—and to help you answer all the little questions in between.

Note that, as with your banker, an individual insurance agent—who knows how to handle your car and home—is different from a business insurance agent, who can handle your E&O (errors and omissions) insurance, workers' compensation, life insurance, fleet auto insurance, and so on. There are so many different business policies that it makes my head spin! This is why you need a good agent, someone who knows you and your business (type/model included—see if you can find a specialist).

What kinds of questions and considerations should you keep in mind when looking for a business insurance agent?

- ✔ When you are interviewing an agent, she or he should have the heart of a teacher, not a salesperson.

- ✔ What companies does the agent represent? What is the agent's A.M. Best rating?

- ✔ What is the agent's Better Business Bureau rating?

- ✔ Does the agent have references you can talk to in similar or different business areas?

- ✔ Has the agency ever had an errors and omissions claim filed against it?

- ✔ Is the agent's business with a company she or he represents?

- ✔ How hard will it be to talk to the agent after the sale?

- ✔ Is the insurance agent a salesperson? Or a professional making recommendations and letting you decide?

- ✔ Is the agency big enough to handle your insurance needs, but small enough to remember your name?

- ✔ Most important, many agents talk about the level of service they provide and how they will be there before, during, and after a claim. Ask the agent for a cell phone number for an emergency and watch for her or his reaction. The reaction and response will tell you how serious the agent is about service.

What types of insurance do businesses need (all businesses, not specialty types)?

When new businesses start, they need to consider—at a minimum—the following types of insurance:

✔ *General liability:* This insurance provides the business protection in the event of a liability claim against the company (e.g., if a customer slips and falls in a store). Many of these policies are also known as BOP (business owner policy). A BOP will provide a comprehensive set of coverages that the normal business owner will need, including but not limited to coverage for the building, inventory, business income, theft, vandalism, and product liability (defects in the product or the quality of the workmanship).

✔ *Business auto insurance:* If a vehicle is used in the course of business, you will want business auto insurance. Examples of relevant businesses could include plumbers, electricians, pool cleaners, contractors, and delivery services. Some personal lines insurance companies will allow certain industries to be rated on their personal auto policies. Examples include realtors, insurance professionals, and many more. To save money, always check with your personal insurance agent for your options.

✔ *Workers' compensation:* Businesses with employees are required by the state to have workers' compensation insurance in the event an employee is hurt.

✔ *Professional liability:* Lawyers, doctors, dentists, accountants, and many other professionals should consider this type of insurance in the event a claim is brought against them for service they provided.

✔ *Disability insurance:* In the event a business owner is injured and unable to work, having disability insurance is critical to the successful continuation of the business. For example, if a lawyer were disabled for a period of time and unable to work, the disability benefit would usually allow the law firm to continue until the lawyer's recovery.

✔ *Key man life insurance:* This life insurance will provide immediate benefits in the event of the death of a key person in the business. The insurance proceeds allow the business to continue on until a replacement can be hired.

✔ *Group health insurance:* Depending on the size of the business, the business owner may want to consider health insurance to provide coverage. The benefit of group coverage is an applicant cannot be denied coverage.[26]

✔ *Group life and disability insurance:* These types of coverage are generally very affordable and have a tremendous effect on employee retention. The policies usually provide options for guaranteed issue life and disability insurance for the employees without any medical exam.

---

26. In 2013 the Affordable Care Act went into effect for many businesses. Make sure you that you are checking with your insurance company to determine what you need to do to be in compliance with these regulations. Many of them apply only to companies with more than fifty employees, but there are regulations that apply to smaller, one- and two-person companies as well.

What phrases should business owners listen for that should make them choose a different agent?

Use common sense, and if it seems too good to be true, turn away and go elsewhere! If you hear any of the following, run.

- ✔ Trust me!
- ✔ I guarantee it! But I am not willing to put it in writing.
- ✔ Our prices are just cheaper!
- ✔ My buddy . . .

Sales Coach

One of the most beneficial things I did for my new business—and one I recommend—was to hire a sales coach. Spending money up front on a sales coach may seem financially scary, until you consider what you'll have wasted if the efforts and money you put into "doing your own sales thing" don't result in an acceptable return on investment (ROI). A sales coach doesn't have to cost a lot. You might even have a willing and knowledgeable family member guide you.

Let's get some input from an amazing sales coach here in Arizona, Connie Kadansky:

What are some ways business owners can hold themselves accountable without hiring a coach?

Find someone who will be your accountability partner, but not just anyone. Choose carefully. Look for someone who will support you, encourage you, and actually hold you to the goals you set.

If someone sets a goal and writes it down, their chance of achieving the goal is about 37 percent. However, if someone sets a goal, writes it down, shares it with someone like a coach, friend, or colleague, *and* reports on their progress at the end of every day, their chance of achieving the goal goes up to 76 percent. That is pretty exciting. See the research study below for further details:

> *Matthews, G. (2007). Study Backs Up Strategies for Achieving Goals. http://www.dominican.edu/dominicannews/study-backs-*

RESOURCE

Sales coach Connie Kadansky is known as one of the leaders in getting businesspeople over their cold call reluctance. If you aren't sure how to get yourself or your people out of their own way here, call Connie! (You'll learn more about cold calling in Chapter 11, and you can find Connie's information in Appendix D.)

up-strategies-for-achieving-goals.html. Retrieved February 24, 2011

Why is it beneficial to hire a coach for sales?

No winner ever got there without a coach. Hiring a coach is an investment in your success. Compare two business owners in the same city, same business, same demographics. Business Owner A hires a coach, while Business Owner B doesn't. The odds are that Business Owner A will outperform Business Owner B by a significant percentage. A trained, certified coach helps their clients move from their current reality to their desired result. A coach is much different than a consultant. Both bring value, but a consultant tells you what to do, shakes your hand, and says, Good luck! A coach sticks with you through the ups and downs of building your business. A good coach will challenge you, keep you accountable, and help you move forward toward your goals. They are often the best cheerleaders for their clients. Hiring a coach is an investment, not an expense.

As an expert in helping businesspeople overcome cold call reluctance, Connie Kadansky has a lot of advice for business owners on how to make prospecting phone calls—we'll hear from her about this in Chapter 11.

IT People / "Tech Peeps"

Depending on your industry, an information technology (IT) person can be very important. Like all the other members on your outsourced team, your IT professionals need to be very familiar with your business—what you do, how you do it. A great tech person is a crucial part of my business as a CPA. Without the computers, a working network, secure file servers, remote access to client accounts, and the list could go on and on, my team and I would never be able to work in the way we do. We would never be able to give the service we do to our clients.

Now, unfortunately for most of us, we don't know the differences between a network administrator, a tech person, a webmaster, and other technology roles. So make sure, when you are interviewing your potential tech professionals, that you ask them what they do, why that is important for you, and what their titles really mean. Donald Kupper, one of our tech geniuses from our local CMIT branch, gives us his top five questions to ask before you hire any tech company/professional:

RESOURCE

Don Kupper is my company's favorite tech genius. He keeps us up and running, and we couldn't survive without him!

1. Are you comfortable outsourcing technology?

If technology is not your core competency, but it is important to your business, then outsourcing needs to be considered. Understand your potential partners' expertise—expertise in desktop, server, and network competencies; security (antivirus, anti-malware, backup, spam filtering); e-mail system software; industry-specific software; web development. Do they keep up-to-date on changes in your industry? Do they understand IT best practices?

Outsourcing to the right company can save you lots of time—and save you a full-time salary. Look for a company that is locally owned and speak to their clients. Find out what clients they have lost and why. Ask about the technicians! The salespeople are good at sales, but the tech is the one that will keep you up and running. Do they cross-train the employees that will be servicing you? Do you have a "dedicated" tech that will work with you on budgets, planning, and growing your business? Managed services (monitoring PCs for issues before you have them) is the new standard in IT companies. The managed services model is great for both the IT company and for you, the small business owner. The IT company will be motivated to keep you up and running without any issues, as they can service more clients per technician versus the old "break-fix" model that only allows them profit when technicians are servicing issues.

2. What are their skills, and how deep is their bench?

Something you need to find out is the depth of skills in the areas that you need. Do they have experience in your industry? Is there specialized software for your industry? Do you use contact management software? Do they take a proactive management approach (monitoring your systems and performing preventative maintenance), or do they just come when they are called, when something is broken? Again, managed services is usually a better model for not only the business owner but also for the technician or IT company if you are outsourcing.

Regarding their bench, do they have multiple technicians or is this provider a single-person operation? Aside from their internal resources, do they have additional resources outside their own company? If you plan to hire a full-time IT person, remember that the depth of the technician's expertise is still an important issue to address. Will he or she put safeguards in place? Does the technician document your systems, in case he or she is out? When interviewing and deciding between in-source and outsource, ask these questions and prepare to add training and outside support to your budget. Even technicians need a vacation.

3. What else will they provide?

Of course you want your IT company to fix things when they are broken, but what other value-added tasks can they provide? Will they help with technology planning? Understand your business and assist with technology budgeting?

Budgeting is a need that is often overlooked, and many technicians are afraid to approach the business owner asking for more money. Be sure that any company or tech that you hire is looking at your growth patterns and planning the budgets around your business goals. Bring them into your planning meetings and include them in your growth. Many times business owners forget that if they will be growing and hiring people, IT needs to keep up with the growth and budget for more PCs and other network equipment. If you will be hiring a tech in-house, be sure he or she is comfortable with these discussions as well as skilled with your software and hardware. If the tech is only going to "speak geek," he or she may not be the best fit for your small company. Look for techs that also know business and planning.

4. Certifications and insurance:

What certifications does the provider have? Technical, industry? Are they insured? What is their coverage? If you are outsourcing or hiring for full-time techs, do they know the requirements of your business? HIPPA (Health Information Protection Policy Act), PCI compliance (for credit information and processing), and other industry regulations need to be considered in your hiring process.

If you are planning on hiring a technician full-time, these laws and training on the requirements need to be planned into the IT budget as well. Training needs to include not only new software, but also any new regulations and requirements. It may be as simple as subscribing to a trade magazine or allowing the technician to attend local meetings with other industry techs, but it needs to be planned for and should be part of your interview process. If outsourcing, does the technology company do this? What training do they offer their employees?

5. Are they able to deliver the hard message?

You want your IT provider to be able to deliver the hard message to you, be open, honest, and up-front. You may not always agree, but you need someone to be able to tell you your options, as well as the risks associated with those options, and make an informed recommendation. You also need to be able to work with them if you can't take that recommendation at that time (could be due to cost, timing, industry support, etc.). As part of your vetting process, did they assess your existing environment? Did they give you feedback on what was good and what can be improved? Did they miss things that you know can be improved? If they proposed changes, did they spell out the benefits of the change or the risk of not making the change? Ask them, if you can put off making the changes, will they still support you?

One thing that I have learned about the tech world is that you should protect the security of your own domain, network, passwords, e-mails, websites, and so on. I know, especially after you have some serious trust with your technical person, it seems okay to share your master passwords, log-ins, and so forth. Realize that if you do this, that person can hijack your entire system, taking you down for days or even permanently. A tech can destroy your business in minutes if he or she ever wanted to. I recommend that you always keep the master passwords and final authorization for deleting files, backups, and so on. Always have a backup somewhere safe where the technical person may not know about it. I know it sounds paranoid, but I would rather you be safe than sorry!

During Operations

You will need several additional types of people during the operations of your company. You may not need all of them at the start, but these are positions that you, as the owner, may be handling without realizing and may at some point want to outsource.

HR Professional

One commonly outsourced area is human resources (HR), the "hiring and firing" part of running your business. In some states this is more important than in others. Virtually all U.S. states are "at-will" states—meaning that employees have the right to quit at any time and employers have the right to terminate them at any time, with few exceptions (one of which is discrimination). States vary, however, on the number of exceptions they make to their "at-will" status. Arizona, for example, has fewer exceptions than California, which means that it's easier for an Arizona employer to terminate an employee without fear of litigious reprisal than it is for a California employer to do so. But who wants to be responsible for knowing all the exceptions, especially when to violate them could mean serious problems for their firms? Typically a business owner would be far better off going about her "business" and letting an HR expert take on the day-to-day human resource tasks.

115

An HR professional can help you with not only hiring and firing but also training, development, performance management, systems and procedures, and other matters relating to personnel, whether in-house staff or contractors. Chapter 10 looks at human resources in more detail.

Bookkeeper

A good bookkeeper is hard to find. Many people who call themselves bookkeepers do not really have the training to help you set up and then run your books accurately. What you are looking for in a bookkeeper (especially the one who is going to set up your books to start with) is someone who is a QuickBooks Pro Advisor. You want someone who has at least seven years of experience working with small- to medium-sized businesses with setup and training in QuickBooks. You may want a different person to handle your day-to-day bookkeeping, but this first bookkeeper should be someone with experience.

Now, in many cases, once you find the right first bookkeeper, you will not want some data-entry person in your office—and to this point I agree. I think this is an area where you should pay for and expect quality. This person will be your right-hand financial-numbers person for a while. Alongside your CPA, your bookkeeper will be helping you make management decisions about how you run your business, collections practices, billing clients, almost everything. This person helps you get your cash in the door and make sure that you aren't spending it unwisely. She or he should have some great business and life experience in order to really be an asset to you and your business.

Some organizations offer bookkeeping skills tests. I would recommend using these as well as getting at least four recommendations from *current* clients of this bookkeeper. You will want to ask questions that relate to how the bookkeeper will be working in your business. Some of these important questions could be:

- ✔ How many days a week does your bookkeeper come in?

- ✔ What areas of the business does your bookkeeper handle?

- ✔ What sorts of permissions do you give your bookkeeper?

- ✔ What is the best area for this bookkeeper (reliable, smart, knowledgeable, etc.)?

- ✔ What is an area of weakness that you see in this bookkeeper? (Do not let the reference say none. If the person says none, you need a different recommendation—everyone has at least one weakness.)

Our expert head of bookkeeping, Tina Wahl, has this advice for interviewing bookkeeper candidates:

What are the top questions that a business owner should ask of a potential bookkeeper?

○ How long have you been a bookkeeper?

○ Have you worked with my particular type of business before?

○ Do you have any tax knowledge/experience? Can you help me analyze my data?

○ Are you familiar with QuickBooks?

What are some key phrases that a bookkeeper may say that should scare you away?

○ I'm just learning accounting but the price is right at $___/ hour.

○ I've found that spreadsheets work fine for accounting, so why pay for software?

○ What is a balance sheet?

○ I'm not sure what the difference is between cash and accrual, but it's probably not important.

A note about some operations pieces here . . . I have seen too many people be "taken" by their bookkeepers for thousands of dollars because the owners put too much power, control, and trust into the hands of the bookkeeper. Make sure that you have good internal controls (something your CPA can and should help you design) so that your bookkeeper doesn't have an opportunity to do something like this to you.

Some basic internal controls are:

✔ Have different people open the mail and pay bills.

✔ Always get a reconciled bank statement with a copy of the bank statement attached so you can review for strange checks/charges.

✔ Never allow the person paying bills to have your signature stamp.

RESOURCE

Tina Wahl, our head of bookkeeping, is an excellent trainer in QuickBooks as well as deeply versed in accounting methods and best practices. I may be a Tax Goddess, but she is our Bookkeeping Goddess!

✔ Always have sequentially numbered checks. If something is out of order, find out why.

✔ Always review your bank and credit card statements for strange charges. (This could be vendor error or a sign of something more dubious!)

Payroll Professional

Because the federal government is very aggressive in getting its money, I highly recommend that any business hire a payroll company. With contractors you don't have the procedural worries you do with employees. You can just write a contractor a check, deliver the annual 1099 form by January 31 of the following year, and leave the taxes and other forms to the contractor.

Employees, however, require more effort and far more paperwork and documentation on your part. Payroll taxes are just the tip of the HR iceberg when you have employees. You'll have to submit multiple government forms at various points in the year for various reasons. These are not duties you'll want to stumble through unaided. Even to clients who have long been doing their own payroll I recommend stopping and handing it off to a payroll service firm. It's just too easy to miss a rate or a deduction change and end up with an end-of-year error that could cost you dearly at tax time. I've generally found that the big, well-known payroll service companies are the best choices you can make, though your choice will depend on the level of service you want and need.

Notable firms such as Paychex, ADP, and CompuPay offer fabulous hand-holding services. You call them; they send their representative to you; you give that rep the time sheets; she or he figures the payroll, makes the required deductions for all, and pays all the outside firms as needed, such as the financial services firm that manages your retirement accounts, the health insurance company that provides medical benefits to your staff, and the U.S. government that wants its payroll taxes; and then the rep cuts the checks for your employees. For a high-end payroll service, you'll pay perhaps as much as $100 each payday for a staff of ten.

I'd be remiss in not mentioning one higher level of payroll service, which also includes human resources. A payroll employer organization, commonly referred to as a PEO, not only performs all the employer payroll functions for you but also hires your staff, who remain employees of the PEO, not of your firm. As an example, you might ask the PEO to find you someone to do office work and earn $10 an hour. The PEO does so, and for that person you pay the PEO $17 an hour—which takes care of the wage, the payroll taxes, the benefits, and the managerial work the PEO does to perform all these payroll and HR functions for you. You effectively end up with a contractor but one that you can control as you would an employee.

PEOs tend to be good for business owners who are disorganized or have a very small company. Where it's most noticeably advantageous is when you're trying to find medical coverage for a small staff, especially if one or more employees have a history of a serious disease or disorder. You might have great difficulty finding a group medical plan with rates you and your staff can afford. A retirement or 401(k) plan might be out of your reach as well. A PEO, however, is buying for all its employees that work for all its clients, and so it has the financial benefit of mass purchase. Instead of buying coverage for a staff of five, that PEO might be buying for 20,000. That drives the costs down considerably, which saves you money as well.

If you don't need a PEO and you don't want to pay for a high-level payroll service, consider PayCycle or something similar—what I'm calling mid- or medium-level service. At this level you may have access to telephone support. You'll submit the forms for payroll, and you'll have to remember what to do when. You won't be buying reminders: "Hey, business owner, you sent me the forms for this week's payroll but Joe is missing. Didn't he work?" Your own CPA might be considered a medium-level service provider, depending on how much or how little she or he offers in that area.

The lowest level of payroll service is a simple purchase of software, the best known of which is QuickBooks. This popular payroll software comes in different versions, which have varying levels of online assistance. At its most basic, you load the software, enter your payroll hours, and have it calculate the deductions for each payee and the amount of net pay for each. You then must cut the check, take it to the bank, and pay the taxes. You also must complete all government payroll forms on your own; so, while this no-service payroll option will save you money, it will also put you at greater risk for the dreaded payroll tax audit.

What makes a payroll tax audit so worrisome is that one minor error can generate a federal perusal of all your payroll form submissions for any number of years back that Uncle Sam wishes to go. I think of a payroll tax audit as a termite infestation. You never get just one termite—from the first one, thousands soon come out of the woodwork. Your failure last year at properly reporting and modifying a rate change could have the IRS asking you to prove your documented salary is "reasonable," for example. You don't ever want to have a payroll tax audit.

My recommendation, therefore, is that you don't scrimp on payroll services. The no-service payroll software version of help may save you money up front but could cost you dearly later on. I recommend a level that makes someone other

than you responsible for the required payroll forms. At this level, what you're doing is buying a payroll insurance policy, so to speak—one that protects you from the financial repercussions of a tax audit. In case of an audit you can refer that auditor to the PEO, CPA, or payroll company that you hired to complete your tax forms. They're the ones who get to answer the hard IRS questions—and to bear the brunt of any financially punitive decision.

The one exception is if an error turns out to be in the favor of one or more of your own employees. In that case, you must shell out the money due the employee(s). Should the federal government find that an error has been made in which you stand to get money back from the IRS, you will, but without any interest. Should the error be that you've paid your employees too much (deducted too little for taxes, for example), you won't want to ask them for it back. While you might have that right, it could seriously damage your relationship with your staff.

As in any industry, there are some unscrupulous payroll companies. This is a serious concern because you'll typically be giving that company access to your bank account, with the authority to take out money for payroll and payroll taxes as well as payment of its own fee.[27]

What I especially like about the big payroll companies is that they make three distinct withdrawals from your account, so you can clearly see what they've deducted each for payroll, taxes, and their own fees. Some of the smaller firms will deduct it in one withdrawal, which makes it more difficult for you to verify that what they're doing is accurate and ethical.

The other concern is that the federal government generally lags about three months behind on its oversight of company deposits. Should you—or that payroll company you've hired—fail to make January's tax payment (due in February), you might not get any notice from the IRS until May. At this point, the payroll company has been withdrawing its fee from your account for several months while you were unaware the company wasn't doing its job. Five months down the road, you might get the first inkling that perhaps 20 percent of each month's payroll is missing from your account, taken by a payroll firm that failed to pay your taxes and didn't earn that fee—and, of course, has put you in hot water with the IRS. Nor does the federal government care that your taxes are unpaid because you were swindled. It just wants its money. And you're left having to pay it and to then try to go after that payroll firm that's undoubtedly skipped town by now.

Keep these things in mind as you decide on a payroll company. Claims of being able to save you a few dollars shouldn't outweigh concerns about a company that

---

27. There are lots of cases out there; just Google "payroll fraud" and you will find them! Scary!

hasn't been in business very long and doesn't have testimonials to offer. You want to know that the company's reputation is solid, that it's not going anywhere, and that it has plenty of satisfied customers ahead of you.

When you're interviewing companies to provide your firm's payroll services, I recommend that you ask each one of them: "Am I allowed to call the IRS on my own account?" If they protest, saying, "No, we handle that for you," run away! Run away as well if they tell you not to worry if you get an IRS notice about your payroll taxes. For you should *always* worry if you get an IRS notice—and more so if someone else is doing your payroll taxes on your behalf. The IRS is happy to take your calls anytime and does so 24/7 with the exception of federal holidays. You can ask the IRS just about any question. If, for instance, you just hired a new payroll company in January, you may want to call the IRS in February to make sure your payroll taxes were paid. That federal clerk should be able to give you the check number, the amount, and the date it was paid. She or he should be able to tell you if your payroll taxes are in good standing.

> *The concern over unpaid payroll taxes, or other dishonest activities of shady payroll service firms, is the reason I recommend the larger and better-known payroll firms such as Paychex and ADP.*

The concern over unpaid payroll taxes, or other dishonest activities of shady payroll service firms, is the reason I recommend the larger and better-known payroll firms such as Paychex and ADP. They follow the laws, they resolve any issues, and they always let you know you can call the IRS anytime you wish. They do this because they have massive reputations to protect. One mistake or omission for one client and thousands have to be concerned about the quality of their work.

I've witnessed less-than-reputable behavior by CPA firms as well. A local business owner who has since become my client was the victim of a dishonest Arizona CPA who failed to pay my client's payroll taxes. From hundreds of business victims, this CPA bilked $56 million. My client was out of state when April 15 rolled around. The CPA called her and said, "I've just finished preparing your estimate. You're going to need to pay in about $15,000. Since you're out of the country, I'll pay it with my own money, and you can just mail me a check as reimbursement." The client did just that because the CPA provided her with a copy of the front of the check written to the IRS and all the documentation. While the client had noticed some odd behavior by her CPA, he'd been her firm's accountant for ten years and so she didn't question the process. Until, that is, the IRS sent her a notice about the unpaid $15,000 payroll tax bill. And the CPA disappeared—e-mails and phone calls unanswered, office empty.

Unfortunately this client still owed the IRS $15,000 plus penalties and interest. That's where I stepped in and helped her write a letter to the IRS that resulted in the waiving of an $8,000 penalty fee. The company still must pay the bill, however, plus $2,000, and is trying, probably fruitlessly, to recover the $15,000 from the CPA, who is now in jail. This was not a case of the client's not doing due diligence before hiring someone, either. This CPA had been a trusted accounting professional for many years. I believe that a long-time Ponzi scheme finally caught up with him.

Again, I urge you to choose a payroll and accounting professional carefully and to also get on the phone to the IRS quarterly to verify that your payroll tax obligations to the federal government are being met. It's a time-consuming bit of drudgery to do so, but put on your headset and be ready to work while you hold for Uncle Sam's representative to come on the line. (You can't e-mail the IRS, by the way.)

Marketing and Sales Teams

There are lots of options when it comes to marketing and sales for your new business. You will be approached by many potential consultants who can offer several different ways for you to bring in new clients quickly. Marketing generally relates to the image of your company, and the sales team is to help you bring in new clients to the company.

The consultants that you may want in each category are different but equally important. Below is a short list of potential types of consultants available to a new business.

- ✔ Marketing team:
    - o SEO (search engine optimization) professionals
    - o Social media experts
    - o Print and television/radio media specialists
    - o Public relations professionals
    - o Website developers

- ✔ Sales team:
    - o Sales coaches
    - o Direct sales people
    - o Cold callers

The hardest part for a new business is deciding where to start. You'll find more details about some of these categories—and some marketing and sales tips and strategies—in Chapter 11.

Administrative Help

Help in this area is something I could just plain not live without! I rely on my wonderful administrative assistant to manage the general office, get supplies, make sure everything is running smoothly, run schedules, and handle clients. Without her, I could not do what I need to do.

If you are like me and you need some help with general administrative tasks, an administrative assistant position may be very important for you to have. So read Chapter 10 and make sure you apply all of its strategies to getting this one right—hire slow, fire fast; do testing; do your ninety-day review; make sure that you are both happy and can be honest with each other. I know, it sounds kind of like marrying a spouse, but I'll tell you what: this person, for me, is basically my right-hand woman. I couldn't run my business without her.

There are also some great overseas services for administrative help if you don't want/need someone to physically be in your office. GetFriday and Brickworks are two excellent services. They can handle many tasks for you—it is amazing what they can get done—without even being in town. For a great outline of this, check out Tim Ferris's book *The 4-Hour Workweek*.

Customer Service Team

It is one thing to get customers, and another to keep them. It costs almost seven times as much to get a new client as it does to keep and increase your services with your old clients, who already love you. Having said that, customer service has to be one of your highest priorities. This is how your word-of-mouth advertising will help you grow without the need to spend a ton of money. It's how you build your image in the community so that you always get spoken of with care and pride and are the envy of other business owners.

What sorts of things are most important for your customer service?

✔ Be honest and open with customers.

✔ Say what you are going to do; then do what you say you are going to do; and then repeat back how you did what you said you would do.

✔ Treat your customers as you would want to be treated if you went to their business.

✔ Watch other businesses for excellent customer service practices and try to emulate them in your own business.

✔ Remember that if there is a problem, you will be judged most on how you fix it.

123

These are just a few, but I think they are some of the more important ones. Most people just want their service done right, at the price they were told, and in an efficient manner. How can you build your business to do this? Here are some key questions you should ask yourself when determining what you want your customer service to look like:

- ✔ What are my favorite stores for customer service? And what do they do that make them my favorites?

- ✔ When have I received customer service that really wowed me? What elements of the service were the ones that wowed me?

- ✔ What systems can I implement my own business to create that "wow" factor for my clients?

- ✔ Is there a system built into someone else's customer service that I can use without having to reinvent the wheel?

- ✔ Can I take the owner of that business out for lunch and ask him or her about how the system was implemented? Can I learn best practices from the business owner?

Financial Planner

A financial planner is someone who, for you personally or for your business, will help you put aside money toward whatever your goals are. Financial planners are integral to offering retirement benefits to you and your staff, creating the proper plans, and helping you determine how your business will fit into your retirement plans. Having a good financial planner now, even if you start with only $100 in an account, is a great way to keep your eyes on the prize of where you want to get to—the real point of starting your business in the first place.

When I first got into business, my uncle told me that the most important thing he had ever done was to take 10 percent of his gross revenues, every time he received a check, and put it into an account at a different bank. I have followed this practice ever since I opened the doors and have always had more than enough savings to handle anything that was thrown at me. I believe this to be an excellent practice for anyone opening a new business.

Real Estate Professional

One of the most overlooked team members for any new business is the commercial real estate professional. Many businesses get into a lease very quickly on start-up and don't have anyone who is representing them to find the space for their business. A great real estate professional can help keep you out of a bad lease and make sure that you get into a place where you really want to be—one with lots of foot traffic (for a restaurant), or that's quiet and peaceful (for a doctor's office), or has great views (for an artist's gallery). Unless you personally know the real estate market where you are very well, you may not be getting what is best for your business. See Chapter 12 on "Location, Location, Location" for more information on this.

Others

While we discussed in general the professionals you'll need to gather on your company team, each industry will have its own specific professionals as well. Medical clinics and physician's offices, for example, will need medical billers. These billers typically work for three or four doctors' offices. A physician opening his brand-new practice does not want to have to see patients at the office, make the rounds at the hospital, and then end his day by sending out bills. This is a specialty that any doctor will want to assign elsewhere. While it might seem a costly alternative when just starting out, the right billing specialist can get the job done more quickly and efficiently than that doctor could, and this leaves the medical care specialist free to give more medical care—and thus have more patients to bill. In the long run, it's worth every penny spent on that outsourcing.

Remember, in the midst of the ongoing recession and more so than ever before, people with very specialized skill sets are out job-hunting. Perhaps you have only a few hours of work a week to offer them. Most would be happy to help you and take in that extra pay. When it comes to finding labor, it's a buyer's market right now. You can get quality, experienced, skilled professionals and tradespeople at far less cost than you might have prerecession. Not all areas will be ones you can outsource, but many of them will—so keep your eyes open for those opportunities!

CHAPTER 10

Human Resources

Chapter 9 noted that a human resources (HR) professional can bring great value to your business team and that small businesses often outsource this role. How should you decide whether to outsource, delegate in-house, or take on the HR tasks?

As I've mentioned before, the three facets of business management are technical, managerial, and entrepreneurial, and most owners are primarily technicians or entrepreneurs at the start of their business ventures. It bears repeating that if this is the case with you, the day-to-day managerial tasks of your business should be hired for or contracted out. If you're not sure, doing a self-assessment or two can help you identify your best skills; see the section later in this chapter on testing options.

I have outsourced HR services for my CPA firm. As a CPA, I have not been trained in the areas of hiring and terminating employees, writing employee handbooks, and so forth. I don't understand all the ramifications of employing people in a right-to-hire state. Other issues that an HR specialist can help with are what you can legally say to your employees in particular circumstances, when employees or contractors are advisable and how they differ, and so on.

This chapter lays out several HR functions you'll want to have covered, including hiring and firing employees, establishing HR documents and procedures, and working with contractors. First, let's learn more about how an HR expert or hiring manager can make your business life easier.

Starting Your Own Business

HR Management Help / Hiring Manager

I have found that for me—because I am better at being the technician and the entrepreneur—that if I work with a talented hiring manager, such as Ginny McMinn of McMinn Business Solutions, my hiring headaches are gone. What Ginny does is handle all matters related to hiring, firing, and general staff issues. She will review candidates via résumé, testing, and interviewing. She will review them with her trained HR eye for facts and features that may or may not fit with the culture of my organization and the job description. After meeting my current staff and interviewing us, Ginny always has a great idea of who would be our perfect fit. I find her talent incredible and extremely useful. The following are some insights from Ginny on how hiring an HR manager for your business would be most useful for you.

Why is hiring an HR professional helpful when growing a small business?

Adding a human resources professional to your team of advisors will help your small business grow in several ways:

o   This individual will save you time. Instead of investing a lot of time debating hiring, training, and performance management decisions, this individual will guide you through these decisions.

o   This individual will provide you peace of mind. You will prevent errors and avoid problems by getting this professional guidance.

o   This individual will set up concrete and workable HR systems for you to follow in your business. Changes in the way HR is handled can be disruptive both to you and your employees. Avoid this by setting up good procedures and policies in all aspects of HR.

Since there are many aspects to managing human resources within a business, it is important that you find the most appropriate individual to help you in yours. Not all HR professionals have experience in every aspect of the HR profession, and still fewer have experience with small business and a variety of industries. Without this experience, you will receive advice based on limited experience instead of broader experience and knowledge and how those apply to your particular business and employees.

RESOURCE

Ginny McMinn of McMinn Business Solutions is our go-to person for anything HR. We enlist her help with hiring, firing, personnel questions, and everything in between.

What are the top questions a business owner should ask to determine if an HR professional is the right fit and has the right knowledge for the business?

To determine whether an HR advisor or employee is a good fit for your business, determine the following:

o   Is the experience in the field broad, specialized but deep, or both broad and deep? Ask these questions: What areas of HR have you worked in? How involved have you been in broader areas of HR? Have you been involved in recruiting and hiring? Payroll and recordkeeping? Orientation, training, and development? Handbooks, policies, and procedures? Pay and other compensation? Benefits? Employee relations, work climate, and communication? Workplace culture development? Legal compliance, poster, and storage requirements? Safety and security? Organization design and optimization?

o   Is experience accompanied by formal training? Have you studied HR in a university setting, learned on the job, or both? Are you certified as an HR practitioner? How many years of experience do you have? Have you been promoted? What industries have you worked in? How has your approach changed once promoted, and from industry to industry?

o   Is the approach to HR work theoretical or practical?

o   Have you created different solutions for similar issues in diverse organizations or applied the same approach to each organization? Have you worked with small and large organizations? Do you prioritize concerns and develop a step-by-step plan or do you recommend major initiatives?

Depending on your work environment, budget, and level of HR concerns, determine a best-fit advisor for your organization. HR help is available in a variety of forms: part-time employees, full-time employees, HR consultants, and HR advisory services. Pick the one that fits your organization best.

Hiring People

One of my favorite quotes on this subject—which I have been using for many years and, to my unending pleasure, has never let me down—is: "Hire slow, fire fast." This adage is so old that who first said it is unclear. All I know is that every time I have not followed this advice, I have gotten bitten by something I wasn't expecting.

Now, I don't mean to put a negative spin on this portion of the book. I only want business owners to know that, no matter whom you hire, no one will ever work as hard as you do—because it is your dream. You can get others to buy into your dream, and that will certainly help. But be prepared, as a starting business owner, to be the one who stays late, works hardest, and produces the most. On some days, you will feel like taking back all the jobs because you can "do it better." Most technicians who go into business tend to have this feeling. At this stage, you either need to hire a manager or grow into your manager skill set. You can find many amazing books on the subject; some of my favorites, in no particular order, are:

- ✔ *The E-Myth* by Michael Gerber
- ✔ *The One Minute Manager* by Ken Blanchard
- ✔ *The 4-Hour Workweek* by Timothy Ferris

When you determine that your new business needs more staff, you have two options: you can hire or you can contract with someone. If you hire staff, you must pay half of their self-employment taxes (FICA, Medicare). While these employees are not self-employed, the IRS refers to this tax as a self-employment tax because you, the self-employed business owner, must pay it all yourself. (Half comes from your employees' salaries, the other half comes from you.) Employees also typically get a number of other benefits you won't be offering contractors, such as paid sick days and vacation.

You could instead hire contractors. These are specialists with their own businesses and to whom you subcontract work. An outside medical biller for a doctor's office is one example. Contrary to the demands you'd typically make of an employee, a contractor shows up, or works at her own location, at the hours most convenient to her and uses her own tools and equipment.

For more information on the contrast between employees and contractors, see the section later in this chapter about working with contractors.

Documents Needed

Several types of documents are necessary when you hire staff. Below are just a few—those that I find many businesses lack but, I feel, are *must-haves* before you hire anyone. These include recommendations from one of our favorite outsourced HR managers, Ginny McMinn, as well as other documents I have found valuable. To start us off, here are some notes from Ginny:

What are the top five documents an employer should have before beginning to hire employees?

Before adding an employee, a business must be prepared to manage the employee through a life cycle of employment that begins with hiring. Make sure you are prepared by having these documents ready:

1. Job description
2. Hiring documents
3. Orientation checklist, training guide
4. Employee handbook
5. Performance management system, including coaching and discipline materials

Having each of these documents in place assists you in hiring the right employee to do the job, tracking employee data and paying appropriately, providing relevant orientation and training, guiding employee performance and behavior through expectation-setting, and providing for the correction and management of performance, behavior, consequences, and rewards.

In addition to Ginny's list, I suggest you consider non-solicit and non-compete agreements, if these apply to your business. Let's explore what all of these documents are and why they are important.

Job Descriptions

Job descriptions are number one on my most wanted list for HR documents. It is so rare that I see any business, unless it is a franchise, with job descriptions. A job description tells your potential staff member what it is that you really want him or her to do. Often a small business owner will start by hiring one person to do the "other stuff" that the business owner doesn't have time to do, can't do, or doesn't want to do. However, when this person has no clearly defined direction, the employee can often end up doing things you don't want, didn't give permission for, or didn't give any direction on how to do (so it ends up having to be redone). Sometimes, this second person can start to feel like an owner of the business and not really a staff member. I have seen cases where this leads to employee theft ("the money in the register is half mine"), lack of productivity ("well, if the owner gets lunches off, so do I . . . I'll just close up shop for an hour or so"), and other problems. It never ceases to amaze me what can happen in this type of scenario. As Tim Ferris states in his book *The 4-Hour Workweek*, you cannot delegate unless the task is clearly defined, with deadlines and permission levels set. This is what a job description does.

Here is Ginny's advice on creating and using a job description:

> Define the job, its duties, skill and ability requirements, reporting relationships, limitations on decision making, physical requirements, and effective performance characteristics. Don't advertise or select employees before you have a job description; this can result in mismatches of a candidate to the job, or employee frustration from changing expectations. Until you know what the employee will do for your organization and how, you are not ready to add staff members.

One of the things I really like about Michael Gerber's *The E-Myth* is that the book asks you to diagram what your entire organization would look like if it had a person for *every* job in the business. This means you include a person for customer service, maybe a manager over three customer service reps, maybe an accounts receivable person and an accounts payable person. What about the VPs, the CEO, the widget builders? Once you have all of these jobs drawn into an organizational chart (start at the top and work your way down), then you want to put your and your staff members' names next to each job. For each job, you will then want a job description. Whom does that position report to, what does it do, what are the goals, to whom does that employee go for help, and so on. As you can see, this process may take a while; it took me about three days straight to create my chart, my job descriptions, and my position statements for each of my staff members. Once I did it, I had a complete organizational chart, with everything I needed to start hiring people and giving them direct tasks and duties in their areas of responsibility. It was *so* much easier once I had it all laid out. Everything was so clear. All employees had their duties; they knew what they needed to do and, more significantly, *why* it was important to the organization (because my hires see my chart as well—they know exactly what parts they play).

Basic Hiring Documents

Per Ginny, here are the basic hiring documents you will need:

> You will need an application form with appropriate waivers and releases, a reference-checking document, and payroll-related forms such as a timesheet, payroll input form, tax withholding forms, new hire notification form, employee history document (to track important dates, pay rates, and changes), and I-9 and E-Verify documents and instructions.

Orientation Checklist and Training Guide

Ginny also recommends having materials for orientation and training:

> Before adding an employee, know how you will bring the person on board, what the employee will need to know about the organization, and what unique systems, processes, and software the employee will need to learn. Use a checklist for orientation; this will increase consistency and ensure that new employees are oriented carefully and consistently. Add a training guide to make sure employees are trained in all relevant job duties. These tools will make sure the employee is productive and comfortable as early as possible. They will also create an impression that you and your business are professionally managed and under control.

Employee Handbook

An employee handbook (or HR manual) tells your employees what you expect of them relating to behavior, general company requirements, and culture at your organization. Not only is it important for this document to cover the company-specific regulations (how to dress, what time work starts, how to ask for time off, what is the meaning of vacation/other benefits), but also it must describe the behaviors you expect (common courtesy, surfing the company computers, use of company equipment/supplies). You should look at this document as your set of commandments and directions for how you want situations handled and the staff members to conduct themselves.

Here are a few notes from Ginny on having an employee handbook:

> Once the employee is working consistently within your organization, questions may arise about various policies, benefits, and expectations. Providing each employee with an employee handbook covering these topics will provide good communication, consistent guidelines, and clear expectations.

> Have the employee sign a receipt for the employee handbook.

My employee handbook is about twenty-five pages long and contains all of the scenarios I have run into with employees over the years (you would be surprised at some of the problems that arise due to a lack of what I always thought was either just common courtesy or basic common sense!). If you would like a copy of our company's handbook to see what yours should contain, please don't hesitate to contact us at info@taxgoddess.com.

Do *not* use our handbook/other documents as your only examples. Laws are different from state to state as well as from industry to industry. It is important that you have a labor attorney review your documents so they are correct for you.

Performance Management Materials

The final items on Ginny's list relate to having a performance management system, including coaching and discipline materials. Here's Ginny:

> The job description, interview, orientation, training, and employee handbook will assist in setting expectations for job performance and professional behavior on the job. However, questions can still arise and performance may not match expectations. Having a performance management system (not just an employee performance appraisal form) will ensure that employees
> o   know what is expected;
>
> o   receive feedback about performance;
>
> o   get training, coaching, and counseling if performance or behavior are not meeting expectations;
>
> o   have consequences (discipline or other) if performance or behavior does not improve to meet or exceed standards; and
>
> o   receive rewards for performance and behavior only when they meet or exceed company expectations.

Non-Solicit

A non-solicit is a document that explains to your staff that they cannot solicit your client base. Some of these documents will also cover any prospective clients that you have had contact with within a certain time frame (ninety days or less, typically). In order for this document to be upheld in courts (if it ever comes to that), you are going to want to have a document that is specific in its terms so that it cannot be out-ruled in full. Make sure you have this document reviewed by your labor attorney.

Non-Compete

A non-compete, in its coverage terms, is very similar to a non-solicit. However, it covers the areas of your business that you perform. One thing to make sure of is that your areas and lengths of time are specific. Another thing to note is that in most cases you cannot draw up a non-compete that will stop someone from earning a living; this agreement would most likely get thrown out as nonvalid by any court (here in Arizona, at least—so check with your attorney on your state's details).

Costs of Hiring

Current Hard Costs

When you calculate the costs of employing someone, don't forget to add another 25 percent over her or his wage to cover the costs of benefits, workers' compensation, and taxes. Should you decide to offer health insurance, pension or a 401(k) match, and other benefits, those costs also need to be budgeted in. Keep in mind that whatever benefits you offer to your employees you can offer to yourself as well, as an employee of your own company.

Typically, retirement and benefit plans fall into groups—manager, executive, and worker—with each group having its own sets and levels of benefits. Each employee gets categorized by group, and each state varies its tax structure depending on the group as well as classification of full or part time employee. Here in Arizona, for example, as I write this in the midst of the U.S. recession, the state's Department of Revenue is considering raising unemployment rates. This is a result of added costs, as companies take full-time employees to part time in lieu of layoffs. The benefit to the employer is that they get to keep the employee; the benefit to the employee is that she or he gets to qualify for unemployment.

Intangible Costs

Benefits: Hiring staff will give you many benefits—you can split work times, you may finally get some sleep or more time with your family, and you can process more orders to bring in more money and, hopefully, a larger profit. There are many, many more potential benefits, specific to each owner; I am sure you can name a few of your own. As the organization gets bigger (and, of course, you will have to decide if it should/will get bigger), staff members can be a bigger blessing or more of a curse, depending on how you structure your business to start with.

Headaches: Some of the headaches that you may encounter are staff not showing up for their shifts, theft, personal issues at work, relationships in the workplace, and so forth. I have run into all of these and many more. Having staff is always a double-edged sword, one that you must agree to work with—to both reap the benefits and live with the costs.

Future Costs

So, what will you do when it comes time for raises? Additional benefits? Perhaps losing a valued staff member if a demand isn't met? You will want to ponder all of these issues and decide how you will want to handle them. I can give you one piece of advice: remember that the business is yours. If you have a plan, and you know where you want it to go, you will have already foreseen these costs and will be ready to handle them. And if you really feel lost, remember that you have a business coach and an HR expert on your team to back you up and help you make decisions, right?

Look at businesses similar to yours. What do they do? How do they handle staff? What does their treatment of their staff look like to customers? Can you talk to others who own businesses like yours to discuss some of the issues, good and bad, that they've had and how they've handled those issues? Find someone you can trust, in an industry similar to yours, who has lived through what you are about to embark on and is not a competitor. Someone in a different locale, or who fits into a different niche in the same general industry, or who has similar types of employees would be perfect.

New Hire Testing

To help you in your "hire slow" mode, you can draw on several tests to assess your potential hires in areas such as personality, work skills, and team skills. No test should be used as a way to judge the whole person, but testing can help you weed out applicants who may not fit your job description or company culture.

DISC

DISC is one of many assessment tools that can help you determine a potential employee's fit. I also believe that having a DISC assessment of yourself is an important tool in your toolbox. It allows you to see where you excel and perhaps where outsourcing to an employee/vendor could help you fill in gaps in areas where you are not as strong.

Here is some information from our DISC expert, Dale Wernette of SHERPA & Associates, on why DISC is so useful:

RESOURCE
Dale Wernette of SHERPA & Associates is the expert to contact for assessments and education on what they mean. Without him, we would be lost regarding issues of our staff, potential candidates, and understanding each other!

Why is DISC such a great tool?

An understanding of people gives you an edge in any interaction with them.

Once you understand *how* you do it, it becomes easier to recognize, understand, and appreciate others.

The DISC tool is "validated," which means it does what it says it can do.

Since it is easy to understand, you are more likely to utilize it in improving your personal and professional life.

In what circumstances would a small business want to use DISC?

The applications for the DISC model are numerous, including:

- *Communication*
- *Job selection*
- *Social relationships*
- *Conflict resolution*
- *Team building*
- *Sales*
- *Customer service*
- *Career planning*
- *Time management*

What can DISC tell you?

How do you respond to the problems and challenges you face on a daily basis? How do you accept these challenges and go about solving them?

DISC measures four distinct factors of your behavioral design:

[D factor]—How do you influence and interact with other people?

[I factor]—How do you respond to the pace of the environment and react to change?

[S factor]—How do you respond to the rules and procedures set upon you by others?

[C factor]—How do you react when you need to be cautious and calculating?

What are the top five reasons a small business owner would want to run a DISC profile?

- How can you "develop" yourself if you don't know who you are?

- To be aware of his/her behavior profile and how it may be different from that of his/her prospects and customers

- To be able to manage, motivate, and communicate more effectively with team members o   To understand where and when to "adapt" one's behavior for enhanced communication, increased sales, and improved relationships

    o   To identify an individual's possible limitations and areas for development

Describe DISC.

DISC is a behavioral model, measuring observable behavior and emotions. It is the "how" of your life. It is not a test and none of the profiles are good or bad. It is a method of action *from* you, measured with four factors (D, I, S, C). Some have called DISC a "language." A communication language. It is the language of watching and observing people.

The DISC model is based on the work of William Moulton Marston (*The Emotions of Normal People*) and Carl Jung (*Psychology Types*) in the 1920s. Various companies have advanced that research to what is being offered today.

Now that we've had Dale Wernette's excellent primer on DISC, here's a little more background on its history and method from Wikipedia:

DISC is a quadrant behavioral model based on the work of Dr. William Moulton Marston (1893–1947) to examine the behavior of individuals in their environments or within a specific situation (otherwise known as environment). It therefore focuses on the styles and preferences of such behavior.

Marston graduated from doctoral studies at Harvard in the newly developing field of psychology. He was also a consulting psychologist, researcher, and author or coauthor of five books. His works were showcased in Emotions of Normal People *in 1928.*

This system of dimensions of observable behavior has become known as the universal language of behavior. Research has found that characteristics of behavior can be grouped into these four major "personality styles," and they tend to exhibit specific characteristics common to that particular style. All individuals possess all four, but what differs from one to another is the extent of each.

For most, these types are seen in shades of gray rather than black or white, and within that, there is interplay of behaviors, otherwise known as blends. The determination of such blends starts with the primary (or stronger) type, followed by the secondary (or lesser) type, although all contribute more than just purely the strength of that "signal."

Having understood the differences between these blends makes it possible to integrate individual team members with less troubleshooting. In a typical team, there are varying degrees of compatibility, not just toward tasks but interpersonal relationships as well. However, when they are identified, energy can be spent on refining the results.

Each of these types has its own unique value to the team, ideal environment, general characteristics, what the individual is motivated by, and value to team.

DISC is also used in an assortment of areas, including by many companies, HR professionals, organizations, consultants, coaches, and trainers.

The assessments classify four aspects of behavior by testing a person's preferences in word associations (compare with the Myers-Briggs Type Indicator).

DISC is an acronym for:

o **Dominance** *relating to control, power, and assertiveness*

o **Influence** *relating to social situations and communication*

o **Steadiness** *(submission in Marston's time) relating to patience, persistence, and thoughtfulness*

o **Compliance** *(or caution, compliance in Marston's time) relating to structure and organization*

These four dimensions can be grouped in a grid with "D" and "I" sharing the top row and representing extroverted aspects of the personality, and "C" and "S" below representing introverted aspects. "D" and "C" then share the left column and represent task-focused aspects, and "I" and "S" share the right column and represent social aspects. In this matrix, the vertical dimension represents a factor of "assertive" or "passive," while the horizontal dimension represents "open" versus "guarded."

Dominance: *People who score high in the intensity of the "D" styles factor are very active in dealing with problems and challenges, while low "D" scores are people who want to do more research before committing to a decision. High "D" people are described as demanding, forceful, egocentric, strong willed, driving, determined, ambitious, aggressive, and pioneering. Low "D" scores describe those who are conservative, low-keyed, cooperative, calculating, undemanding, cautious, mild, agreeable, modest, and peaceful.*

Influence: *People with high "I" scores influence others through talking and activity and tend to be emotional. They are described as convincing, magnetic, political, enthusiastic, persuasive, warm, demonstrative, trusting, and optimistic. Those with low "I" scores influence more by data and facts, and not with feelings. They are described as reflective, factual, calculating, skeptical, logical, suspicious, matter-of-fact, pessimistic, and critical.*

Steadiness: *People with high "S" styles scores want a steady pace and security and do not like sudden change. High "S" individuals are calm, relaxed, patient, possessive, predictable, deliberate, stable, and consistent, and tend to be unemotional and poker-faced. Low "S" intensity scores are those who like change and variety. People with low "S" scores are described as restless, demonstrative, impatient, eager, or even impulsive.*

Compliance: *People with high "C" styles adhere to rules, regulations, and structure. They like to do quality work and do it right the first time. High "C" people are careful, cautious, exacting, neat, systematic, diplomatic, accurate, and tactful. Those with low "C" scores challenge the rules and want independence and are described as self-willed, stubborn, opinionated, unsystematic, arbitrary, and unconcerned with details.*

Colors Testing

True Colors Assessment is another way to determine more about someone's personality and the ways they work in teams and by themselves. This tool describes each person by color and describes which colors are most representative of that individual. There are four main colors: orange, green, blue, and gold. Each represents a different set of traits. Some people are very strong in one area, but many people have two that are competing for top spot. Any combination of these will help you, as an owner, better understand someone you are about to hire or work with. I personally find the True Colors Assessment very helpful once I've hired someone, to better understand how they communicate and work at peak performance. If you are looking to do this with your team (or potential new team members), I would check the True Colors International website for a professional near you who can help you with this assessment.[28]

---

28. http://truecolorsintl.com/

Skills Testing

In many businesses, specific skills are required for a position. Your industry association can direct you to firms that have tests for these skills, or you can create your own skills test—although I would only recommend this if you cannot find a professional who does the testing (otherwise you could skew the results by your input as a nonprofessional tester).

Remember to also look for intangible skills: Does this person need to be able to communicate to clients in layman's terms? Does this person need to work alone or in a team? What about promptness, reliability, ethics? These are all considerations when hiring someone as well.

Test Yourself

Many businesspeople have never taken a self-assessment test. If you're among this group, I highly recommend you remedy this. The most common of these tests consists of 200 questions that determine what your skill set is. You may even want to take two different tests. Having outsiders who are trained to make these skills assessments advise you on where your strengths lie can be very helpful in determining the business tasks you can take on and the ones for which you need to hire or outsource. Knowing who you are will help you in hiring your staff and those you choose to work with.

Nor do these tests simply determine skills. They provide personality assessment as well. That's important. In my own example—the aforementioned outsourcing of HR tasks for my own firm—it's not only that I don't know the HR rules. I could learn the rules, certainly. But by nature I'm a big softie when it comes to relating to other people. I like making people happy. I'm less inclined than I should be to be tough with subordinates who get out of line. This personality trait indicates I'm not the best person to oversee HR functions, whether I know the rules and legislation or not.

I recommend you read *E-Myth Mastery: The Seven Essential Disciplines for Building a World Class Company* by Michael Gerber. This fabulous book is available online and will be worth far more to you as a business owner than the few dollars that it will cost you. As previously mentioned, a Gerber theory from *The E-Myth* is that of the three different types of entrepreneurs—the technician, the manager, and the visionary/entrepreneur. No one is all three. Some business owners fit into two of the three categories; most dominate in one of the three types.

Fit Testing: Technician, Manager, Entrepreneur

What I mean by "fit testing" is looking at the skill sets of a candidate and knowing what questions you can ask to try and draw out where someone is most comfortable. Depending on the job you are hiring for, and which level you want this person to work in (technician, manager, entrepreneur), you will want to determine where his or her strength lies.

Let's turn again to HR professional Ginny McMinn for a few questions and strategies to help you determine the skill set for a candidate.

What interview questions or testing can an employer use to distinguish among employees with different work personalities and goals? How can an employer distinguish among workers, leaders, and entrepreneurial spirits?

To obtain information before hiring an employee, it is important to use methods that are both job-related and consistent. Based on the job needs identified in the job description, an employer should prepare for an interview process that will collect the necessary information. It is also critical that the process be consistent and that documentation be kept that will support both hiring and refuting any challenges.

Plan the Process: Lay out a plan that will enable your organization to get the information it needs. Begin with a job description listing duties and skill requirements. Consider your workplace culture, and whether the position and culture are aligned on requirements. Ask yourself whether the position requires

o   someone who follows directions and completes tasks;

o   an employee who makes decisions and leads others; or

o   an individual who enjoys risk-taking and will help to drive your business forward.

Different positions will require different strengths and personalities. A mismatch can be frustrating to you and the employee, as well as damaging to results.

Gather Information

Questions: Develop an interview plan to use with all candidates. Ask a variety of questions to determine a fit with training, experience, job knowledge, skills, and abilities. Keep all questions job-related. Utilize the same plan for each interview to maintain the consistency of the process and obtain the most efficient information for decision making.

Questions that will assist in determining worker personality and preferences include the following:

o   How do you determine priorities in your work?

o   How do you organize your workday?

o   How is your job performance measured?

o   What part of your current job do you enjoy most, and why?

o   What frustrates you about the work you do?

o   Have you changed or modified methods or procedures in your job? If not, what were your ideas for doing so?

o   What questions or concerns would you typically take to your supervisor? What would you expect to result from that discussion?

o   Have you ever owned or worked for a small business?

o   What gives you the most satisfaction about your job?

Depending on job, work culture, and personality requirements, you may also wish to use testing or assessments.

o   **Testing:** Testing should relate directly to job skill requirements, such as keyboarding or software usage. If the job requires math skills, for example, test math skills with samples of the work, or at least the same type and level of math used. Tests of general intelligence are not job-related and should not be used. Use the same testing for each candidate.

o   **Assessments:** Employers may also wish to utilize assessments to help determine the employee who best fits the job, work culture, and worker characteristics. If you decide to use assessments, plan to utilize outside resources to administer and interpret the assessment for you. Insist that the assessment be a validated and reliable assessment based on job and worker criteria. And look for a resource that is experienced in administering, interpreting, and explaining results.

Compare Apples to Apples: If you stick with your interview plan and gather the same information and test results on each candidate, comparing candidates will be much easier. Being consistent is important legally but also for effectiveness.

Make a Hiring Decision: Review the job requirements and candidate information before making a hiring decision. Select the candidate whose interview, test, and assessment information is the best match for the position.

> **Something to Note Across the Board:** It is very important that if you decide you are going to test candidates, you test them all at the same point in the interview process. Meaning, if you give anyone who applies a colors test, you need to do that with *anyone* who applies. In most cases, you use these tests post a primary interview so that your costs of testing are lower overall.

Working with Contractors

We've talked already about the differences between an employee and a contractor, but to review the official definition of contractor, it's someone to whom you pay a specific dollar amount to perform a specific task for a specified amount of time. It contrasts with an employee, whose role is to do whatever you tell her or him to do in the way in which you tell her or him to do it, and generally without an ending date of the work relationship in mind.

As an example, compare an administrative assistant to a medical biller for a doctor's office. The administrative assistant works Monday through Friday in the doctor's office from 9 a.m. until 4 p.m., using the doctor's computer to perform her office tasks. She interacts with the patients in a manner dictated by the office manager, in a wardrobe dictated by the office manager, and she takes a lunch break during the one hour assigned to her by the office manager. The doctor's medical biller, in contrast, works out of her home office or in the doctor's office based on her decision of what works best, keeps the hours she decides on, uses her own equipment most of the time, and dresses as she wishes. The administrative assistant is a W-2 employee; the medical biller is a contractor.

The IRS has its own set of guidelines to determine if a person working for you is a contractor or employee. You can access this information on the IRS website (as of the publication of this book) using IRS Form SS-8: www.irs.gov/pub/irs-pdf/fss8.pdf. (Note: *Do not file* this form with the IRS—it is for your purposes only, to help you determine whether someone is an employee or a contractor!) See also the IRS's 20-Factor Test on Employment Status in Appendix C of this book. But essentially, the difference between a contractor and an employee is the amount of control the business owner has over the person completing the tasks. The more control you exert, the less likely that person is taking on the role of contractor.

Hiring Contractors

When hiring a contractor—what you'll hear me refer to as a "1099 employee," named after the IRS form that you provide the person for work documentation—it is crucial that you have a strong contractor's agreement signed by you both. Your contractor's agreement must make it clear that you're not exerting enough control over the schedule, hours, and how-to's of completing the work to have that worker be deemed an employee by the IRS. You'll also want to make it clear in the agreement that all tools and equipment needed to complete the assigned job are to be provided by the contractor. While you want to clearly state the repercussions of the contractor not completing the work in the fashion and time frame that you require, the only things that need to be noted are the dollar amount you will pay the contractor and for what work. That's about it for documentation, from a *tax* standpoint (note that I am not a lawyer!). Should the contractor wish to work on the assigned project at 2 a.m. on a Saturday, she or he is free to do so. You want to make it clear that you don't care about means and method—you only care that the job gets completed satisfactorily by the deadline.

As with just about anything else in the business world, nothing is ever as cut-and-dried as you'd like. There are circumstances under which a contractor would be allowed to use your equipment and still be a contractor. What is black and white here in Arizona, however, is your inability to consider an administrative person a contractor if he or she is working in your own office.[29] Exceptions would be virtual, such as outsourcing firms and virtual assistants. If that person is completing administrative/clerical tasks in your office for your company, I advise you not to quibble and just pay them as you would any employee, taking out payroll taxes and providing them with a Form W-2 at year-end.

Temporary and temp-to-hire staff are not employees—at least not until or unless you decide to hire them outright when the opportunity arises. Until that time you are actually hiring the temporary agency as a contractor, who in turns hires its own employee(s) to come to work for you on a temporary basis. Each temporary worker is paid wages by the temporary employment agency, which bills you for its services. If the worker gets any benefits, such as medical coverage, those have been provided by the temporary agency. For a temporary agency worker, you prepare no payroll, provide no benefits, and prepare no year-end W-2. Nor do you give them a 1099. Your relationship is with the temporary agency, with the exception of greeting the worker and guiding her or his completion of the duties you've requested.

Ideally, a business owner would benefit from having everyone who does work for the business to be a contractor rather than an employee. The workers would then be responsible for their own equipment, taxes, and just about everything else. Your obligation to them would be simple: pay them for what they do for you. Their obligation would be to do the work.

---

29. Make sure that you check your own state's regulations on this particular issue, as I've heard it can be sticky in other states.

In contrast to what's ideal for the business owner, the IRS would like all workers to be employees, as it's much easier for contractors to skip out on their self-employment tax, and they are less likely to file and pay on tax returns. The IRS knows this from experience with contractors and, in general, the IRS goes after contractors in full force to make sure they report each penny earned and declare as few expenses as possible.

If the worker is a temp-to-hire and at the end of the designated "temp period" (usually sixty to ninety days) you opt to keep that employee, she could become your employee or contractor, depending on the arrangement you make with the worker. If, for instance, you hire her for one project at predetermined total of $5,000—to create digital files from your manual files—and you provide a key to the office to come and go as she wishes until the job is done, she's a contractor. In contrast, if you keep that worker on as your office manager, having her do payroll and other office tasks each day from 9 a.m. to 5 p.m. in your office, in business attire, she is your employee.

Tax Forms Needed for Contractors

The aforementioned 1099 forms for your contractors must arrive at the contractor's address by January 31 of the year following the tax year for which you're filing. Work done for you in 2014 must be mailed to each contractor in time to arrive in his or her mailbox by January 31, 2015, for example. Large corporations do not require a 1099, nor do contractors to whom you've paid less than $600 that year. You need only provide a 1099 to specific people, including but not limited to:

✔ Contractors who are sole proprietors
✔ LLCs taxed as sole proprietors
✔ Professionals such as architects, lawyers, and accountants

Of course, there is going to be some confusion about who is what. The best way to resolve the confusion is to require up front from each contractor a completed W-9 form (provided by you; see Figure 17) before you pay him or her any money for the work. The W-9 makes it clear that the information the contractor provides is under penalty of perjury. Included in that information is the business type. Getting the form up front also saves you a last-minute scramble at tax time to determine who needs a 1099 before you can file taxes.

The best approach to John, the contractor, for example, is, "Okay, I'd like you to do the work for me. All I need from you to hire and pay you is your completed-in-full IRS Form W-9, including your social security number or company EIN, your basic information, and your signature on the form."

In all my years as a practicing CPA, I've never known the IRS to come after a company for not completing a 1099 for a contractor, but that's not an assumption I want my clients to make.

What generally happens is that you're being audited for something else and the auditor says, "Okay, you say you've been paying Mary Jane this amount for the last X years but Mary Jane hasn't been reporting the income, so can you prove to us that you actually have this deduction?"

And you say, "Yes, I have the checks," or "Yes, I have my payroll documentation."

That auditor is going to counter that with a request to see your 1099s. If you can't come up with them, not only do you lose the deduction, but also you incur the penalty for not filing the 1099s. That could destroy your business. And, by the way, if they're auditing you, they're probably auditing Mary Jane, too. In fact, anytime an audit strays into the area of contractor and client, both will be audited. To protect yourself, make sure that all contractors provide you with W-9s—and that they know that the tax obligation is theirs, not yours.

I add a paragraph on my contractor agreement that explicitly describes the obligation of the contractor to pay her or his own taxes. Often I include that the contractor needs to pay her or his own self-employment taxes, what the tax rate is, and the fact that they have to report every dollar. If I as a business owner were ever to get audited and the IRS agent said, "Show me your 1099 form," I would be able to show them that and the contractor agreement attached to it, in which I said, "You, contractor, are responsible for your own taxes." If someone doesn't report $500 of income the IRS isn't going to come back to that person, but if it's $10,000 or more, you'd better believe the auditor is coming knocking.

Should the IRS decide to penalize a company for not providing 1099s, the cost to the company ranges from $50 to $100 per 1099 for each year the forms are not submitted. Typical small companies have fifty to one hundred 1099s required for each year. One year's penalty, therefore, could cost your firm at least $5,000—and that's just for one year. With no statute of limitations on the penalty, ten years of not complying could cost you a lot of money indeed!

One important thing to remember, especially since your company might not only use the services of a contractor but also at times *be* the contractor, is that while a company doesn't have to file a 1099 for any contractor to whom they paid less than $600, that contractor does still have to report the income. If I pay you one dollar for the pen you're holding in your hand, or for talking to me for one minute, you must report that dollar to the IRS.

Form **W-9**
(Rev. August 2013)
Department of the Treasury
Internal Revenue Service

**Request for Taxpayer
Identification Number and Certification**

**Give Form to the
requester. Do not
send to the IRS.**

Print or type
See Specific Instructions on page 2.

Name (as shown on your income tax return)

Business name/disregarded entity name, if different from above

Check appropriate box for federal tax classification:

☐ Individual/sole proprietor ☐ C Corporation ☐ S Corporation ☐ Partnership ☐ Trust/estate

☐ Limited liability company. Enter the tax classification (C=C corporation, S=S corporation, P=partnership) ▶ _____

☐ Other (see instructions) ▶

Exemptions (see instructions):

Exempt payee code (if any) _____

Exemption from FATCA reporting
code (if any) _____

Address (number, street, and apt. or suite no.)

Requester's name and address (optional)

City, state, and ZIP code

List account number(s) here (optional)

Part I   **Taxpayer Identification Number (TIN)**

Enter your TIN in the appropriate box. The TIN provided must match the name given on the "Name" line to avoid backup withholding. For individuals, this is your social security number (SSN). However, for a resident alien, sole proprietor, or disregarded entity, see the Part I instructions on page 3. For other entities, it is your employer identification number (EIN). If you do not have a number, see *How to get a TIN* on page 3.

Note. If the account is in more than one name, see the chart on page 4 for guidelines on whose number to enter.

Social security number

☐☐☐ – ☐☐ – ☐☐☐☐

Employer identification number

☐☐ – ☐☐☐☐☐☐☐

Part II   **Certification**

Under penalties of perjury, I certify that:

1. The number shown on this form is my correct taxpayer identification number (or I am waiting for a number to be issued to me), and

2. I am not subject to backup withholding because: (a) I am exempt from backup withholding, or (b) I have not been notified by the Internal Revenue Service (IRS) that I am subject to backup withholding as a result of a failure to report all interest or dividends, or (c) the IRS has notified me that I am no longer subject to backup withholding, and

3. I am a U.S. citizen or other U.S. person (defined below), and

4. The FATCA code(s) entered on this form (if any) indicating that I am exempt from FATCA reporting is correct.

Certification instructions. You must cross out item 2 above if you have been notified by the IRS that you are currently subject to backup withholding because you have failed to report all interest and dividends on your tax return. For real estate transactions, item 2 does not apply. For mortgage interest paid, acquisition or abandonment of secured property, cancellation of debt, contributions to an individual retirement arrangement (IRA), and generally, payments other than interest and dividends, you are not required to sign the certification, but you must provide your correct TIN. See the instructions on page 3.

**Sign
Here**

Signature of
U.S. person ▶

Date ▶

General Instructions

Section references are to the Internal Revenue Code unless otherwise noted.

Future developments. The IRS has created a page on IRS.gov for information about Form W-9, at *www.irs.gov/w9*. Information about any future developments affecting Form W-9 (such as legislation enacted after we release it) will be posted on that page.

Purpose of Form

A person who is required to file an information return with the IRS must obtain your correct taxpayer identification number (TIN) to report, for example, income paid to you, payments made to you in settlement of payment card and third party network transactions, real estate transactions, mortgage interest you paid, acquisition or abandonment of secured property, cancellation of debt, or contributions you made to an IRA.

Use Form W-9 only if you are a U.S. person (including a resident alien), to provide your correct TIN to the person requesting it (the requester) and, when applicable, to:

1. Certify that the TIN you are giving is correct (or you are waiting for a number to be issued),

2. Certify that you are not subject to backup withholding, or

3. Claim exemption from backup withholding if you are a U.S. exempt payee. If applicable, you are also certifying that as a U.S. person, your allocable share of any partnership income from a U.S. trade or business is not subject to the withholding tax on foreign partners' share of effectively connected income, and

4. Certify that FATCA code(s) entered on this form (if any) indicating that you are exempt from the FATCA reporting, is correct.

Note. If you are a U.S. person and a requester gives you a form other than Form W-9 to request your TIN, you must use the requester's form if it is substantially similar to this Form W-9.

Definition of a U.S. person. For federal tax purposes, you are considered a U.S. person if you are:

• An individual who is a U.S. citizen or U.S. resident alien,

• A partnership, corporation, company, or association created or organized in the United States or under the laws of the United States,

• An estate (other than a foreign estate), or

• A domestic trust (as defined in Regulations section 301.7701-7).

Special rules for partnerships. Partnerships that conduct a trade or business in the United States are generally required to pay a withholding tax under section 1446 on any foreign partners' share of effectively connected taxable income from such business. Further, in certain cases where a Form W-9 has not been received, the rules under section 1446 require a partnership to presume that a partner is a foreign person, and pay the section 1446 withholding tax. Therefore, if you are a U.S. person that is a partner in a partnership conducting a trade or business in the United States, provide Form W-9 to the partnership to establish your U.S. status and avoid section 1446 withholding on your share of partnership income.

Cat. No. 10231X

Form **W-9** (Rev. 8-2013)

Figure 17: The W-9 Form Currently Being Used by the IRS

Firing People

Once you've hired employees, you have to be prepared to fire them. Hopefully, all of your terminations will go smoothly. This section covers some tips and things you need to know regarding firing someone.

Issues to Be Aware Of

When it comes to what occurs when a worker is terminated, the pros and cons to that worker, of employee or contractor status, varies by state. Arizona, for example, is an employment-at-will state. If I hire you as an employee, for any reason I can fire you on the spot. Now, of course, you the business owner wouldn't ever fire someone for religious preferences, ethnic background, or sexual preference, as these would get you into federal hot water. Let's say, however, I tell my administrative assistant to put addresses on white labels, and instead he puts them on red labels. I could fire him for something that simple.

Being an employee in Arizona, then, is a more precarious position than in states where employees can only be terminated for "good cause," sometimes referred to as "just cause." Of course, as an employer you're much happier to be in an at-will state, because if you want to get rid of any employees, you just get rid of them. It's that easy. In contrast, an employer in a just-cause state must have sufficient human resource documentation to fully back up its claim of a problem with the employee. The documents must show that the direct supervisor and/or human resources representative went through a warning process with the employee to try to resolve the issues before resorting to termination of the troublesome worker's employment. The red tape for the process is extensive, and the discharged worker can take you to court for unreasonable dismissal. Solid documentation, including reviews that indicate your dissatisfaction and the requirements for improvement along with consequences of failure to do so, are crucial to protecting your company from litigation.

I once hired someone who had moved here to Arizona from her home state of California—a "just cause" state. Dissatisfied with her work, I gave her one warning, which she failed to heed. I then terminated her employment. A few days later she contacted me by mail, demanding a one-month severance package, continued health insurance coverage, and other perks. My attorney and I advised her she would get nothing, as Arizona was an at-will state and she wasn't eligible for any of what she was requesting.

Before you start employing people in your new small business, make sure you know if your state is at-will or just-cause. Additionally, be sure you know the precedents of prior employment-law decisions. Just because your state is at-will does not mean, for example, that it won't look askance at some less-than-fair employer practices with regard to termination of employees. Montana, for example, while identified as an at-will state, as of this writing will only honor an employer's right to terminate at-will during a ninety-day probationary period for each employee.

As an employer, you—or the person to whom you give HR responsibility—must know your state's regulations for employers and contractors. Find out what agreements you must have in place and what you have the right to request in the areas of confidentiality, nondisclosure, and non-compete, for example. If you're in a service industry or an industry for which intellectual property and contact databases are a part of your day-to-day activities, these issues are paramount.

While online legal resources such as LegalZoom are helpful and a great place to start, they shouldn't ever take the place of advice from a local attorney who specializes in employment law. Littler Mendelsohn in Phoenix is a specialist firm, for example. They concentrate their services on drawing up employment contracts and overseeing human resources manuals. These are crucial tasks for your business. As noted earlier, when it comes to employee relations, your HR manual (a.k.a. your employee handbook) is one of your company's most important documents. In it you'll describe work dress code, work hours, vacation and sick leave policies, tuition reimbursement, smoking regulations, drug policy, sexual harassment definition and process, and so forth. Should you fail to include an issue that arises, its resolution would fall to a judge, so you don't want any glaring holes in your manual. You need to sit down with an employment attorney or HR professional to draw up your manual. This document is your employer/employee prenuptial. Before the first moment of that new employee's first day of work, she or he needs to read and sign off on its contents.

One of my clients—a directory publisher with a staff of about forty—wrote a Right to Free Speech agreement for her office about ten years ago, one she shares with prospective employees. If they don't consent to go along with the agreement, they don't get hired. It came about after she was successfully sued for offensive language in the workplace. My client is loud, boisterous, and sometimes profane, although she doesn't use or tolerate sexually explicit or harassing language or behavior. Prior to writing the agreement she hired someone who was offended by my client's language in the office. Because the publisher didn't have anything in its employee handbook or its HR manual that told a candidate prior to acceptance of a job offer that profanity was acceptable in the office, the offended employee won her case against my client.

The one-page agreement now in place basically says, "I understand that in this office the staff says words such as [all the words she likes to use] and as an employee or contractor of the firm I may well be hearing such words. By signing this I agree that this is an acceptable working condition." Any prospective employee or contractor unwilling to sign the agreement, and thus open my client up to more litigation, does not get the job.

According to my client, there is now a higher level of joviality in the company, with people more comfortable about what they can and can't say. Joviality in an office is very important—keeping your staff happy is the key to keeping your staff and keeping them productive. In fact, some firms actually have departments of joviality or merriment, dedicated to playing funny practical jokes on the staff, taking them out for a day at the movies, or otherwise keeping them happy and amused. For more on this, I recommend *Catch Fire*, a book by Peter McLaughlin that teaches us to ignite energy, reduce stress, and bring happiness into our lives.

A good rule of thumb, as you consider company policies, is that the more hot water a situation can land you and your firm in, the more you need the advice of an attorney before you take action.

Here, from our HR expert Ginny McMinn, is advice for firing someone (from a business owner's perspective):

What are some tips for firing an employee in Arizona?

The State of Arizona is an at-will state, meaning that employers and employees can end a working relationship with or without cause or notice to the other. This should not be used, however, as a reason to fire an employee for an otherwise illegal reason (like discrimination) or as a substitute for good hiring and management practices.

In order to avoid potential liability under other laws and employee relations problems, here are recommended steps an employer should take in the management of performance:

Set expectations from the very beginning of the work relationship. Define the job in a job description, then use that description as the basis for advertising, interviewing, training, setting work expectations, and managing performance. If you speak with an employee about performance, keep notes about why, when, the expected change, and any consequences discussed for not achieving the change(s).

Monitor performance expectations and results early and often; problems are easiest to correct early and when small. Document performance results and discussions. If there are issues with performance, consider the training given the employee. Was it well delivered? Can it be supplemented with additional training, preferably by someone different or in a different manner? Keep notes about what was done, when, and by whom to provide additional assistance.

If performance issues continue, advise the employee of the overall performance issue, expectations for change, and consequences for failing to improve. Keep notes. You may also want to initiate a formal Performance Improvement Plan.

If performance concerns are not resolved within a reasonable time based on complexity of the job duties and sufficient time to improve, consider your next action carefully. Consider whether the employee

o   can't do the job at all due to skill, training, or experience deficiencies;

o   can't do the job yet because he or she needs additional training or practice time; or

o   won't perform the job due to a lack of motivation or interest.

Your response will vary depending on which of these conditions best describes the employee situation. In the first instance, your choices are to terminate the employee or to transfer the employee to a job (if available) that fits the available skill, training, and experience. In the second instance, consider whether your organization can sustain additional training time or must proceed to termination and training someone else. In the last instance, if the employee has performed the job at some point but doesn't perform the job currently, review the coaching notes you've kept. If the individual understood the issue and potential consequences and did nothing to improve his or her performance, a termination is in order.

Analyze before making a final termination decision. Review what your organization has done in similar situations. Review your notes and documentation of issues and results. If you feel the employee has been trained, coached, and warned appropriately, proceed to sever the working relationship. If you have doubts, consider repeating a step or consulting with an outside advisor about the best next steps to take.

If you must proceed to terminate the employee, it should not be a surprise to the individual. Given your training, coaching, and warning, the individual who is not performing should anticipate the termination.

During the termination meeting:

o   Treat the individual with respect; failure to do this reflects on you, not on the candidate, and may impact current employees who hear about the treatment. Ensure privacy during the meeting with the employee and while escorting the employee out. This is best accomplished at the end of a workday, preferably midweek.

o   Keep the termination meeting short; don't rehash the entire history of performance issues. Summarize, and share your decision.

o   Ask for equipment and work materials to be returned; allow the individual supervised time to remove personal things from his or her work area or locker before leaving. Remove the individual immediately from computer and facility access.

o   After the termination, share with coworkers that the employee is no longer working with the organization. Never share why or discuss private information with others; move on to coverage issues and forward progress. If the employee was not a good performer, others will have seen this coming.

Hire Slow and Fire Fast

So, we've already talked about this, as it is one of my favorite, good ol' standbys. If something isn't working out, and you've tried to fix it, coach about it, and work on it, and you've looked at yourself and the staff member to determine who really has the issue (you or the employee), and still it cannot be worked out, it's time to terminate. No questions, no emotions, no drawn-out dramas—just rip it off, get it done, and move on. Everyone will be happier for it.

I have been told that this can sound kind of harsh. No one likes firing people. The real question is, when each hour of time that employees who should be fired costs you money (see the below statistics), can you really afford to spend that money on them? You will need that money to hire and train new people. So, doesn't it make sense to just get on with it?

✔ **Statistic #1:** It costs 2.5 times an employee's salary to hire someone new (so hire right the first time).

✔ **Statistic #2:** The cost of keeping a bad employee—tangible costs only (not including all the intangibles)—for employees making under $75,000 annual wage is 2.3 times the hourly wage; for wages over $75,000, this jumps to 4.6 times the hourly wage.

Additional statistics from expert,and business coach Fred Kroin:

> When asked about statistics like this my best reference source is Brad Smart's book *TopGrading: How Companies Win by Hiring, Coaching, and Keeping the Best People* (published by the Penguin Group 1999, 2005). The book outlines in detail why the costs of not terminating an employee that should have already been fired are, in fact, staggering. Furthermore, the costs go up substantially the higher the compensation of the employee.
>
> Consider both tangible and intangible costs such as pre-hire interview costs (i.e., time for your recruiting staff to process paperwork, arrange interviews and perhaps lodging and travel, as well as labor costs for the time it takes to conduct interviews and evaluate the candidate as well as those candidates who were not hired this time), on-boarding costs (i.e. orientation, training, and getting the employee up to speed and at full productivity), overhead costs (facility cost allocations, the costs of their equipment and/or tools of the trade, benefits, taxes), and the inherent salary costs (including vacation, sick, and personal time off). This fails to mention yet the costs of the employee's interaction and eventual disruption of other staff members and managers. The list goes on and on.
>
> Based on several hundred case studies, the cost of a mis-hire of someone whose annual compensation is below $100,000 is approximately . . . are you ready for this . . . 14 times base salary! So even a $26,000-a-year employee (i.e., $100 per day), if they're a mis-hire, costs you $1,400 every day you keep them beyond when you realized you should be firing them!
>
> The story gets worse for those above $100,000. Because they tend to be often in management and customer-facing positions (sales, customer support, etc.), this seemingly high figure actually doubles to 28 times base salary. Why, you ask? The answer is obvious it seems. These people not only cost you quality employees (who deteriorate and quit because they can't get along with the OBT), but also alienate customers and prospects. So when you consider the impact, don't forget to include this opportunity-lost cost, as well.
>
> The lesson here is fairly simple; once you know someone isn't going to work out, let them go. Sometimes, if they are really unhappy in their job, they'll even thank you for it. Good leaders seldom regret firing someone too early, but many lament taking too long to do so.

Never Deal with OBTs – On-Board Terrorists

An OBT, mentioned above by Fred Kroin, is someone who sabotages your organization from within. The person can do this in many ways: spreading rumors, causing dissent among other staff, or something as simple as not doing what you ask, when you ask it, as a means of defying the chain of command. All of these things can cause issues among the rest of your workforce that you don't even see until you terminate your OBT. Hopefully you quickly recognize these or other issues that will lead you to fire fast. When you do finally terminate the person, you may receive many thanks from the rest of your staff, as they were the ones feeling a lot of pressure from this person and their terrorist activities.

Here is more from Fred Kroin on OBTs:

o   What do business owners need to be on the lookout for with regard to on-board terrorists?

o   What types of behaviors?

o   What types of speech/comments?

o   What types of attitudes?

Let's start by building a basic definition. Paraphrasing some simple Webster's definitions, a terrorist is one that inspires fear; an appalling person; a cause of anxiety; one who coerces. Further, while on-board typically has, in the media, referred to such perpetrators of airline disasters, in the corporate world on-board merely means they are part of a company's staff either as employees or even contractors. So in our context an on-board terrorist (OBT) is a person in a company that causes anxiety or fear through their behaviors, attitudes, or outright coercion.

Though you might intuitively think otherwise, more typically and perhaps surprisingly, OBTs are often a company's top performers—perhaps the salesperson who generates the most revenue, or the project manager or technical person whose superior skills enable them to accomplish difficult tasks with great efficiency. Perhaps it is their very success that is the root of their behavior, in that this success feeds their already healthy egos and they cultivate a sense of outright superiority to their peers (if they even think they have any). This in itself does not personify the OBT, until it is coupled with disrespect or even a disdain for others and shirking of the company's defined values. If these patterns begin to be exhibited, red flags should start going up in the minds of the leaders. Additional observed behaviors and attitudes might include:

- Exhibiting a cavalier attitude toward company policies (e.g., disregard for normal working hours, required status reporting submissions, or meeting attendance)

- Expecting or demanding special treatment regarding business expense allowances or personal time

- Demonstrating an adversarial attitude toward working or cooperating with team members

- Making demeaning remarks toward, or showing disrespect for, their peers, coworkers, or subordinates

- Blatantly undermining others (to make themselves look better)

- Bad-mouthing the company's policies, performance, or leadership (behind their backs)

- Outright showing of disrespect for their bosses or even customers

- And an—in general—I'm special, I'm the best, the-rules-don't-apply-to-me attitude

While they might not actually come out and state the above, one might hear comments like:

- The boss lets me make my own hours; I can come and go as I please.

- If that were my client, I would have closed that deal a week ago.

- I could have done that task in the time it took John.

- I shouldn't/don't need approval to spend $250 on a round of golf with a prospect.

- Oh, those weekly status meetings aren't meant for top performers like me.

- And, in the extreme, my personal favorite:

- I'm irreplaceable—you can't fire me, this business would go under without me!

As CEOs of Fortune 500 companies and rainmakers all over the world find out every day *no one* is irreplaceable!

How do you best deal with an on-board terrorist?

The simple answer to this question is *quickly*. And that's for everyone's benefit—including the OBT's!

The sooner, the better. It's not about saving face or placing blame. Let's face it, there's enough blame to go around—you included, in all probability. The person you hired was not an OBT when they applied for the job, they gradually deteriorated into the role. Think back, and you in all likelihood saw subtle changes along the way but did nothing about it. It's very important for any leader in a business to remember: What you don't confront, you condone! (As my colleague Kevin Davis, president of TopLine Leadership, says.)

So, in a perfect world, the first time you see signs of any OBT-like behavior, you step in and nip it in the bud. If it's someone who had been a person of solid values, you may want to start with exploring what's changed; is there something going on in their lives that has caused their attitude to erode? Maybe they've got a problem at home or they don't enjoy their job anymore. If you can discover the underlying reason behind the behavior, you may be able to save them. But don't wait too long. Confront the attitude or behavior with the person head on, being sure to explain why it's not acceptable in our organization, that it won't be tolerated, *and* that further occurrences may be cause for remedial action or **even** dismissal. That's often enough to set things straight, and if so, great. If it's a more firmly established behavior, the situation may require some formal leadership training (there are many good programs available for different symptoms).

Do remember that you cannot allow the unacceptable behaviors to linger unresolved. And, if you can't resolve them, you *must* take action! Of course, make sure you start with a well-documented paper trail of his or her activities, the conversations you've had, and the actions you've taken to try to resolve the situation. At least begin by mentally developing a plan for what changes need to be made in the organization to enable you to terminate the OBT with minimal disruption to the business and the company's culture. If it's a key salesperson, make sure you personally have or build a relationship with their clients, so it'll be more difficult for the OBT to take them when they go. If it's a technical person or project manager, make sure their work is documented and you figure out what knowledge transfer is needed before the termination. Think also about to whom and how you'll transfer their responsibilities (and customers if the OBT is involved with them). Once you decide on the plan, implement it. And that includes setting a timetable for moving on, the sooner the better, but certainly not more than ninety days (see the discussion on the costs of a mis-hire). Whatever you do, do *not* listen to that little voice in your head that keeps saying: I sure hope this works itself out. *Hope* is *never* a strategy!

Reminders and Additional Advice

Document everything.

In some states, those that are not right-to-work/employment-at-will states like Arizona, you need to have some pretty hefty documentation as to why you are terminating someone. Even in Arizona, where the right-to-work laws apply, you still want to have backup and history for any termination. You just never know when something might come back to haunt you.

The best way to document any of the following items is to have it in written format, signed by both the manager/owner and the staff member. If this is not possible, just make sure that you keep a file folder with notes, dates, times, and pictures (if applicable) of the incidents.

Typical items that you will want to have documentation on:
- ✔ Conversations
- ✔ Reviews
- ✔ Training moments
- ✔ Issues that arise
- ✔ Warnings

The final termination package should include a request for all property, tangible and intangible, of the company to be returned, as well as the reminder of any company policies that may apply (non-solicit, non-compete, etc.).

You will always want to check with your attorney or appropriate HR professional for your locality and state, as the rules may be different.

Have ninety-day review periods with all workers on the jobs they do for you.

Vendors, employees, contractors, clients—everyone!

I feel that this is one of the most important feedback sessions you can have with your staff/vendors/everyone. It lets them know where they stand with you, and vice versa. It is always better to know how your relationship is doing and be able to fix issues early if they arise, as well as to know that both parties are on the same page about the work being done.

Hire out what you do not do well, but always know what your delegates are doing.

This comes back to the idea of only delegating if you have a clear path for the delegation—a clear idea of what needs to be done, how, and by when. Items you delegate or hire for must be clear; otherwise, how will you know if the job was well done or not?

How do you know when and what to delegate? Look at Figure 18 for some guidance. This diagram was drawn based on my understanding of Tim Ferris's work in his book *The 4-Hour Workweek.*

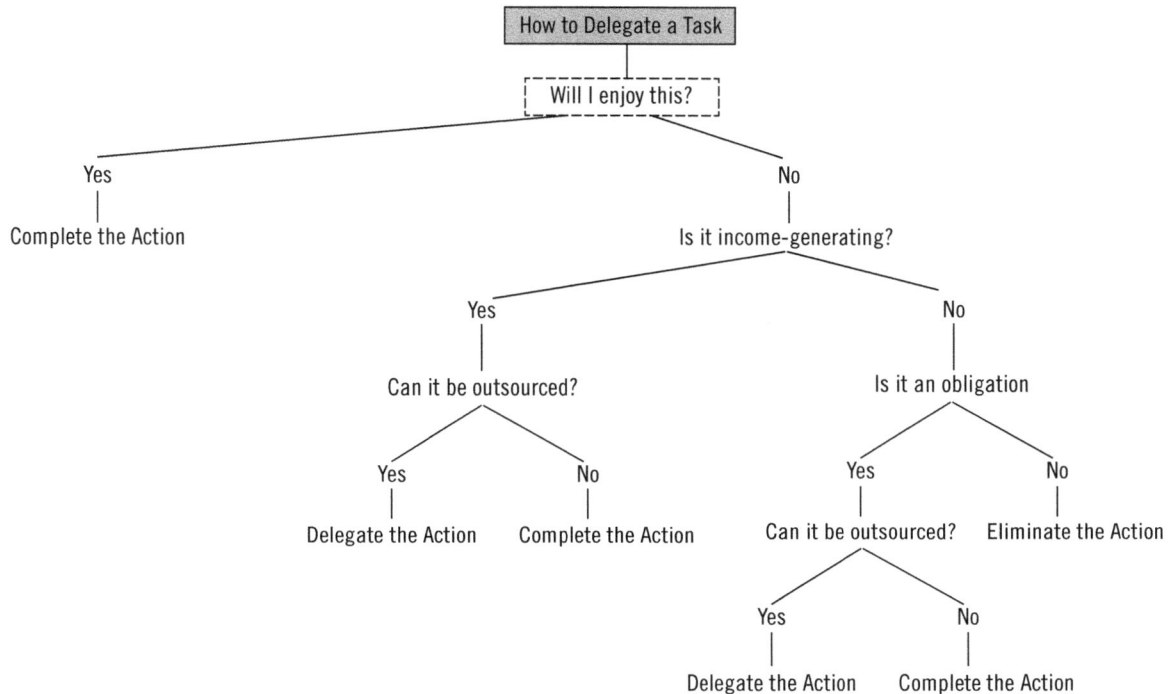

Figure 18: What Do You Need to Know to Delegate?

Tell people what you mean and what you can and cannot do. Be honest. It's better to be up-front about everything than to think you can "get there" or "fix it" later.

Honesty is the best policy, isn't it? Some things you as the owner will need to bear on your own. For instance, your staff doesn't want to hear that there are cash flow problems or that you are having a rough day; to them you are a superhero—an amazing and awe-inspiring person who can do it all. (After all, you started a business didn't you? Many people can't even dream of doing that!) Some things you should share, such as how the business is growing, what duties are expanding, and when you need help from someone responsible who is up for the job. Be honest, but don't share it all!

Chapter 11

Marketing and Sales

If you are really going to make a go of owning your own business, you are going to need to know how to sell, how to close, how to make your product or service enticing to new clients, and how to get some cash in hand.

Many new business owners have never had to deal with marketing or sales. They have always had other people doing this work for them. This can be one of the hardest parts of starting a new business, as it can mean getting out of your comfort zone, talking to new clients, and—better yet—*helping them solve their problems*. Remember, as one of my favorite sales gurus, Michael Goodman, once told me: Selling is not pushing your product/service down someone's throat. A sale is helping someone solve a problem if your product/service can help that customer.

Marketing

Business owners who excel as technicians or managers are wise to outsource their marketing, and many do. Marketing has so many facets in today's world that it is hard to keep up with each new one and which ones you should be using as they appear.

The job of the marketing professional is to guide your business down the path most useful for your industry, style, and fit. Often what works for one business—let's say a restaurant giving away a free appetizer on a coupon—wouldn't work for a doctor's office, which can't really give away a free shot! When hiring marketing professionals, you will want to ask questions about their background, industries they've worked with, and what their specialty is (traditional, online, social media, etc.). You will want to get references to speak to about the accomplishments for those owners.

Below are some tips from my own marketing professional, Susie Timm with Girl Meets Fork, on what to look for in a marketing professional for your business.

Ten questions to ask when interviewing an independent marketing executive:

o   Please tell me how you define a successful marketing plan (look for specific benchmarks, goals met, other methods of accountability, etc.).

o   How many clients do you currently have? How will you fit me into your schedule?

o   How often shall we meet to discuss how the plan is going?

o   Tell me five specific success stories from your marketing efforts. (Look for success with advertising, social media, PR, and events.)

o   Tell me about your experience with other clients similar to me.

o   Tell me what motivates you to make your clients successful.

o   What is one thing about yourself you'd like to change (as it relates to your professional career)?

o   Do you work with any specialized subcontractors (PR specialists, people to help at events, etc.)?

o   What time frame can you be contracted for? Thirty days? Ninety days? What is your cancellation policy?

o   Tell me about how you expect to be paid (retainer or bill at end of month). What are my options (retainer vs. project fee)? (Remember, 99 percent of marketing pros get paid on retainer, at the beginning of each month.)

A comprehensive marketing plan entails traditional marketing and advertising efforts combined with new media, such as social influence marketing, and a strong public relations strategy. All of these types of marketing have their place in a plan of any small business; the key is to budget for marketing (in good times and bad) and to understand that no

RESOURCE

Susie Timm with Girl Meets Fork is our company's amazing marketing and public relations (PR) expert. She has helped us build our Tax Goddess brand in many ways and is someone I would recommend to almost anyone!

type of marketing is a quick fix that will save a failing business instantly or drive traffic immediately to that particular business. It's a slow and steady process that, if executed with consistency and at the correct target market, will result in everlasting dividends paid back to the company in the form of increased exposure, awareness, and revenue.

What Is the Difference Between Marketing and Advertising?

Often the terms marketing and advertising are used interchangeably by those of us who are not in those industries. However, they have major differences, as you can read below from the Wikipedia definitions (as of November 2011). In my mind, the major difference is that with marketing you devise a plan; you determine *whom you are trying to reach, why, and how.* Advertising is the *how* portion of the marketing plan—this is how you reach your customers.

The Wikipedia definition of marketing:

> *Marketing is the process used to determine what products or services may be of interest to customers, and the strategy to use in sales, communications, and business development. It generates the strategy that underlies sales techniques, business communication, and business developments. It is an integrated process through which companies build strong customer relationships and create value for their customers and for themselves.*

> *Marketing is used to identify the customer, satisfy the customer, and keep the customer. With the customer as the focus of its activities, marketing management is one of the major components of business management. Marketing evolved to meet the stasis in developing new markets caused by mature markets and overcapacities in the last two to three centuries. The adoption of marketing strategies requires businesses to shift their focus from production to the perceived needs and wants of their customers as the means of staying profitable.*

Advertising is one place you'll see your business money go, and rightly so. With business, as with your personal life, it's ever so much easier to spend money than to make it. You might spend advertising dollars on TV, radio, print, Internet, search engine marketing, social networking, grassroots marketing, direct mail campaigns, promotional materials, or e-newsletters. What's hot right now—and what costs you the least money, though may cost you the most time—are social efforts such as a company blog, a company Facebook fan page, a LinkedIn company page, and a regularly scheduled e-newsletter.

The Wikipedia definition of advertising:

Advertising is a form of communication used to persuade an audience (viewers, readers, or listeners) to take some action with respect to products, ideas, or services. Most commonly, the desired result is to drive consumer behavior with respect to a commercial offering, although political and ideological advertising is also common. Advertising messages are usually paid for by sponsors and viewed via traditional media, including mass media such as newspapers, magazines, television commercials, radio advertisements, outdoor advertising, or direct mail; or new media such as websites and text messages.

Traditional Media

Traditional media marketing and advertising venues are such outlets as newspapers, radio, TV, direct mail, coupons, flyers, and directories (Yellow Pages). Virtually all of these now include online components, and while some may be out of your price range early on, don't write off their value because they seem a thing of the past. Most are evolving themselves into multimedia products that include online components, directories (sometimes even free), and search engine optimization.

Don't forget that best method of all free publicity: the press release. You can find plenty of help, including templates that help you write your press releases. There are free press release sites as well, such as YourStory.com and FreePressRelease.com, though I don't recommend that you use any of what's posted there by others as your guides. Some of them are awful—really amateurish. Do take a look at PublicityHound.com. While this website features some products that you'll need to pay for (though not much), it offers free help too, including an e-newsletter that I highly recommend. You can also get a free cheat sheet on "89 Reasons to Write a Press Release" that is terrific.

So, when would you want to use traditional media marketing?

In some industries, traditional marketing is going to be more valuable than some of the new social media or electronic marketing methods. A great example of this would be mattress sales stores. Having a good social media campaign will definitely increase their referral sales and potentially their new client sales, but more likely than not—at least as it stands in this day and age—having a television or print media sales pitch will be equally as helpful.

Typically, where the customer is going to be of an older generation, it is appropriate for those businesses to use the traditional media outlets.

Online Media Outlets

There are even more ways to market online these days. With more and more of the marketing going this direction, is it any wonder that there are always more venues?

Websites

Your website is the face you show to the international community. Often it can help or hurt you, depending on what is on your site and how your pages are designed, appear, feel, and interact with your customers. In the past, a web page was simply an online business card. Now it is an entire interactive universe that can either help you draw customers in or can make them hunt for some other provider.

Even if your website is a simple landing page, it will make sure that your customers know you exist. Many times, if the customer does not see a website, especially these days, the customer can believe that you no longer exist or are not a reputable store.

Note that with today's high rates of mobile Internet users, whatever you do online, you should make available via mobile as well; create a mobile-accessible website.

Blogs

If you're a novice to the world of online marketing and social networking, you'll want to become familiar with certain providers for blogging: WordPress and Typepad. These were created with the novice in mind, and both have plenty of online help available. Before you start, however, understand that if you're going it alone with either, you'll need to set aside several uninterrupted hours to learn their ins and outs by trial and error. Once you have a handle on the world of blogging, it gets much easier; and what you and your business will gain in the way of recognition and followers or subscribers will be well worth the effort you put into it.

WordPress has two divisions: wordpress.com and wordpress.org. While the first is easier, and perhaps the only one you'll be able to create on your own, it has the disadvantage of disallowing features that will let you monetize the site later on. You can't, for example, add any Google AdSense ads to help defray the cost of the blog, and there aren't as many features to allow you to totally customize its look. If you don't care about that, then go ahead and create with wordpress. com. The worst that will happen is that later on down the road you'll change your mind and you'll pay someone a small amount to create a wordpress.org blog and move your blog over.

Other blog platforms are available, some of which have more bells and whistles but are also more of a technical challenge to create. Performing a Google search for reviews of blog platforms will always bring you great data and current information on who the public believes is the current front-runner for blog platform products.

Many people now use blogs as a way to find new followers and new potential customers, as well as to exchange ideas with others in their field. I will leave it to my expert, Dave Barnhart of Business Blogging Pros, to explain why a blog is so important these days as a part of your online marketing campaign.

> In the last ten years there has been a paradigm shift in the way your customers ask questions, get answers, and make buying decisions. Ten years ago, many business owners did quite well with no marketing activity other than a Yellow Pages ad. Today almost no one even owns a copy of the Yellow Pages.
>
> For example. not long ago I purchased a new automatic dishwasher. As a foodie, I spent time on several foodie blogs and forums talking with friends, educating myself, and choosing the make and model of the dishwasher. Then I went to Yelp to read the reviews of all the appliance dealers in my city who carried that brand. As a result, when I walked into the appliance dealer my conversation with the salesman consisted of four words: I want that one. In order to survive in these economic times, it is mandatory that business owners learn to think like twenty-first-century marketers.
>
> There are thousands of social media tools (sites), but a blog should be the foundation of all of your social media activities. It is the place where you tell your story:
> o   Who you are
> o   What you do
> o   The problem(s) you solve for your clients
>
> Your other social media activities (typically outreach and relationship nurturing) should draw people to your blog where they can learn more about you.

RESOURCE

Dave Barnhart has been an expert in social media for many years (basically, since social media was born as a term!). He knows his way around and is the only person I trust to tell me what to do, how to do it, and what does and doesn't work.

What You Should Write About on Your Blog

Think of your blog as a symphony orchestra, and each blog post is an individual instrument. As the conductor, your job is to make this collection of blog posts work in harmony and deliver a rich message to your audience in a way that makes them want to read more.

So what do you do if your orchestra sounds like a couple of kazoos and a banjo? (No offense to banjos, I play one myself.) The instruments in a symphony orchestra are divided into four groups:
o   Strings
o   Woodwinds
o   Brass
o   Percussion

Similarly, you should be writing four kinds of posts in your blog:
o   Describing problems you solve for your clients
o   News and trends in your industry, education, and information
o   Behind-the-scenes activity in your business
o   Personal anecdotes that humanize you and your company

A symphony orchestra may have as many as thirty-two violins but generally only one bass drum. Used at specific moments, one single bass drum can have a tremendous impact upon the audience. However, if the sound of the bass drum is the only thing the audience hears, they will probably be shaking their heads and walking away.

The point is that proportionality is important. A few posts about the antics of your cat are endearing and provide a point of connection for your animal-loving audience. Too many such posts and it's a blog about your cat and not about your business.

Describe Problems You Solve for Your Clients

This is the most important group and by far the hardest one to get right. Classic marketing texts call it your USP, or Unique Selling Proposition, but it's more than that. Your blog is not about you or how you efficiently and effectively integrate a wide range of resources and core competencies to provide flexible, scalable, groundbreaking industry-standard, cutting-edge solutions. Instead, your blog posts in this group must be about:
o   Me, your reader
o   My problems
o   Conveying to me that you really do understand my problems
o   How you solve my problems

The most important—and most difficult—part is to articulate it the same way your customer does, not the way you would do so. Look at their problem through their lens. Frame it in language they would use. For example, a personal growth coach might be working with people who are living too timidly, but her client would never say it that way. Her client would say something like "I keep wimping out."

If making this shift in thinking is difficult (you're not alone), try calling your most recent dozen or so customers on the phone. Begin with "Hi, how are you doing?" Let the conversation be open-ended and non-directed. After the conversation has warmed up a bit, simply ask: "So tell me: I'm curious why you chose to do business with me instead of my competitor." Then listen. Really listen. Take notes.

Write about the problem in a way that doesn't bury it halfway down the page. Get it right up there in the first sentence so that your reader doesn't have to invest a lot of time to learn that you are talking about his problem.

Most of us get too formal in our blog posts. When you are writing, imagine yourself sitting across the table at a coffee shop from your client who is an old friend. Write like you would say it.

Your objective is for your readers to think, "She really understands my problem."

News and Trends in Your Industry—Educate and Inform

You are an expert. The more you share that expertise, the more you will be considered an expert by others. The objective of this group of blog posts is for your readers to think, "She is eminently qualified to solve my problem."

For example, if you are a tile installer, explain the process of installing tile in a shower stall in such a way that it stays intact for twenty years instead of falling down in three. Educate your reader. Strive to help your readers be informed consumers.

Behind the Scenes

Everyone loves to get the inside scoop. If you are a printer and the new printing press arrived today, blog about it (better yet, include some pictures!). Blog about getting it set up and calibrated. If you are an auto mechanic, blog about the new diagnostic machine. If you are a janitorial company, blog about your handheld airborne particle counter. You have clients who are your fans. These are the ones who drive past six of your competitors to buy from you. Make them feel like they are part of your inner circle.

Personal Anecdotes that Humanize You and Your Company

Now that your reader recognizes that you understand his problem and knows that you are qualified to solve it, there is one more thing you want him to think:

"She is the kind of person I am comfortable doing business with. I can trust her."

People don't do business with your company, they do business with you. You want your readers to know that you are not a big, cold, impersonal company. Write about your hobbies, kids, pets, and personal achievements. Readers who are your future clients will connect with you.

Video is a great way to accomplish this. With YouTube, an inexpensive video camera, and some free editing software, anyone can include video in their blog.

One caution: It's easy to get carried away and let the volume of posts in this group overwhelm the rest. The objective is for posts in this group to act as that one lonely French horn in your orchestra that gives the whole thing an emotional tug.

Top Three Tips for Business Owners About to Start Blogging

Start by thinking about your goals and objectives. What do you want your blog to accomplish for you? How are you going to use it to accomplish that goal? Some common goals are to

- o Educate
- o Build brand awareness and exposure
- o Increase Google rankings
- o Build your reputation as an expert
- o Provide industry news
- o Build loyalty
- o Gain direct access to your audience (bypass media gatekeepers)
- o Humanize you and your company, build trust
- o Create conversation with your market
- o Polish your image

Next, think ahead two to five years and envision the features and functions you might want your blog to have, then pick a blogging platform based upon that vision. There is nothing worse than needing to move an established blog containing years of content to a new platform.

Finally, establish an editorial calendar and a schedule. If you start out by writing in your blog once a week, then your readers are going to expect you to continue publishing once a week (or more). If you miss a few weeks, they'll think your blog is dead and they'll move on. By establishing an editorial calendar you'll be thinking weeks or months ahead about topics to write about.

When you're coming up with topics, don't be afraid to repurpose content you've already written. White papers, public presentations, e-books, e-zine articles, and so on all make terrific ingredients for new blog articles.

Pay Per Click

Pay per click (PPC) is one of the many forms of advertising that is meant to help get people from the search engines to your website. It can be very expensive or very cheap, depending on how you utilize the programs available. So, if you decide to go this route, I suggest speaking with a professional such as Lee Steele at Strategic Insight, LLC, in Arizona. Here are some pointers from Lee on how to make an ad campaign work for you.

Here are the three things you must do to ensure your PPC ad campaign is a success:

Do your research before you begin. You want to use the Google Keyword Tool to identify the most-searched keywords relevant to your product or service and their associated cost per click. This will ensure a maximum volume of traffic from clicks and help you to set your maximum bid prices for each keyword. You'll also want to research what other competitors are saying in their Google ads so that you'll know what to include in your own ads that will make them more compelling versus competitors' ads.

Write ads that are clear, concise, and compelling. Your ads should clearly state what you are offering and why someone should buy from you. Because Google ads are limited in the number of letters, spaces, and punctuation you can use, you want to be concise in the words you choose to use for your ad. And finally, your ads must be compelling—they must "speak" to your target audience and provide a powerful reason for them to click on your ad.

Ensure proper design and content of your landing page. Design the landing page for your Google ads to ensure that the page will convert "visitors" into "sales leads" or "customers." Every landing page should include (a) Who We Are, (b) What We Do, (c) Why You Should Buy from Us, and (d) What You Should Do Next (the Call to Action).

RESOURCE

Lee Steele is our expert in online marketing and strategy. We don't make a move without him, and we consider him an invaluable tool in our arsenal!

Here are some of the pitfalls that Lee recommends you watch out for:

> Pay-per-click search engine advertising can be a very powerful, affordable, and effective way to generate a steady stream of prequalified sales prospects to your website—if done correctly. As pay-per-click specialists, we're often asked by new clients to take over the management of existing search engine ad campaigns that have been previously managed in-house by the client. So, we're very familiar with the most common mistakes made by nonprofessionals.
>
> Here is a partial list of the top ten mistakes you'll want to avoid if you're currently managing your own PPC ad campaigns. For a complete list, visit www.StrategicInsight.com.
> o   Running a campaign on "default" settings
> o   Using only "broad" keyword match types
> o   Not using "negative" keywords to avoid paying for clicks you don't want
> o   Not writing clear, concise, and compelling ad copy
> o   Sending click-throughs to a poorly designed landing page

Social Media

Although I love social media, I don't believe it is as strong as your face-to-face presence. Once you have that face-to-face presence, having things like a blog, a Facebook profile, and a Twitter account is fabulous. It takes a lot longer to build up a relationship via non-face-to-face tools than going to an event where you can relax, have fun, and be excited about what you're doing. Everybody wants to be around people who are passionate about what they do. If that's you, and you can bring that across in your demeanor when you talk to others, they will love you. They will start calling you the Tax Goddess, for example.

"Taxes Rock!" says the Tax Goddess

That being said, face-to-face is time consuming and social media can reach so many more people in one fell swoop than you could ever meet and greet at a face-to-face event. A mix of the two, therefore, is essential. One of the best success stories I've ever heard was at a real estate conference where a group of realtors/ bloggers talked about how they got new clients through their blogs. More than one said that people started reading their informative blog about the local real estate industry, the neighborhoods, legislation, or tips on finding or selling their homes, and got to "know them" personally. Instead of what usually took two face-to-face meetings before that buyer or seller contracted with them, people were now e-mailing or calling them and saying, "I've been reading your blog for a while now. I really like what you have to say. Please come over and list my house."

What's crucial to remember about your social networking, whether it's on Facebook or Twitter or your own blog, is to obey the 80/20 rule—for every two posts or tweets that are of the self-serving "here's my great special, buy it" type, you must have eight messages that are helpful, or amusing, or entertaining, or inspiring, or just informative. If you break that rule, you'll find yourself unfollowed and socially friendless. The exception is on sites such as LinkedIn, designed for business networking. Even there, however, you'll still want to give away helpful advice, answers, tips you heard, and so forth much more often than you promote your own firm.

Multiple forms of social media are currently available: Facebook, Twitter, Myspace, and the list could go on and on. The question is which one(s) should you use for your business? Below is a story from a good friend of mine, Sharon Hill, regarding a little restaurant and how they are using social media:

Lingering over a great meal at a local Italian restaurant recently, my friend and I found ourselves in conversation with the owner, who was also the chef. In response to his concern over the scarcity of patrons, I recommended social media—Facebook, Twitter, and Myspace. I told him of another local restaurant that offers free dessert to its Facebook fans. He said he didn't have the time to spend on social media. I suggested he get his staff involved, asking them to spend fifteen paid minutes before or after work posting about the restaurant.

"My employees don't really care about my business like I do," said the owner. I agreed that no one cares about his business like he does, and that's one of the drawbacks of delegation or outsourcing. "But your job when you outsource or delegate anything is to find someone who can do the best job that they possibly can for the money that you're willing to pay them," I told him. In the case of these 18–25-year-old food servers at his restaurant, who better to ask to socially network than those who live and breathe it day in and day out? They're the ones with the devotion to social, the ongoing comfort with it, and the vast networks of friends, fans, and followers to best get the word out.

I told the owner that he might segue this into a contest, or a share in the profits that their efforts bring in. "The staff member who brings in the most friends for this half-price offer gets four hours' paid time off" or "Any time ten or more of your friends dine here in any given month, I'll give you a free dinner for two to take home to your significant other" or "When your Twitter follower dines

---

with us, you get 5 percent of the bill as a bonus." In addition to motivating his staff, keeping them happy, and growing his business revenue, he will have set in place an excellent tracking system that will tell him which of his marketing campaigns work and which do not.

I outsource my own company's marketing to a fabulous expert, a 1099 contractor I call on irregularly, as needed. I simply call him and tell him what I need him to do, and he does it. He then sends me an invoice. I pay him $25 an hour and I've always been pleased with his work. While there are times you may be tempted to forego a $25 per hour expense, I must say that as a CPA, when I'm in the middle of taxes, I'm thrilled to pay him to accomplish what it would take me so much longer to do—if I even could.

E-Newsletters

I have found that e-newsletters are a great way to stay in contact with your clients in a nice, easy, drip-method of marketing. Keeping your name in front of your clients on a monthly basis helps them remember to refer you and use you on a recurring basis. One of the great providers of this is a company by the name of Constant Contact. They have created a very easy-to-use, simple-to-learn program that helps you create professional-looking newsletters in minutes.

Meetup.com

Meetup.com is a website where you can organize groups based on interest.

You could also start your own Meetup event or group, putting yourself out there as the expert in a particular field. If, for example, your business is a hobby shop, you might start a model airplane enthusiast club, helping others build their own planes. You could even have a drawing each week for a free kit or give half-off coupons to the first ten people who sign up to join your group. When you're on a strict budget, grassroots marketing and participation in community events and fund-raisers are great ways to get your name out and spread the word that your company is a good neighbor, too.

For ongoing training in business technology and online marketing strategies, my top online subscription recommendations (both free) are paidcontent.org and mashable.com. And, for both learning business marketing strategies and networking with other local businesspeople, I highly recommend you go to Meetup.com and do a keyword search of area groups and events. Here you're almost sure to find meetings that will help you learn about online business strategies, technology, and marketing; network with potential business customers or fellow entrepreneurs; and just enjoy your favorite pastime with others who enjoy it as well.

Sales

Sales are the lifeblood on the operations side of any business. Without sales, you would have no income, no customers, and no profit for you!

Return on Investment Principle

Whenever you are trying to make a sale—to a customer, to a vendor, to your employees—remember that everything in life is on a balanced scale. Why would they choose something different if what they have now is working for them? This is where we get into the return on investment (ROI) model. Without a perceived return higher than the perceived investment required, a sale will never move forward.

Think about it this way: when your return is greater than your investment, you are motivated to move forward. When you buy a new piece of clothing, it is because you believe that the money you are paying for this particular piece is worth less than the other benefits you will receive from having the item (such as *I will look great in it, I will impress someone I care about, it will keep me warm/ cool, it is soft and it makes me feel comfortable,* etc.).

Cold Calling

When I first started my own company, my business coach at that time told me that if I wanted to be a full-fledged business, I must make one hundred client-prospecting phone calls twice a week for ten consecutive weeks. After that was accomplished, she and I would assess the results. Most new entrepreneurs, especially those who excel in technician-type tasks, have never made prospecting calls in their lives. They may well be terrified of doing so. They need to bite the bullet, however, and make that first (and always worst) call.

Those who are experienced in the art of cold calling will tell you two things. First, assume that the first few calls you make are throwaways. You should start with "cold" prospects—people and companies you know you have only the remotest chance of luring to be your clients. Don't waste your learning experience on hot prospects. The fact is, you're almost assuredly going to mess up, say the wrong thing, and get off the phone thinking, "Boy, did I sound stupid. Why did I say that?"

Don't worry about it. Jot down what you did wrong and what you should have said, and perhaps ask your coach how it might have gone differently, before you get on the next call. You might also consider doing some role-playing with your coach or a business-savvy friend or family member. Ask this person to be the prospect and make the call to him or her. Make several. Then switch roles so you can see how you would react if someone approached you and your business as you are approaching your prospects. Record your role-playing. You might even record your "real" calls, though bear in mind that you cannot record a conversation without advising the other party on the call that you are doing so, unless you and your prospect are *both* in what is known as a one-party state.

In one-party states only one of the people on the call needs to know the call is being recorded. In two-party states, both must be aware of it. While this could change after this book is published, as of right now the only two-party states are California, Connecticut, Delaware, Florida, Illinois, Maryland, Massachusetts, Michigan, Montana, New Hampshire, Pennsylvania, and Washington. And let me reiterate that if you are in a one-party state, that doesn't always mean you can record. You must first determine that the person you are calling is also in a one-party state.

The second thing a polished cold-caller knows is that it takes approximately ten "no's" to get one "yes." In other words, you'll probably have to talk to nine business people who hang up on you, or give you reasons they're not interested, or tell you "don't call me, I'll call you" before you get that one person who says, "Yes, I think I need your services. Let's talk." When you're starting out, the ratio may be even more lopsided. But if you keep in mind that the seventh person who tells you he or she doesn't want your business product puts you that much closer to talking to the tenth person, who *will* want your services, you can keep from getting discouraged. That's vital. Otherwise your voice will convey your discouragement to the next prospect and can hurt your results. People buy from people they want to be around—happy people, and people who are obviously excited about what they offer. Keep your voice happy and upbeat. Keep a smile in your voice.

Nor does cold calling necessarily mean phoning. E-mail addresses and cell phone numbers (for texting) of prospects, with their opt-in, can be obtained in many ways—*only* with opt-in, though that's a topic too extensive for this book. Make sure that before you make any calls, send any e-mails, or so on, you check with federal and state regulations on unsolicited communications.

In Chapter 9 you met Connie Kadansky, sales coach and expert in training businesspeople to get over their cold call reluctance. Here is some excellent advice from Connie about how to do cold calling:

What are the top three tips on getting over cold call reluctance for a new business owner who has never had to do cold calling before?

Formulate a laser-sharp valuation proposition from your customer's perspective. Conviction about your value and your ability to articulate your value will help you override fear.

Start asking for testimonials and LinkedIn recommendations from your customers so that you recognize and acknowledge the value you bring them. This exercise will help you recognize your value.

When you experience anxiety about prospecting, it's not the prospecting that is causing your anxiety; it's how you're thinking about it. A shift in perspective will reduce the anxiety.

Shift your perspective to embrace the fact that you are a salesperson and reaffirm that it's okay to sell. The world is driven by sales, and nothing happens until something gets sold.

Decide to wear your sales and marketing hat at all times—yes, even to the grocery store.

Sales success is 99 percent mindset. The *how* will come to you once you have adopted a positive selling mindset.

Can you give the top three things you *must* do to get from a "no" to a "yes" on a call?

Recognize that sometimes no is the best thing a prospect can tell you. You do not want everyone as your client or customer; you want to work with your ideal prospect. Make a list of five to seven characteristics of your ideal prospect. Make a second list of where you are willing to deviate from your first list. Make a third list of those who are definitely not your ideal prospect. Etch these answers deeply in your mind and work only with your ideal prospects.

Realize that a no can simply mean it is a timing issue. If your prospect tells you no three times during your conversation, ask if you might keep in touch with them from time to time. At least 80 percent of your prospects will agree to this.

The only way to engage a prospect is by asking them questions. Develop savvy, strategic questions that force the prospect to answer and engage with you. Use open-ended questions; avoid asking things that can easily be answered with one word.

When making a prospecting call, do not quit until you receive three no's. With practice, you will be able to do this effectively and confidently.

If these suggestions sound pushy to you, you may have Yielder Sales Call Reluctance and need to get assistance immediately.

My business coach—the one who made me do all those initial cold calls—said that you have to be told no or turned down at least one hundred times before you're really ready to make cold calls. A lot of being an entrepreneur and making cold calls is knowing what you're going to say when someone asks you questions such as "What do you do?" This is the elevator speech, your thirty-second commercial, which you should have prepared to deliver for any occasion or event, face-to-face or by phone.

Other common questions, the answers to which should roll easily off your tongue before you make your first call, include the following:

✔ **How much do you charge?**

When you first start out, it could be very productive to have some flexibility here that makes that prospect feel special. "I usually charge $50 for that service, but since you're a friend of Bob's, I'd be happy to give you a good break." Or: "Well, my usual fee is $50, but how about I give you my fellow-tennis-player special (said with a laugh)?"

✔ **Will you come to me?**

There's really no right answer here. You have to assess the cost and the time involved in traveling to a client as opposed to their coming to you. When you're new, it might be worth it if they're close by; or perhaps you charge a small fee to cover the gas.

✔ **I already have a CPA or a landscaper or a . . . ?** Why should I switch to your company? (Or other versions of "Why are you better than your competition?")

Each person's response is going to be different. (Ours is "Because we are CPAs that you can talk to, have a personality, and *love* what we do.") You need to determine what makes sense for your business.

✔ **How do I know you can do what you say you can?**

This is where you start sharing testimonials and references and discussing your training, experience, and education. Remember, as you service a satisfied customer, to ask for a testimonial. People are nearly always willing to give one, especially if they're in business and you're going to be mentioning their name and company in your marketing materials. That's free publicity for them as well.

✔ **How long have you been in business?**

Don't shrink from the fact that you're new. That could mean you just learned the very latest techniques, or have the newest state-of-the-art equipment, or can charge a lower fee, or can be more flexible with your hours and spend more.

It's been said that when you meet someone for the first time you have seven seconds to catch his or her attention and to leave either a positive or negative impression. So, what are going to be the words out of your mouth for those first seven seconds?

Networking

Networking is crucial in building your business; you need to start networking before you even start your business plan and well ahead of opening your business doors. You want to find people who know lots and lots of other people who can help you build a solid network. What you don't want to do is be single-minded and self-serving about it, however.

Creating relationships for the sole sake of building your business—and acting with a "What can I sell you?" and "What can you help me with?" attitude—will be clear to others soon, and it will hurt you. Like you, other businesspeople need help and need to grow their own businesses. With all networking, business or personal, you must take a "you scratch my back, I'll scratch yours" attitude. You should help others at least as often as they help you. Take a lesson from early online businesses, whose growth was spurred by their willingness to give away tons and tons of free information, advice, and sometimes even products and services. The idea that it's better to give than receive is true nowhere more than in business networking, where being seen as a helpful and well-informed entrepreneur—and most importantly, an expert others can turn to—can get you positive viral marketing and new business clients far faster than your blowing your own horn on social network sites.

LinkedIn is a terrific business networking site and a great resource for showing your expertise. I recommend that you join LinkedIn at the business level, join (and perhaps create your own) groups, grow your network slowly, build out a profile that also brings in posts from your own blog and includes a Twitter widget, and answer questions of other members that earn you "best answer" status. LinkedIn is also an excellent source for contract help or employees.

A quick Google keyword search for online communities in your own industry will suggest some other good social places for you to hang your online hat as well. There are AdGabber for advertising and marketing professionals, AutomotiveDigitalMarketing.com for auto dealers, and Stylists411 for hair stylists, as just a few examples.

Many industry-specific websites for consumers have social communities within their pages. A prime example is the Trulia Voices community on Trulia.com, where homeowners and prospective buyers can interact with real estate agents and brokers.

Finding a social site where you can talk to others in your industry is helpful indeed, but finding one where prospective customers can come to you for advice and information about your industry expertise is even better. A little time spent searching online should give you at least a couple of options in your own industry.

Of course, networking shouldn't be only online, especially if your target market is local. Getting out and meeting other entrepreneurs and prospective customers face-to-face is a wonderful way to grow your business. Your local Chamber of Commerce, Small Business Development Center, and state- or local-level small business association are excellent places to seek out for these events. Meetup is another good resource already mentioned. LinkedIn and other social sites are starting to hold face-to-face events as well—gatherings that give you a chance to meet in person people you've already "met" online.

Another good resource, not only for networking but also for building your public speaking and presentation skills, is Toastmasters. This wonderful organization will typically have five or more different local clubs in any good-sized city, with choices of meeting times that vary from early morning or lunchtime to evenings and weekends.

The point of Toastmasters is to hone your public speaking and extemporaneous speaking skills, but the folks who join are generally business decision makers who need to speak in front of groups. These may well be your business's ideal target market. Not only that, you choose the topics of each of your speeches before this group, so you have a captive audience for the message about your expertise and your business services.

While you don't want to keep badgering them week after week with the message that they ought to buy from you, you can creatively let them know you have expertise, dependability, and a quality product. One week you might talk about yourself and how your early life brought you to an interest in your new creation X. Another week you might tell a funny story about your most difficult customer project and how it all fell apart—or not. You might even do a presentation on choosing the best hairstyle for your lifestyle and climate (if you're a stylist) or how even a mechanically inept homeowner can fix some plumbing problems (if you're a plumber) or "ten things you must do to maintain your car in good running order" (if you're an auto mechanic). Done well, these are the kinds of entertaining presentations that get you remembered as the expert and get you invited to speak elsewhere—in front of yet more prospective customers.

You don't have to have an event or gathering to meet people, however. I meet people on the street, at the grocery store, at the bookstore, and elsewhere. Not everyone is garrulous with strangers (though this can be learned with practice), but if you are, take full advantage of it. I met a woman who turned out to be one of my best clients, and referrals, in the parking lot of the Home Depot.

Upselling and Cross-Selling

Upselling and cross-selling are terms used for when a current customer of yours purchases additional products or services. This is one of the best ways to increase your profit in the cheapest way possible. Remember, your current clients love you, they already buy from you, and you don't have to spend money advertising to them; they already need or are using your services, but maybe some of the services you offer are ones they're currently getting from somewhere else. They may not even realize that you offer these services! Your job in this scenario is to help them see that you can service them with the same great customer service you've always given and at a price at least comparable to what they are paying now.[30]

Things to watch out for when attempting to cross-sell:

- ✔ Take care that you are not damaging a relationship with one of your vendors by going after their customers.

- ✔ Ensure that the client's level of service will either increase or at least maintain its current levels.

---

30. A very easy way that I've found to do this in a rather passive manner is to put new services, or just a change-up of your services, in the thank-you line of your e-mails. Mine goes something like "PS—Did you know that we offer flat-rate bookkeeping services? Ask me about it if you are interested in learning more or getting a quote today!"

✔ Implant the seed of cross-selling items when the customers purchase the first item. Example: "You know, if you buy this hot tub with the additional jets, you can also work on your neck muscles for relaxation!"

✔ Make sure that your initial sale is solid. Otherwise, you risk confusing the customer with too much information.

Referrals

Getting a referral from a client or a vendor—or anyone else, for that matter—is the highest form of compliment. It is extremely important that you treat referrals and the person who referred you with great respect and care. These people are acting as your salespeople, and they are doing your sales job for you! Make sure you thank them with a small token of your appreciation (e.g., a $5 Starbucks card).

In my opinion, a referral is the strongest of all ways to get new business. This is what you are striving for, as it will allow your marketing efforts to work on their own to earn you new business.

Physical Tools of the Trade

A business card scanner is probably one of the most important tools that I have at my disposal. It allows me to input and track the mounds of data I gather when I meet new people at networking events.

Always carry lots of business cards! Remember that every person knows at least 256 people, so *always* have your cards on you. (I have been asked at the grocery store, at the bank, at the Starbucks—so be prepared!)

A tablet PC: This fabulous device allows you to show video or pictures of whatever it is that you do. Remember that 70 percent of all people are primarily visual learners; pictures are extremely helpful in getting that first appointment or even closing the sale on the spot.

Honestly, the best thing I can tell you to do is go out and get 'em, tiger! Selling is hard stuff, and very few people have the initiative or drive to force themselves to do something that gets them out of their comfort zone. So go the joys of being a business owner. One of my favorite quotes (of all time, by the way) is from Yoda: "Do or do not. There is no try." If you want to be a business owner, get out there and do it!

CHAPTER 12

Location, Location, Location

Not every business needs a brick-and-mortar office or building. Some businesses start from the owner's home or garage and only require a separate business location after outgrowing the home location through increases in the number of clients, the number of products produced, and/or the number of employees or contractors needed to fulfill client or customer needs.

Some businesses remain work-at-home or virtual enterprises for as long as they remain a going concern. Some businesses are mobile, such as mobile dog grooming or home health care. A mobile business, unlike work-at-home businesses, totally eliminates the need for an office location to meet clients. Some work-at-home professionals, such as freelance writers, recruiters, photographers, Web designers, graphic artists, and the like, may from time to time require a professional-looking private location. These needs, if occasional, can well be met by various executive suites companies such as HQ Global Workplace and Regus. At times, meeting someone in a coffee shop is okay; and, as more and more businesses become virtual or people work from home, this becomes more acceptable.

Still, sometimes you just need the professional, thriving, stable look of a business office location. And, of course, some businesses cannot manage without a day-to-day office. For these firms—especially those who rely on walk-in customers, such as retailers or food and beverage providers—location is very important.

Negotiations

Before you sign on the dotted line to lease office or warehouse space, remember that everything in life is negotiable. Just because you walk into the rental management office of an office complex in a highly desirable location and the rental agent tells you the office of your dreams is $1,000 a month, this doesn't mean you must pay $1,000 a month for the office. You might offer to sign a more extended lease; you might offer to do the painting yourself if they supply the paint and knock off half the deposit; you might negotiate a discount off of the first few months' rent. Be creative. Especially during a down economy, when commercial as well as residential rental and purchase properties are lying vacant, you should make a good effort to save yourself some money. The worst that could happen is that rental agent will say no.

If you don't feel you have the time, the knowledge, or the comfort level to negotiate, you could hire a lease negotiator instead. Just the fact that you have gone to the trouble and expense—and have shown that you have the savvy to know lease negotiators are available—may well tip the dicker scales in your favor. A lease negotiator will cost roughly $250–$500, but what she or he can save you over the course of the years of your lease will typically be several times that. A lease negotiator is tasked with finding your business the right rental property and then negotiating with the owner or property manager for the best deal possible.

Many business owners set themselves up with a commercial realtor, perhaps to buy, but to lease as well. Not quite the same as lease negotiators, commercial realtors are nevertheless practiced negotiators—though their primary assignment is to help you complete the lease transaction.

Let's hear a little from my favorite commercial broker, Susan McCall, on the mistakes that entrepreneurs make when looking at real estate:

> Many new business owners make a common mistake when getting started by taking on the job of finding space for their business without the aid of a focused commercial broker who is looking out for their benefit. These entrepreneurs are often in the "do it yourself" mindset and think that approach could apply to the selection and negotiation of their space.

RESOURCE

Susan McCall, CCIM, is the amazing commercial broker who helped Tax Goddess Business Services buy a building in Scottsdale, Arizona, for our corporate headquarters. Her advice has been invaluable and we respect her and recommend her to anyone in need!

Whether leasing or buying space, the commercial real estate transaction is fraught with traps and pitfalls that in many cases last as long as you own or lease the property. Generally speaking, the savviest of business owners, who have leased or purchased commercial property many times over, use a commercial broker; and for the very active investor, they often have one on staff.

So frequently I'll meet with a new client who needs to move from a space where they had negotiated their own contracts. Often they are moving because they can't continue to live with the bad choices they made on the space they are in. Had they had proper representation, they could have avoided the expense of relocating. This is true for both leasing and purchase transactions.

Some examples include:

1. A jewelry store owner wound up paying three times the going market rate on a shopping center lease because she assumed the building owner's broker was also looking out for her best interests. This was compounded when, during the great recession, the center occupancy waned and management began leasing to anyone who could pay. The jewelry store owner found herself next to a thrift shop, and there was nothing she could do about it because there were no provisions written into the lease to protect her.

2. A physical fitness user leased space in a center and didn't think to include a non-compete clause in his lease. Another fitness center moved to the same center, and while I was there visiting with him the other fitness company was conducting boot camp fitness exercises directly in front of his shop!

3. An office user didn't think of asking for a few months of free rent. She realized later she had left several thousands of dollars on the table.

4. A buyer for an industrial building, who was paying cash, got a general inspection but missed having an environmental phase 1 done and was stuck with a property whose soil was contaminated and that he, the new owner, had to remediate. A simple environmental study would have uncovered this before it was too late. But he didn't know.

5. A buyer of an office building discovered long after purchasing his property that his neighbor was using part of his land for the storage of equipment and it had been going on so long that the neighbor had a claim to the ownership of that part of the land.

185

6. A strip center sold to a buyer who discovered after the fact the parking ratio was not sufficient for potential high-traffic retail uses. This severely limited the owner's ability to lease suites to retail users with any sort of high-traffic use. Actually, I've seen the same thing in medical office developments where there simply wasn't enough parking for patient parking.

Why does this happen? Because the unknowing entrepreneur thinks they are saving money on commissions for the owner by negotiating the deal themselves and are convinced this savings will be passed onto them. Not true. If there is an owner's broker, then a commission for the buyer/tenant's broker is already agreed to by the owner. If there is no buyer/tenant's broker, the owner's broker keeps 100 percent of that commission. There is no reason why a buyer/tenant shouldn't have representation.

In commercial transactions, it is common for one broker to represent both parties. However, that needs to be stated up front and disclosures must to be signed that confirm the broker is indeed representing both parties. For this to work, the owner of the property must agree that his/her broker may also represent the buyer/tenant. Sometimes an owner only wants their broker looking out for them, in which case a responsible broker will disclose this early in the transaction. Often an inexperienced buyer/tenant doesn't really understand the conversation or its implications, and terrible, sometimes long-lasting mistakes are unknowingly made.

Lastly, when selecting a broker to represent you, check their credentials. There are a lot of agents out there who are new, unsupervised, and hungry for business. Why should a new agent learn on your dime? With a little investigation, you can determine how long they have been in the business, whether they spent much time working in your product type (office, industrial, retail, multifamily), and if they have the commercial designations which indicate a focus in commercial real estate. Do not use a residential broker for a commercial transaction.

What Is in a Lease?

All leases are not created equal, and before you try to sign a lease agreement on your own, be sure you understand terms such as *net*, *double net*, and *triple net*.

You need to be aware, up front, of what you are required to pay and to care for, and what the property manager or owner is going to pay and care for, so you can appropriately budget. Some of the more common, and even odious, terms and issues to watch out for are prepayment penalties, late fees, common area maintenance fees (CAMs), building maintenance charges, utility fees, and responsibility for repair and replacement of fixtures. A lot of minor and some-times not-so-minor technical things can get buried on page ten of the lease. As with any other contract, don't sign it until you understand it fully. This points out all the more reason to have the help of a lease negotiator or commercial real estate agent. Should you get a verbal promise or explanation of something not fully explained in the lease document, you should require that that verbal agreement be added to the written document before you sign.

I learned the lesson of written agreements the hard way when I moved my business into its previous leased location.

I chose the building because the manager agreed verbally that I could bring my dog to work with me, and so I did for the first eighteen months of my lease. Then the property manager arrived at my office one day to say my dog had gotten too big and too scary and could no longer be on the property. I immediately perused my lease agreement, feeling sure that my right to bring my dog to work was written there. It was not, and my dog had to then stay home. Of course, even putting in writing that my dog could come to work with me wouldn't have said it could enter the office building. When something is important to you, it must be in writing, and it must be clear.

Another lease clause you should request has to do with renewing your lease upon expiration. If the area is highly desirable, the property manager or owners might not want to renew your lease. They might have a prospective tenant from whom they think they can get a better price. To protect your interest, get it in writing that renewing the lease is *your* option, not the property manager's. You might wonder why not, then, just ask for a longer lease when you first sign. The answer is because you don't know how long that location will work for you. You don't know if your business will thrive or fail. You don't know if you might do so well that you'll want to expand. You might even find a property to buy that makes better financial sense for your company. Additionally, the building management or owner might change, and the new person you have to do business with might not be to your liking. Still, you want to have the renewal option available should you need it.

Most commercial leases are written for one, three, or five years. In Arizona, the longest term for which a lease can be written is ninety-nine years. I'm a fan of the three-year lease. My last lease was for three years with two additional three-year

options, which ensured that the office building I was in would be the home of my company for the next nine years, if I so chose.

I also learned my lesson about getting lease options the hard way. In the lease at one office building I was in for a time, I had no option. One weekday, while I was in the middle of meeting with a client, a man I'd never seen before walked right in and announced he had purchased the building. "You have twenty days to get out," he said. I was in shock. I went back to my contract and discovered it didn't address this. This awful situation brought me to my next location. Its appeal: it had been owned by the same local company, which was eighty years old, for thirty years. They were not likely to sell, and if they had, I had two options written into my lease contract that protected my company from a move for a total of nine years. Not only was my firm in a permanent location but I was leasing from people I trusted.[31]

Buying a Building

Of course, as mentioned before, you can choose to buy a building for your business rather than leasing one. As with house hunting, you must consider many issues before buying the "building of your dreams." Don't get head over heels in love with what you first glance at and fail to look logically at all the ramifications of your choice. The building might seem perfect for your business needs, but what about the neighbors? Do you know what types of businesses are nearby—how noisy, smelly, or off-putting to your clients they might be?

One of my clients bought a building after checking it out several times. That might seem like the thing to do, but because he was busy during the day he only perused the property during evening hours. It wasn't until after he'd made the purchase and moved in that he discovered he and his staff were working next door to a very smelly printing plant. He sold the building three months later, after his staff members were continually falling ill and failing to show up for work.

What he should have done before buying the building—what any business owner should do—is drive by the location at various hours of the day, talk to the neighbors and see if they're friendly, and find out if the neighborhood is safe. The local police will provide you with information on how crime-ridden an area is, as will several real estate websites. You also need to know if your property requires a CAM payment.

---

31. We bought our new corporate offices in June of 2013 and are very happy with our new home. ☺ Come in and check us out—we always love visitors!

If you're a retail or other business that requires walk-in sales traffic, you don't want to purchase—or lease—a building that is difficult to find and out of the way of regular and consistent traffic patterns. While it's great to have loyal customers, you'll still want to prospect for new customers and clients, and part of that process involves being visible to passersby. The right location is crucial. Even if you offer a service that doesn't rely on walk-in traffic, you still need to offer your staff a convenient and safe place to work.

I've recently seen firsthand what a poor location choice can do to a business, when a friend and I dined at a new Italian restaurant. The food was great, but I almost didn't get to find that out. The directions I had were "on the northeast corner of Street X and Avenue Y." I wasn't told that I had to drive behind the Discount Tire store. My GPS was saying that I was there, but I couldn't find it. If my friend hadn't told me where it was and planned on meeting me there, I would have given up and dined elsewhere. Ten minutes later I found the restaurant in a corner on the back side of an L-shaped building.

We talked a bit with the owner of the restaurant, who is also the chef. He said business was very slow. In addition to the restaurant being difficult to find, the other stores in the strip mall are daytime offices and services, so they fail to promote any walk-in traffic for dinner. This business is probably going to fail.

The fact is that restaurants fail a lot. Have you ever noticed how often a restaurant closes, to be followed by another restaurant in that same location, which closes not long after, to be replaced by yet another restaurant? This is an indication that the location is simply not right for a restaurant, and new restaurant owners are just not getting that. They see a reasonably priced spot with a kitchen already in place, and they think savings. But nothing is a good price that causes you to spend money only to fail. If your business requires walk-in traffic, you need foot traffic, drive-by traffic, and plenty of free parking.

Making sound decisions is especially important when you buy. For, once you've bought the building, you've bought the building. You've probably also bought a lot of hard work and expense to ready it for business. Unlike having a leased space, you may have to install walls, carpet, and lighting fixtures and do some painting and wallpapering. You may have to landscape the outside or install outdoor lighting to keep people safe after dark as they leave the building and enter their cars. You may have to hire a consultant to help design the interior and/or exterior. It all takes time and money.

As you start looking at the various buildings for sale or lease, think about what you like to find in the stores and other public places or dining establishments you frequent. What about the aesthetics of one makes it more of a pleasure to frequent than another? Do you like the music that's being piped in, the height or look of the ceilings, the painting or papering, the floor covering, the parking area? I have a friend who will drive a considerable distance to find a Barnes & Noble when she wants to enjoy a good cup of coffee and a good book. She'll pass right by the more convenient home of a well-known national coffee chain, even though she likes their coffee. Why? Because she'd much rather sit in a comfy easy chair then one of those stiff-backed wooden chairs that the coffee chain offers. She's there to relax for a bit, and she can't do it in what she calls a "kitchen-table atmosphere."

One thing that's important when you consider the purchase of a building, or sign a lease, is the length of time it will serve your purposes. While you don't want to spend a great deal of money on a facility that you won't grow into for a very long time, you also have to weigh that against the possibility of growing a clientele only to have to direct them to a new location after a short period of time. Inevitably, a move loses customers no matter what you do. About the only time this isn't the case is if your business is Internet-only or completely mobile. But even with the latter, it may be that people who were in your "no delivery charge" area might be far enough away now that a move might cause you to spend more funds on transportation or even require the initiation of a delivery fee to those who have come to expect it for free. There are all sorts of ramifications to a business move.

If you must move, throw a grand-opening party when you relocate. Invite your current customers (perhaps to a before-party gathering, too, to show them they're special) and people in your new business neighborhood. Don't forget to announce your new location on your website and any social networks to which you belong.

Funding Options and Arrangements

While there are all sorts of funding needs for a new business, let's first take a look at the purchase of a building for your company, and the funding options for that purchase. You might, for example, simply apply for a business loan through a bank. You could ask the SBA for a real estate property loan. Another attractive option is the willingness of banks to accept money gifted to you by family or friends to create a partnership of several people for your building purchase.

You'll recall that I explained how a partnership is a separate entity. When it comes to buying commercial real estate, it's actually the most common entity.

The flexibility inherent in a partnership makes it easy for ten people to invest $25,000 each, for example, and buy commercial property. Were friends or family members to do this for you and your new business, that would not make them your business partners. Most people, when they do this type of arrangement, set up a separate entity that holds the building. This arrangement would make the people who contributed the money partners for your property only, not your business as well.

Multiple entities can work toward a common goal, in fact. The most common example of this is a doctor's office, in which several doctors each contribute an equal share of the purchase price of the medical building. For purposes of explanation, we'll call this property partnership the ABC Partnership. The medical practice itself—the actual care of patients—is a separate entity. We'll call this DEF Partnership. To have a business home, a "tax home" as the IRS calls it, DEF Partnership will lease the medical building from ABC Partnership. The same doctors might be involved evenly in both partnerships, but perhaps not. You, Doctor K, might own 25 percent of ABC, along with Doctors L, M, and N, and then own 25 percent of a completely different partnership, EFGH Medical Partnership, with doctors P, R, and S. Partnerships are fabulous for flexibility and ease of use.

Why, you might wonder, don't you just own 50 percent of one partnership? The reason is to protect you from liability. Were you to have a medical malpractice issue that ended in litigation, the plaintiffs could only take funds from the medical practice itself, Partnership DEF. They would have no right to any profit, cash, or other assets from ABC Partnership. In fact, you could go even further with this, creating a third entity—Partnership WXYZ—that owned the costly medical equipment such as X-rays and other machines used in the performance of your medical services. DEF would then lease from WXYZ. Once again, were DEF to be sued successfully, the plaintiffs might get proceeds from your medical services but could not take or sell off any of your medical equipment. They couldn't because your medical partnership does not own that equipment.

A loan for commercial property is quite different from that of residential property. Except for FHA (Federal Housing Administration) and a few other unusual loans, the standard residential loan requires a 20 percent down payment from the purchaser. Commercial sellers and financers, however, typically require that the buyer provide 40 percent of the sale price up front. Where both commercial and residential are similar are in the items the lender peruses to determine your suitability for the loan. These are your income, your expenses, and your outstanding loans/assets.

Of course, if you're a business, you have other forms to share that aren't part of a residential transaction. These are your company's balance sheet, profit and loss (income) statement, and statement of cash flows. Your prospective lender will want to see all three, to see your business health. What the financial institution is normally going to look at is whether your current profits and cash flow indicate that you are going to be able to repay any loan they provide you. Unlike with a residential purchase, where the bank just wants to make sure you can make your house payments for the next month or two (though note that this requirement is getting tougher as we speak), a commercial lender wants to be assured that your company has enough profit and cash flow to pay the loan for the next few years at least. The reason behind the increased stringency for the commercial loan is the decrease of emotional attachment to your commercial property as compared with your residential property. As a rule, people will fight tooth and nail to keep their homes, while a business crisis might drive a commercial building owner to default on the commercial property without a comparable fight to keep the building.

There's one more serious matter that you must take into consideration before purchasing commercial property rather than leasing space for your new business. In many states, Arizona included, residential loans are nonrecourse. What this means is that if you default on your mortgage, your lender cannot come after you for the balance. Nowhere is that true of commercial loans. Just because you can't afford to make those payments on the commercial property you bought, doesn't mean you can walk away from that bill because you walk away from the building. That bank or other financial lender will come after you (or whomever guaranteed the loan) personally for the balance. And while we've talked a lot about protecting your personal assets through a wise entity strategy decision, if you default on a commercial property loan, your personal assets and funds will be in jeopardy. This happens because normally a new business owner will have been required to sign the loan papers as an individual cosigner for the new firm. This also happens in commercial leases. In fact, it's rare that an individual owner avoids this problem if the business is less than ten years old.

My recommendation to all new business owners, therefore, is that you lease before you buy. Since statistics show that 90 percent of all small businesses fail in the first five years, I suggest you lease for the first five years. This doesn't mean one five-year lease; you might lease for a considerably shorter time period, with subsequent options as discussed earlier. The point is to lease until you know and you can show that your business is viable and profitable enough to handle any commercial building purchase payments. It takes a while to be that sure. The economy or your industry can change suddenly, or unexpected circumstances can cause unexpected expenses. It's best to know you can survive a harsh short-term 33 percent drop in profits before deciding on the purchase of a commercial building for your business.

Keep in mind there are two sources of money for your business: your cash flows and your cash reserves. If you have plenty of one, your firm is generally okay. If you have plenty of both, that's better yet. If you have neither, you're in trouble and you had better resolve the problem right away. What's most troublesome is that far too many business owners don't even know when they're in these dire straits. They don't read or take the time to learn how to interpret their company balance sheet, profit and loss statement, and statement of cash flows. The balance sheet tells you what you own and what you owe. What you own is your cash reserves. The statement of cash flows tells you how much money is coming into the business and how much money is going out at the end of the day. It describes where that money went. It's important to be able to see at a glance that your business is experiencing a positive cash flow (spending less than it's bringing in) or a negative cash flow (spending more than it's bringing in). While seasonal businesses might well have regular periods of negative cash flow, those trends have to be well understood, and the busy season profits must make up for those negative time periods and more.

> *It's important to be able to see at a glance that your business is experiencing a positive cash flow (spending less than it's bringing in) or a negative cash flow (spending more than it's bringing in).*

A business that sells Christmas trees or one that sells pumpkins is seasonal. Each has only one or two months of profit. The rest of the year each would realize a negative cash flow, though it would tend not to be a big money loss. Expenses during the off-season might be phone bills, website hosting fees, and some seed and/or sapling purchases. Once that sale season hits, however, the profits should well offset the negative cash flow for the off-season months—otherwise, why be in the business?

I talk a lot about cash flow in Chapter 13, "The Money," so if you are concerned about this type of seasonality I recommend that you read through that chapter as well as speak with your CPA, your financial planner, and your banker to see how they can help you manage this type of business cash flow.

The Money

The two categories you must concentrate on to make your business successful are your cash flow and your cash reserve. Of course, when we think of success, we don't just think of a positive bottom line. We think as well of things such as lifestyle flexibility, a healthy work/life balance, and "being our own bosses." But let's face it: you're not going into business to lose money; rather, you want to make money.

Determining if you are making money in your business is not a simple matter, however, and many business owners don't evaluate this in the right way. If, as many owners do, you look only at your company's top-line gross revenue to determine if your company is succeeding, you might draw the wrong conclusions. Gross revenue does not necessarily translate into bottom-line revenue and a nice flow of cash into your own pocket. If, for example, you expand the number of clients you have, you may or may not make more money. If more clients were to translate into additional staff—that are perhaps less efficient staff—you could actually decrease your net profit as a result. So it's important that you know what you're looking at when you review your finances and how to use that information to make decisions.

Now, I typically recommend that you outsource the bookkeeping and financial areas of your business unless you are an expert in them. Remember the point Michael Gerber makes in *The E-Myth*, and the point I've been stressing as well, that you should always surround yourself with people who are smarter than you in the key areas of your business in which you do not excel.

However, outsourcing or delegating does *not* mean abdicating. If you release control completely, someone could pull the wool over your eyes—and when it comes to your money, you certainly do not want that! You need to know the basics and stay on top of things. To help you do so, this portion of the book covers accounting methods as well as basic financial statements, their components, ways to utilize and analyze them, and what you, as an owner, should be looking for in your own set of books.

Accounting

You can choose one of two methods for your business accounting: cash or accrual. If you are using a cash basis, you are accounting for the actual proceeds you take in and spend within that given time period. In your cash basis income statement for January through December of 2013, the $10 you received on December 31 would count as income for 2013. If you write a business check on December 31 that doesn't clear your business's own bank until January 5, you wouldn't consider it an expense for 2013; it would be an expense in 2014, when the check clears. Neither accounts payable nor accounts receivable exists in a cash basis accounting system.

Accrual basis, however, considers both accounts receivable and accounts payable; the money you take in or spend for any given year is not based on the money in your hand or the money you pay out. Rather, it is based on (1) the money you earned and can expect to receive at a later time and (2) the bills you owe and know you have to pay at a later time. Even if you, the plumber, haven't billed the family whose sink you repaired, you've earned income when the work is done. If you have to first go to the hardware store for the sink fittings to complete your customer's repair, once you purchase those items on your charge account, you've incurred an expense even before you get the invoice from the hardware store.

Before you choose which of these accounting systems you're going to use, be aware that once you make the choice, your company is stuck with that basis for the life of the firm, in most cases.

Most small businesses choose cash basis accounting because it's the simpler method of the two. Companies that choose the accrual method of accounting do so as a tax-planning technique. Accrual can be beneficial during the first few years of a business, when you typically spend more than you make.

If, for example, you were to have two businesses, you could set up the first on a cash basis and the second on an accrual basis. The assumed loss of the first business, if it were to suffer from having more expenses than revenue early on, would offset the profit of the second business. The problem with using the accrual business is that, while it's beneficial for the years when your expenses exceed your revenues, it might very well raise your business's tax bracket in later years, when you're realizing a profit. Another disadvantage of using the accrual method of accounting comes into play with late-year unexpected client commitments. If, for example, you had a new client commit on December 31 to a major work agreement with you, your choice of accrual method would require that you report that commitment as revenue for the current year. What a major financial problem it would be to have an unexpected $100,000 profit to report for the year, unless you could quickly incur expenses to offset it. Accrual, while not always a bad choice, is not a choice you should make without a planning session with your CPA or other accounting adviser.

Because it is very difficult to change accounting methods once you've committed to one or the other, you need to contrive some sort of sliding-scale method of determining your current and future tax brackets, to help you decide which of the two accounting methods would be most financially beneficial for your business.

Another thing you'll need to decide is your accounting year. Businesses, depending on what they do, can ask for a fiscal year. In other words, you might for some reason want your year to start in February and end in January. All you're doing is shifting the twelve-month period. This sometimes happens in an effort to follow seasonal business activities. A perfect example is a Halloween store. The bulk of the business's sales are probably in August, September, and October, so the beginning of its year might be August, because that's when the bulk of the costume sales and rentals start for the year. Most businesses are on a calendar year. The IRS likes it that way, and having everyone's tax return deadline the same day each year simplifies the procedure for everyone. If your company has a specific reason for requesting a different fiscal year, you may request that from the IRS.

Financial Statements

As a business owner, you may not be the person doing the day-to-day accounting tasks and ultimately creating the financial statements. But to protect yourself from inept or unscrupulous employees or contractors, you should know enough about financial statements that you can interpret what you are reading and know if the figures look reasonable. If you don't monitor the forms continually, you could miss that something is not right—and by the time you realize it, in terms of what your business could suffer as a result, it could be too late.

For instance, what I most often witness, whether through error or deception, is a bookkeeper putting draws—which belong in the equity section of the balance sheet—on the profit and loss (income) statement. The effect of this error is that the business owner thinks she has a $30,000 loss to claim on her taxes, when what she really has is a $30,000 profit. This can be devastating at tax time.

So that you, the owner, can head off this kind of traumatic error, you will need to understand three key financial statements: the balance sheet, the profit and loss statement, and the cash flow statement. The balance sheet tells you what you own and what you owe. The profit and loss statement (also known as the income statement) shows you your gross revenue as well as your expenses, which brings you to your net income and, in many cases, your taxable income. Your cash flow statement, which I believe to be the most important of the three, tells you what cash reserves you have. It lets you know where you *really* stand, in terms of having money to run your business (and your life).

If, for example, you are grossing $100,000 in revenue, and your expenses total $80,000, you might assume your profit is $20,000. If, however, you have credit card payments totaling $25,000 due for that year, your cash flow is actually in the red by $5,000. In other words, you have no cash with which to pay yourself.

Pay Yourself First

I wish I had gotten this advice before I started my business. If you make sure to pay yourself a salary—including a bit for savings—that you can afford to live on, you will make it easier to recognize just how much profit you need to have, how little you have to spend on "stuff" and extras when you first start a business, and how much extra effort you may need to put in to make it all work. I highly recommend paying yourself first and then working to cover the costs of everything else.

You can see, then, why your statement of cash flows is more important than the profit and loss statement, if making money for yourself is important to you.

A big part of making your money is about increasing the gross income, the top-line income. This includes the overview of your marketing and sales efforts. As you look over your plans and the results of those plans, you will need to consider whether you are a good salesperson and, if so, if a sales staff of one is going to be enough to grow your business for the immediate future. You'll have to consider whether you need to hire salespeople.[32]

---

32. Your profit is based on two major things: high income and low expenses. You can move either of those numbers to end up with higher or lower profit. Just be warned that sometimes there is only so much you can cut; the rest you need to grow as more sales for the top-line revenue.

Another reason you prepare financial statements, beyond knowing if you're actually making a living and understanding how to plan for the future, is to have something tangible to show a potential lender, should your business need to borrow money. Banks and other lenders rely on your financial statements to gauge whether or not lending your company money is a good risk for them.

To determine its risk and your creditworthiness, a financial institution uses a set of comparison ratios, according to industry and locale. There are performance ratios, activity ratios, financing ratios, and liquidity ratios. Each of these categories has ten to fifteen category subdivisions, each enabling a unique look at your business.

The performance ratio category, for example, will include ratios applicable to the performance of equipment-heavy companies and other ratios that apply to service firms. The latter don't have assets that produce income, so the performance ratio of cash flows to assets wouldn't be applicable to those companies.

It's not necessary to know the complete set of ratios; later in this book I provide some of the more common ones. Although you're not a lending institution, the better you know the criteria banks use to decide whether you can have that all-important loan, the better your chances are of getting it.

This is where my philosophy of working *on* your business and not just *in* your business is crucial. For my own business, I spend every Friday from 9 a.m. until noon looking at its financial statements, collections, staff time sheets, and any productivity indicators. I look at the results of our marketing campaigns, one of which is an ongoing monthly wine-tasting party. Sure, I could be completing client tax returns during these hours, but I am convinced that using this time for working on my business is a must.

If you can't take a few hours out of each week to do as I am doing on Friday mornings, then make at least a monthly commitment to do so. If you don't, you won't know where your business is going. Without direction, you'll never arrive at your business destination. If, when you consider the three types of business owners—technician, manager, and entrepreneur—you determine that your entrepreneurial spirit is not up to this farsighted task, hire or contract with someone else to do it for you. Schedule it with them. Don't leave the process to a haphazard, when-I-get-to-it time frame, whether it's for you to do or for someone else to whom you assign it. As with any other business task—and perhaps any other life task—if you don't schedule the "job," it's far less likely to get done.

> ## *Analyzing Your Profits*
>
> I recommend a software program called ProfitCents, which helps small business owners analyze their profit. It is available by annual subscription. Especially helpful if you are looking for financing or investors, ProfitCents gives you access to a gigantic database of businesses, through which you can search by Standard Industrial Classification (SIC) code, zip code, revenue, number of employees, and other sorts.
>
> To use ProfitCents, you enter your company data anonymously. If, for example, you own an auto body shop in Scottsdale, Arizona, and your gross revenue is $100,000 for the year, you can compare your business with other body shops whose revenue and locations are similar. You can see how your cost of goods sold and other expenses, and their percentage of profit, compare to like companies. You can compare all three of your financial statements to those of other shops. You can even determine if what you pay your staff is more or less than what other comparable body shops are paying.
>
> If, in using ProfitCents, you discover that you are ahead of the competition, your next step is to determine why. Succeeding by accident is not going to help you succeed the next time. It's in learning what led to your success that you can repeat the success. Of course, if you find out that your competition is ahead of you, it's even more important to determine why that is.

Something important to note: different sets of books are kept in different ways. Your set of books—that is, your balance sheet and all your other financial statements—might be kept on a generally accepted accounting principles (GAAP) basis, for example. That would be unusual for a small firm, however. GAAP is usually used by large companies.

As a small business, you'll more than likely keep your books on a tax basis—that is, the way in which your tax returns are prepared. Most small business owners simply want to know at the end of the year how much tax they must pay and how much of the company's revenue will return to their own pockets.

Books are also prepared according to the type of entity a business is established as. As an example, let's look at a partnership. Should you have multiple partners, a variety of types of contributions can be made to the company. As we discussed earlier, one partner might contribute cash, another could provide services, while a third gives the company land. Yet all three of these partners may be treated equally if each contribution is valued equally. This partnership's books would be kept on what is known as a 704 basis, which is different from a GAAP basis or a tax basis.

Not keeping books correctly has caused companies to collapse. Enron and AIG are two such examples. Your company might end up with three, four, or five sets of books, each producing a different set of figures depending on what you're working with, who you're reporting to, or several other pertinent circumstances. It can be scary for you or any other investor, since you can't be sure which set of books the preparer is showing you. If you don't know how to read financial statements, you won't have a clue what you're looking at or if/when something is wrong. Just because someone is preparing your company's books, and he or she shows you those books, don't assume that all is as it should be with the finances of your business unless you can interpret the general meaning of what you see in the financial statements.

The financial statements are interrelated, all working together to show you and other interested parties, such as financial institutions and potential buyers or partners, how well your company is doing. It's imperative that you have a decent understanding of all three of the financial statements to guide you in management decisions.

In addition to the general information in this chapter, there are several ways to further your understanding. Most community colleges and some small business organizations offer courses that will teach you, or you might just sit down with your CPA for basic lessons. Should your CPA be unwilling to teach you the basics, look for another CPA. One of the tasks of a committed CPA is to help you learn your data and how to analyze it. The benefit of learning from your own CPA, as opposed to through college or other courses, is that you are learning the basics while absorbing your own company's data. That's a twofold benefit you won't get any other way.

Even if you are capable of, and have the time for, keeping your own books, it's often a good idea to have an external financial professional such as bookkeeper or CPA review them. A second, objective eye can help assess what your books are saying about your business and watch for any errors or telling figures.

Now, let's delve into more details for each of those three important financial statements—your balance sheet, your profit and loss (income) statement, and your statement of cash flows.

Balance Sheet

Your balance sheet is where your company reflects and itemizes what it owns and what it owes. This is perhaps both the simplest and most complex of the financial statements; most people are clear in their minds about what is owned versus owed, but often the equity section can become very confusing. We'll talk more about equity in a bit.

The balance sheet is the form that banks, your potential lenders, look at when they decide if they will lend you money or lower your interest rate. The balance sheet provides a good view of the health of your business. It gets its name from the fact that the "what you own" portion must balance with the "what you owe" portion. That's pretty simplistic, but it's enough to help you understand the basic premise. For example, let's assume you have $100 in your bank account and you don't owe anyone anything. This means that your business has equity of $100. If, instead, you have $100 in your bank account but a $10 balance on your business credit card, your company's equity now drops to $90.

We can divide the balance sheet into its top (assets) and bottom (liabilities and equity) portions. As you'll see, each of these sections includes specific items.

THE ASSETS SECTION
The top section of the balance sheet is the "what you own" part—your assets. These assets are broken down into current, long-term, and fixed assets.

- ✔ *Current assets:* These are liquid, which means you can cash them in within one year or less (or your assets can be cash itself!). They can also include accounts receivable.

- ✔ *Long-term assets*: *Long-term* means it will take more than a year to cash in these assets. Within this category, you might have a subcategory for amortizable assets. These are intangibles, such as goodwill, customer lists, signage, website marketing, your website domain, a non-compete with an old employee, or a client list. Intangible assets are basically things you cannot touch.

- ✔ *Fixed assets:* These are tangible assets, the things you *can* touch, such as buildings, equipment, and vehicles. It refers to anything that is used in your business for making money. This could be equipment, vehicles, computers, furniture, and so on.

THE LIABILITIES SECTION
The bottom section of the balance sheet is the "what you owe" portion, which is divided into two parts, your liabilities and equities.

Your liabilities section may include:

- ✔ *Current liabilities:* These are items that you have to pay on in less than one year. Examples are credit cards, short-term notes, accounts payable to vendors, or the upcoming year of loan payments on a vehicle or equipment loan.

✔ *Long-term liabilities:* These are loans that you owe money on with terms longer than one year. Examples are an SBA loan, a longer-term loan on a vehicle, or a building mortgage.

Also in your liabilities section, you'll include something called "loan to or from shareholders." While your business may start, as small businesses often do, with your initial stock input as owner, and that figure is what the stock or membership interest is worth, you may have to make another loan to the company at some point. You might, for example, have to lend it an additional $50,000 to hire employees. Unless you are a sole proprietor with no LLC, you are a shareholder, owner, or partner. As such, you and your business are two separate entities. If, then, you (entity A) lend money to your company (entity B), you must have a signed loan document. It might seem odd to sign a loan agreement between yourself and yourself, but that's what you must do. And when you do, it becomes a liability to the company and, as such, goes into the liabilities section of your company's balance sheet.

> *It might seem odd to sign a loan agreement between yourself and yourself, but that's what you must do.*

Your business loan must include a fair-market interest value—what the IRS refers to as applicable federal rate (AFR). You can find this figure on the IRS website. Additionally, your loan to your company must have regular terms. Setting up a loan with terms that aren't reasonable in the eyes of the IRS will not stand up to IRS scrutiny at tax time. You can't, for example, lend money to your firm with a 0 percent interest rate and a due date of 100 years from now. The general rule of thumb is that if a bank would never issue such a loan—one with the terms and due date that you're about to propose from you to your company—it's not reasonable, and you shouldn't do it.

To clarify, let's assume you're ABC Cleaning, and you need a $50,000 bank loan. Your company is brand new, without financial statements, history, creditworthiness, or client lists. Thus, you're going to pay a higher interest rate than would a company with a long, solid business history and proven profit. That only makes sense. So, if you are the bank for your own ABC Cleaning, you must charge your company a higher interest rate, too. You would want to start the loan by requiring no payments for the first three months. In the fourth month, however, your firm should start making the payments just as you would if you had borrowed from a third party, what the IRS calls an "arm's length" party. When you lend money to your company, therefore, you should act as you would in an arm's length transaction.

Shareholder loans fairly precipitate IRS audits and lawsuits. A company that has received a loan from its shareholders and has not been making payments back to them, has not been paying interest or late fees, and is in other ways not acting as it would in an arm's length transaction may well end up with the entire loan being reclassified as capital. With capital, as opposed to a loan, the money is contributed to the company with no expectation of its return to the shareholder. To have the IRS reclassify the loan you make to your firm would tie up your own money until the company is sold. Your company could end up "taking" money from you that you had counted on having returned to you. You could lose this money for decades, with its value decreased by the due date instead of increased through regular interest payments. In this way your "loan" may be reclassified as equity in the company.

In contrast to equity, to be described next, the liabilities portion of your balance sheet is easy to understand. Simply put, liabilities are anything you owe. It might be a credit card, a line of credit, a loan from a family member, a vehicle loan, or even something called "liability for things unknown." To explain the last, let's assume your company is being sued and the case has not been decided yet. Let's assume further that you expect to lose and to have to pay $5,000 in damages. That $5,000 is a liability, simply because you expect that you will have to pay it.

Of course, knowing (or thinking you know) whether you are going to win or lose a lawsuit is iffy. Having a good feel for whether or not you'll win a lawsuit hinges on the type of books you are keeping—GAAP, tax, or 704—and the reporting you're doing as a result. Your decision on how to keep your books should be based on what helps you manage your business. You need to be able to see if your liabilities are getting too high, if some of your credit cards should be paid off, and so forth. Once you understand the statement of cash flows, for example, you'll then be able to tell if your company has the cash to pay off any of those credit cards.

THE EQUITY SECTION

Equity in the company is what you have, as a positive or negative, after you take all the assets (items you own) and subtract all the liabilities (things you owe). This balance, the remainder, is your equity in the company, similar to an individual's net worth.

In the equity section you also track any "draws" that you, as the owner, may have taken. Remember the earlier discussion about the basis account and how that was affected by draws (going down by money you take out)? This is where the money you've drawn is reflected in your financial statements.

A side note: As a balance sheet rule of thumb, your company's capital stock category should be as low as you possibly can make it. One of the ways to assure this is to follow arm's length transaction guidelines for any loan you or any shareholder makes to your firm. This point needs to be made for auto loans as well.[33]

Stock is a common word that can be used to describe many parts of common equity categories. These can be divided into opening stock (also called opening balance stock), additional paid-in capital, capital stock, preferred stock, and the various distributions within these categories.

Opening stock is your initial contribution to your new business. The word *stock* can be confusing, as it technically only applies to an Inc. or an LLC being taxed as a C or S corp. A full-out partnership or an LLC taxed as a partnership would use the term "membership interest" or "capital account" rather than referring to stock. Seldom does it matter what term you use on your financial statements, and with programs such as QuickBooks (which I highly recommend), you can change the term as needed.

The additional paid-in capital category refers to any contributions you make to your business after your start-up contribution.

Preferred stock is typically only seen in C-Corporations and represents a form of stock that has more benefits than normal common stock. These benefits usually include voting rights and, potentially, dividend rights.

Each owner, depending on the taxation type of the entity, may be eligible for distributions. One of the most typical is related to S-Corporations and is commonly called owner's distribution or owner's draw. This category is generally broken down on the balance sheet as a subcategory of opening stock or common stock and is reported as a separate line for each year of distribution. This is one of the ways you can pull cash out of your company based on its future value at time of sale or closing.

Capital accounts are confusing. At the start of your business, your capital account is similar to your retained earnings, a category that also goes into the equities section. Your retained earnings and your capital account together track your profit and loss over the life of your business. Going back to our earlier example, let's assume you're a brand-new business with a capital account at zero. You

---

33. I'll quickly mention here that a good strategy for your acquisition of a business vehicle is to lease it from yourself—but make sure that you are checking with your CPA for the best route to do this legally. You can also consider creating a separate entity that holds equipment and leasing the equipment from that entity. (If you don't have the signed documents to lease equipment from some other entity, it's not a lease, and now you have all sorts of IRS problems.)

have earned nothing as yet. When you put your first $1,000 into your business bank account, your company's capital account goes up to $1,000. Should your company lose $400 that year, your capital account drops to $600.

Now, let's jump ahead to when you sell your business. Let's assume you're going to sell the business for $2,000. You'd have a $1,400 gain because your business was "bought" for $600. You may tend to think you bought it for $1,000, but with a flow-thru company, the amount that you bought it for changes each year. Any time you take money out of or put money into your company, the value of what you started and what you purchased changes. This account is generally crafted by your CPA, but it's also reflected on your balance sheet. You must track these figures year to year to know at any given time what your basis is.

A business sale in the eyes of the IRS can refer to the actual closing of the business, its sale to a third party, or a buyout from a partner. In other words, several things could kick your company's capital account into effect.

Keep in mind that any time you draw money out of your company, you lower your business's capital account. You're basically pulling money out for yourself against your business's future sale.

Most business owners fail to track the capital account. It's on their shoulders to do so, and they must be vigilant about doing it or seeing that their accountant is doing so. A CPA who will do that for you is going above and beyond and is to be valued. If the CPA is not going to do so, she or he needs to at least teach you how to do it yourself. You only need to do it once a year, and tax time is the most logical choice. Since you must track draws by year, here's how the account would appear on the balance sheet:

✔ Partner A
  1. Contributions
     2012
     2013
     2014

  2. Distributions
     2012
     2013
     2014

✔ Partner B
  1. Contributions
     2012
     2013
     2014

  2. Distributions
     2012
     2013
     2014

The draws and distribution category is also important for maintaining your taxing structure, as we talked about earlier—especially for a partnership or S corp. To demonstrate the flexibility of partnerships: Partner A can take a $5,000 distribution in 2013, while Partner B opts for a $10,000 distribution. That's okay to do. If the company is an S corp and the shareholders are 50/50 owners, however, Partner A's distribution of $5,000 would necessitate an equal $5,000 distribution by Partner B. Your balance sheet, if done correctly, would give you a clear look at whether your S election was in jeopardy, for example. Your balance sheet makes it much easier for you, the business owner, to manage your capital accounts, your partner distributions, and your tax plans if you report and separate each category clearly each year.

Profit and Loss (Income) Statement

The statement of profit and loss, also known as the income statement, consists of sections that describe your business:

- ✔ Income
- ✔ Cost of goods sold
- ✔ Gross profit
- ✔ Expenses (also referred to as overhead expenses)
- ✔ Net profit
- ✔ Other expenses
- ✔ Other income
- ✔ Final net profit (To be absolutely technical, the final net profit line is net income before interest and taxes. Very large companies include interest and tax estimate figures prior to giving the final net profit figure.)

Each of these areas reflects different but important information about your business and how it is operating, as a whole and in its pieces.

INCOME

Income can be referred to as normal income or gross income, but no matter what name it is given, it means the money you take in from your ordinary business transactions prior to deducting all the expenses involved in earning that money.

Keep in mind, however, that were you to be asked for an income figure by an outsider—a lawyer, tax preparer, or financial institution—you'll want to clarify if that request is for gross (and not net) income.

Note as well that I said it is money from "ordinary" business transactions. If you own a laundromat, for example, the coins that your customers feed the washers and dryers and the money they pay you to dry clean their suits are ordinary income. If, however, you have a friend who closes his printing shop and asks you to help him get rid of copy paper and other printing supplies, and you say "sure" and display those items at your laundromat's customer service counter for a couple of weeks, the money that anyone pays you to buy those supplies would not be "ordinary." As such, it would not be considered a part of your gross income; rather, it would be a part of the "other income" category. You can't count that income in your gross income because your financial statements are supposed to be guides for you and others, such as your potential buyers, partners, or lending institutions. Including as part of gross income something that occurred once for a very short period of time—and is not expected to occur again—inaccurately skews the perception of your business's health and operations, which can lead to serious errors and/or missed opportunities in business decisions later on.

COST OF GOODS SOLD

The cost of goods sold (COGS) section is often the most difficult part of the profit and loss statement for new business owners to understand—so don't feel bad if you feel lost! Always ask your CPA.

Included in cost of goods sold are the figures for the expenses involved in producing and selling your company's products. If, for example, you own an ice cream store, the money you spend to buy the ice cream, the cones, the sprinkles, and the scoops is all part of your cost of goods sold. That's fairly obvious, even for a novice entrepreneur. If you hadn't spent money on these items, you wouldn't have been able to sell your goods (the ice cream).

Where it gets a little more difficult to comprehend—and what a lot of business people miss when they compute their cost of goods sold—relates to the wages paid to those employees who scoop, dish out, sell, and ring up the cash register during the sale of the ice cream. These jobs are *directly* related to the ice cream sales. On the other hand, cleaning the tables, sweeping the floor, balancing the cash register at the end of the day, and washing the dishes aren't employee tasks that directly contribute to ice cream sales. So when determining COGS, the business owner must add those employee tasks—and *only* those tasks, and the time they took out of an employee's week to complete them—that helped sell the ice cream. If, for example, four employees each worked 25 hours in a week (100 total hours), but each employee spent only half of every day waiting on customers (50 of the total hours), and each earned $10 an hour, the cost of goods sold for that week would be 50 employee hours at $10 per hour, or $500 a week.

The software program ProfitCents allows you to benchmark this issue, providing you with a look at the cost of goods sold in the financial statements of similar firms in your local area.

Gross profit, which may also be referred to as gross margin, is often how the sales price of your business is determined. Gross profit—that is, the difference between the gross income a company generates and the expenses directly related to the sales (your COGS expenses)—tells a potential buyer about the health of the company. A potential buyer needs to see not only the overall net profit of the firm but also the margin on each product the company sells.

So, assuming that you have an ice cream store you'd like to sell, let's say that:

✔ You're selling your ice cream cones for $1.50 each.

✔ Your cost of goods sold includes
  o The amount you spend on each cone: $0.30

  o The cost of the ice cream you scoop inside it: $0.50

  o The cost of your employee to scoop the ice cream: $0.50 per cone (assuming that the employee scoops 20 cones per hour, you pay her $10 per hour, and that's the only task she has during her work hours)

Your profit margin/gross margin would be $0.20 per cone—which may or may not be enough to appeal to a prospective buyer.

Depending on your type of business, your margin may be high or low. In an ice cream store model, you can have a low profit margin because you have a high volume (lots of sales each summer day). However, in a mechanic's shop, where you may work on only two or three cars each day, the profit margin would need to be much higher to be able to cover your other overhead and general expenses. Each prospective buyer will be looking for his or her own acceptable profit margin for a specific type of business, so it is important that you know what your profit margin is and how it compares with other similar businesses in your industry. This push drives some business owners to "fudge" their COGS figures, and therefore their profit margins, on their companies' income statements.

In fact, many companies keep separate sets of books—one for themselves and one to show potential buyers or lenders. They keep a set of books indicating what they believe to be their true costs for managing purposes, so they can figure out on their own if they are making a profit or need to lower prices, get rid of an employee, and so forth. A business may also keep an external set of books. These are what the buyer is looking at, though they are not necessarily a true and accurate representation of the business's health and wealth. Many business brokers are often not familiar with the detailed workings of financial statements so, if you are considering the purchase of a business, you should make sure that you review the statements with your CPA or CFO. And don't forget: if it feels funny, it most likely is!

Note: Normally this is *not* an acceptable practice, and the IRS certainly does not approve of your having two sets of books! This commentary is only meant to demonstrate that there may be a difference between the truth and what the books reflect, so only if you prepare the numbers yourself do you know that they are close to truth.

Also, please note that sometimes general administrative and overhead figures get included in the cost of goods sold, which causes some fudging as well.

One big concern is that the COGS number can be so easily altered. Whether the owner says that an employee spends 30 or 80 percent of her time scooping ice cream, for instance, will have a considerable impact on the cost of each cone sold. As another example, the purchase of an ice cream case is an expense that would not have to occur were that company not selling ice cream. Its purchase price does, therefore, get included in the cost of goods sold. Whether you purchase the top-of-the-line ice cream case for $10,000 or the standard case for $5,000 will significantly impact your cost of goods sold. Depending on who owns the business, these choices may or may not be the same for a potential buyer.

Subtracting cost of goods sold from gross income gives us the gross margin/ gross profit/profit margin figure that potential buyers study to determine the offered purchase price for your business.

The next income statement section (my favorite) is called overhead expenses. It's what we might call the "catch-all" section—where all the expenses that don't fit in any other category are listed. In overhead expenses, you would put your own salary and the money spent on water, furniture, utilities, janitorial supplies, and employee wages, for example. I frequently hear the question "What can I write off?" My best answer is to understand what the IRS uses to determine business expenses. Uncle Sam uses two qualifying words: "ordinary" and "necessary." If it's not ordinary or necessary to your business, it's not a business expense you can claim as a tax write-off.

To revisit my favorite example, let's assume you are a rock star. To maintain your popularity and your image, you need to maintain your gorgeous/handsome body. You also need a big travel trailer for touring the country. And when you fly commercial, you can't ride in coach—that would ruin your image—so you need first class. You need to keep your nails and your hair in healthy and attractive condition and you need something, beyond your talent, to differentiate you for the fans. You might, for example, become known as the star that loves M&Ms, or has a charm bracelet collection, or doesn't perform unless the facility provides you with plenty of pre-concert burgers and beer from Germany.

So, while that ice cream shop owner we talked about earlier wouldn't be able to write off the price of a first-class plane ticket or a pedicure, you, the rock star, could. And the theater owner who paid an arm and a leg to make sure you had plenty of burgers and beer before your rock concert could include the cost of those provisions and their delivery in its overhead expense category on its own income statement. It would, as well, be tax deductible.

So, just what could that ice cream shop owner write off? Of course, the cost of the ice cream. Marketing and advertising costs would be deductible, as well as dining with potential clients (if the owner were invited to bid on a corporate ice cream party event, for example). The IRS has an excellent list of regular expenses; I suggest you read through the list and, as you go through each business day, be conscious of the money you spend. Each time you reach for your wallet, think "Is this an ordinary and necessary business expense, or a personal expense?" Once you've determined that, you know which card or bank account check should be used to pay for the item(s).

Statement of Cash Flows

The statement of cash flows is a form that's easy to understand. It simply describes the cash that came into and went out of your business during the designated time period, as well as the amounts of that cash that went to or came from each of three categories: operating activities, investing activities, and financing activities.

- ✔ The operating activities category lists your company's monetary day-to-day activities. In its income cash subcategory, you'd note the money brought into the firm through sale of your products or services, while in the outgoing cash subcategory, you'd list the various costs of maintaining your business, such as salary, rent, and utilities.

- ✔ The investing activities category is focused on what you do to rebuild your company's wealth. A cash-positive investing activity might be selling a business asset, increasing your savings accounts, or purchasing a CD (certificate of deposit), while the purchase of a business asset would be a cash negative (draw) against the investing activities subtotal. Generally, you'll have a less active investing activities category than you will an operating activities category.

✔ Your financing activities category includes any monetary activity that involves third parties or the company owner(s). A business loan and an infusion of cash into the company by an owner are positive financing activities, while a payment on a business loan would be a draw against the financing activities.

The format of the statement of cash flows is fairly straightforward. The first figure at the top of the statement is your beginning cash flow for the designated time period. The last figure at the bottom is the cash balance with which you end the time period.

You should look at these statements monthly or quarterly, to help you understand where your company's earnings are going. If you see, for instance, that most of your earnings are going toward operating expenses, with little set aside for long-term growth, what can you do to change this hazardous activity? Perhaps you need to invest more into savings or better equipment.

On the other hand, if, every month, business operations bring in a generous amount of proceeds but a disproportionate amount of the profit is going to financing activities, where is the problem? Are you taking owner distributions? Paying off loans? Can you renegotiate your interest rates to lower your financing costs?

Take a look as well at where the company cash is coming from, beyond the sale of its products and services. If, for example, a ton of money is coming in from financing and a ton of money is going out to financing, the owners are either dumping that money in or borrowing it from a bank. If you're one of those owners, is that really what you want to be doing with your company?

As you see, your statement of cash flows is a good way of looking at different scenarios beyond the balance sheet and the profit and loss (income) statement. You really want to look at all three statements—balance sheet, profit and loss, and statement of cash flows—together to get a rounded view of the health of the company.

While it's easy to understand the statement of cash flows and its importance, people often get confused about what is investing and what is financing. If you find yourself struggling with this or other financial statement how-to's, I recommend the following accounting books:

✔ *Basic Accounting Concepts, Principles, and Procedures,* Vol. 1, by Gregory R Mostyn

✔ *Bookkeepers' Boot Camp: Get a Grip on Accounting Basics* (Numbers 101 for Small Business) by Angie Mohr

✔ *Accounting for Dummies* by John A. Tracy

Ratios

Ratios are important for you, the business owner. They tell you and potential lenders how well your company is doing, and they also help you compare your company's business health against other companies in the same or a similar industry and/or geographic location.

Any time you apply with a bank or other financial institution for a loan, the potential lender will apply ratios to your set of books. It's vital that you've already done the same before showing up there, hat in hand. If you don't know ahead of time what ratios might be higher or lower than the average for your industry, you won't be prepared with an explanation.

Nor are banks the only firms that study ratios. Sophisticated investors—defined as those with liquid net worth exceeding $250,000—look at ratios also. If they're going to invest, they first want to know about the company's health and their potential return on investment (ROI). If you already have a business loan from a bank, the interest rate on that loan is its ROI. So, the sophisticated investors look at that, and then try to determine whether, after you've paid the bank its due, you'd be able to repay them as well. An investor risks more than the bank and so will require a higher rate of interest. You and your potential investors can apply common ratios to your current books or your forecasted (budgeted) set of books.

Once you get the knack of consistently studying ratios, it will be as if you have a crystal ball for what might happen to your firm should the business's proverbial "shit" hit the fan. A couple of my clients use these ratios very frequently. In both cases, they were able to foretell, at the start of the U.S. economic crisis, that they should close their businesses. Their ratios told them that if their profit margins dropped, they wouldn't be able to generate enough cash flow to continue supporting the businesses while making the profits they wanted. Both sold out.

These are but two examples of why knowing your ratios and your company's health are crucial. You might think, "I don't have the time to keep an eye on this—I'm working in the business, not on the business." But, as I mentioned earlier, it's critical that you set aside some time each week to work on your business and assess its financial health. And so every Friday morning, I spend time studying my company's ratios, my customers' satisfaction, my financial statements, and so forth. One of the ways to study ratios is by way of an Excel spreadsheet with a ratio template already created.

WHAT ARE THE TYPES OF RATIOS AND WHAT ARE THEY USED FOR?

There are many types of ratios, but they really all fall into four main categories:

- ✔ *Performance ratios*: These describe how the company is doing.

- ✔ *Activity ratios*: These describe how much of X the company is creating.

- ✔ *Financing ratios*: These describe how the company is financing itself.

- ✔ *Liquidity ratios/warnings*: These describe how the company is handling its cash flow/ability to pay.

In Appendix A, Financial Ratios, is a listing of the various ratios, explaining the type of ratio, the name of the ratio, what the ratio describes, what industry the ratio is most useful for, and how the ratio should be used. As I brought up earlier, ratios are handy for judging your company against the ratios of your competition.

There are three ways of studying ratios:

- ✔ *Vertically*: Cash flow and asset comparisons within your own firm during a specific month

- ✔ *Horizontally*: Ratio comparisons of two time periods within your own firm

- ✔ *Comparative analysis*: As a benchmarking tool to compare your firm's ratios against the ratios of other firms

Of the three, comparative analysis is the most difficult, as you can't just call up your competitor and ask for its ratios. As mentioned before, however, you can get this information from ProfitCents. Although it won't tell you a company's name, it does indicate industry and locale. Should you have only one local competitor, you then know which company's ratios you're perusing on ProfitCents. Some ratios will relate to the company's health, while others will give you a look at debt.

Let's assume for a minute that you notice that your competitor has a huge debt-to-income ratio; in other words, they just might be in trouble, and ripe for a sale or merger. Knowing that, but not disclosing that you know, you might approach your competitor by mentioning your own financial issues and inquire about his or her interest in combining forces. Perhaps you could ask if there is an interest in your buying out the competitor. If the company is truly struggling, this could be a godsend in that owner's eyes.

Tracking ratios gives you a lot of insight—and a better opportunity to find the gem within the competitor rocks. You can determine if you're buying into a lot of debt, or perhaps if the problems you see are ones you are uniquely qualified to solve.

You might find a friendly competitor as well. I have one, a buddy of mine who has a CPA firm in North Phoenix, outside of my general market area but close by. We get together once a month and share financial statements, talk about human resources and other business issues, and generally try to help each other. It's very helpful to us both.

Bookkeeping

Bookkeeping can seem scary, or at best a tedious and unattractive ritual, to many business owners. It is crucial in running your business, however. Beyond the obvious need to know what you sold, what you bought, what money you have on hand, into which category each item falls, and what bills must be paid, bookkeeping is important because it's historical. If you don't know your own business history, you're doomed to repeat your mistakes—and possibly drive your business into the ground. Additionally, if you don't know that you've made a profit, you can't put money in your own pocket or the pockets of your family members.

While there are business owners who wait until year-end to do their bookkeeping, I recommend you do it weekly or, better yet, daily. Unless you're a small, part-time company with only one client, it's difficult or impossible to know where you stand financially unless you do bookkeeping regularly. Bookkeeping is what creates your financial statements—the tracking mechanism through which you form those documents.

Bookkeeping, including the debit and credit system at the root of it, was invented in the fifteenth century by Italian monks who had to find a way to keep track of their wine sales. There are now hundreds of thousands of software programs for bookkeeping. As a small business, however, you need to consider only three bookkeeping methods. Which of the three you choose depends on your business volume.

The old, manual way of doing bookkeeping—the process used from the time of those grape-growing monks until somewhere around the 1300s—was to record figures by hand on a series of worksheets. The monks, for example, would have had a page for each type of winemaking expense. They'd have had a page for the labor involved, another for the bottles, and a third for the cost of the grapes. Each time they completed some monetary transaction, such as buying more grapes or selling bottles of wine, they'd record it. When grapes were purchased in 1336, for example, they'd record it on the grape page: March 13, 1336, purchased 300 grapes, and the cost of the grapes they bought. At the end of the year they could look at the wine page, where sales were noted, and compare that with the grape page to see how much money they had made to keep their monastery going.

This manual-entry bookkeeping process, what I call "legal-pad bookkeeping," does not create financial statements, however. It simply provides you with all the figures you need to compare in order to determine your profit. If you're a sole proprietor who doesn't need a loan, and doesn't need to show prospective partners or buyers that you're solvent, you probably don't have to create financial statements. All you need for quarterly and annual tax returns is in your bookkeeping figures.

A more advanced bookkeeping process than this manual legal-pad procedure involves software or online applications. Excel is the most common and probably the simplest to use. Once you've created your Excel spreadsheet template, you create a column for each month, and then label rows for each income and expense category. Depending on how numerous and how specific your rows, you could end up with an income (profit and loss) statement. While the income statement is the most-used of any of the traditional financial statements, you're still going to need a balance sheet and a cash flow statement as well if you want to look for partners, buyers, lenders, or investors.

What's important to your business, whether it's small or large, a sole proprietorship or other type of entity, a part-time avocation or full-time occupation, is that you get some Excel training early on, if you haven't done so already.

The most complex do-it-yourself bookkeeping process involves using one of several software packages. The most common of these is Intuit's QuickBooks and its less-costly, stripped-down version, Quicken. While Quicken is nice for personal use, it really only acts as an electronic check register and is not complete enough for business bookkeeping. For that you need QuickBooks. Once you've learned how to use QuickBooks, you can create financial statements from your bookkeeping entries in two clicks. Stepping up to the more advanced QuickBooks from your manual-entry system will require several hours of learning and a few hundred dollars, but the time and effort saved will be more than worth the time and money spent.

QuickBooks comes in several versions that vary in price and features, with some versions specific to business specialties or industries. The Point of Sale QuickBooks version, for instance, enables a highly complex and detailed inventory tracking system. As your bookkeeper documents each item sold, the inventory number changes in QuickBooks, so you can be alerted when it's time to order more inventory.

Sage's Peachtree Software is a popular alternative to QuickBooks. Other options include Xero, FreshBooks, and MYOB Premier (which integrates with Microsoft Outlook, a handy feature).

For very large firms, something even more advanced is needed. One alternative is Sageworks software, which, for example, for retailers can drill down into details as minute as the cost of buttons, zippers, thread, dye, fabric, and labor for the production of a pair of pants. It's going to be a while—if ever—before you need anything this massive. For a new small business, QuickBooks or something similar should do just fine.

If you decide to buy an Intuit product, you can even start with its free QuickBooks version, called Simple Start. This will work well until you have more than twenty customers. All you need to do at that point is to upgrade to Premier, Pro, or one of the more advanced QuickBooks versions. Each of these has an annual upgrade, with an additional fee attached, but you are never obligated to upgrade. In fact, I have clients using the 2003 version of QuickBooks, and it's working fine for them. Before you purchase accounting software, ask your CPA or bookkeeper what she or he uses and if she or he will train you on it. In fact, QuickBooks is so popular that many community colleges offer courses. Every version has its own tutorial as well, with videos that you can watch and re-watch as needed.

Accounting is scary for a business owner who doesn't know the first thing about keeping books. It's very tempting to just hire a bookkeeper and then walk away from the accounting process, without ever glancing over your ledgers or financial statements again. Taking this out-of-sight, out-of-mind stance, however, can lead you to the poorhouse as an unscrupulous bookkeeper steals your hard-earned money. Nearly any competent bookkeeper could steal from you, and while most would never do so, it only takes one to ruin your business.

Perusing your books frequently and unannounced is the best protection you can have against employee theft.

Perusing your books frequently and unannounced is the best protection you can have against employee theft. While you don't need to understand every line item or be able to duplicate bookkeeping tasks, you should know how to interpret your financial statements, how to look something up in your accounting software, and how to compare your office check register with what your bank shows is there. Besides, people do quit, get sick, take vacations, and so forth. You should know how to do some simple things on your own, such as writing a petty cash check for staff pizza or paying a contractor. It's crucial that you understand that check writing isn't only about signing a paper form. You must know how and where to enter that debit so that your expense is noted and your bank account balance is accurate.

If, at any point, you suspect that your bookkeeper might be doing something unethical, and you don't feel up to the task of verification, find someone you trust who is competent and have her or him go over the books after hours, or perhaps on the bookkeeper's days off. Inventory is a very complex function, however. I recommend you have your CPA oversee inventory bookkeeping twice a year.

Expenses, Deductions, and Credits

When it comes to documenting how you spend your business money, your expenses, deductions, and credits each have their own category.

Expenses

The items on which you spend your company's funds are documented on your profit and loss (income) statement. These could include

- ✔ office supplies;
- ✔ payments on a business loan;
- ✔ life insurance for you and your employees; and
- ✔ similar costs for running a business.

As expenses, meaning movements of cash out of your business, you may or may not be able to deduct any of these off your taxes.

Although life insurance may be an allowable expense, there is a big disadvantage to claiming it as a deduction on your taxes. If, for example, you deducted payments for your own life insurance as owner of the company, and you were to pass away, all the life insurance that gets paid out to your designated beneficiary would become taxable to your company. Please make sure that you check with your CPA for the current regulations on deducting insurance premiums. These change regularly and you want to make sure you are deducting only what you are truly allowed to.

Deductions

While deductions involve expenses, they fall into a narrower category. A deduction is a reduction that you are able to claim on your tax payment to the IRS because of the type of expense it is. Common business deductions would be fuel for your work vehicle, cell phone charges, and office equipment repairs. No deduction offers a 100 percent reduction of the money you spent on that item. Your taxable rate determines the percentage of that expense you'll be able to deduct from your income tax. If, for example, you are taxed at 30 percent, an expense of $100 for copy paper would provide you with a $30 tax credit.

Two of the most common big deductions for a small start-up business are the home office and depreciation/amortization deductions.

HOME OFFICE

Home office situations are much more common for entrepreneurs than they were just five or ten years ago, and so it's important to take some time to discuss this prevalent arrangement and its tax benefits. Perhaps the most important thing to know about your home office deduction is that the IRS has spent the last decade on a "witch hunt" for home office deduction cheaters. In fact, there is a complete IRS pamphlet written about the home office and taxes. If you're going to take this deduction, be sure and get it right.

First and foremost, your home office needs to be a room of its own. Having half of the kitchen set up for your computer workstation won't cut it with Uncle Sam, nor will moving that guest bed into a corner of your office pass muster for deduction purposes. The home office must be all office and nothing else. One interesting point as well is that, for some reason, there are more legitimate West Coast home offices than East Coast ones, and the IRS is aware of this. If you're east of the Mississippi, keep in mind that the IRS might be a tad more suspicious of your claim than if you lived elsewhere.

Normally you're only allowed to claim one office per business. If you want to write off the cost of the lease for your company's storefront location, you're probably not also going to take a deduction on the office you've set up in your home. About the only time you'd be allowed both is when you are completing job tasks at home that you couldn't get accomplished at your company site. The owner of a noisy auto body shop that didn't have a divided, soundproof office/ administrative room or rooms at the same location could probably legitimately claim that payroll, bookkeeping, marketing, sales calls, and similar administrative tasks had to be completed from the home office.

Another situation that can arise regarding the home office is when personal partners both work from home, sharing an office for two different businesses. One partner or spouse might have a W-2 job and use the home office irregularly to complete end-of-day work tasks, while the other partner might work full time from home, running her own business. In such cases, the IRS typically allows percentages of space write-off. The self-employed spouse or partner might, for instance, take 80 percent of the home office write-off, while the other partner takes 20 percent of the deduction.

Occasionally, an entrepreneur will have two businesses that she or he runs from a home office. In that case, the IRS would allow a full home office deduction for each company *if* each has a separate home office. That's seldom the case, however. Most owners of two or more businesses run out of their home have one office for all the companies. In that case, the deduction would need to be divided up between or among the businesses. On IRS Form 8829, the owner would indicate the multiple businesses and the percentage of deduction claimed for each. Because the situation is not common, however, it's not always easy to find tax software that will readily document two home businesses.

DEPRECIATION AND AMORTIZATION

Not all expenses claimed on tax forms are cash expenses. Depreciation and amortization are the two most common noncash expenses. Whether your accounting is a cash or accrual basis, you can still take either of these deductions.

Through the use of depreciation and amortization, the IRS puts a monetary figure on the drop in value of an asset during a given time frame (usually a year). The example we think of most is depreciation of a vehicle. Just about everyone knows that the minute you drive your brand-new car off the dealer's lot, the car goes down in value. This loss of value, called depreciation, happens because of what the IRS terms being "placed in service."

Depreciation has to do with physical assets that the company owns. You can claim a depreciation expense on your company building, the chairs and desks in the office, and your computers, for example. In contrast, amortization accounts for the depreciated value of intangibles, such as customer lists, your firm's website, goodwill, and the traffic patterns for your location. Of course, it's much easier to recognize and understand those items you can depreciate. All it takes is a look around your office to spot them. Amortization items are more difficult to recognize. Business owners don't always realize what they have and how valuable they are, especially if they have grown a business from scratch. If nothing else, you can begin your amortization process by placing a value on your client list and your name or brand.

Here is a basic list of some of the many types of intangible assets out there:

- ✔ brand names
- ✔ buy-sell agreements
- ✔ chemical formulas
- ✔ computer software
- ✔ computerized databases
- ✔ contracts
- ✔ cooperative agreements
- ✔ copyrights
- ✔ customer contracts
- ✔ customer and client lists
- ✔ customer relationships
- ✔ designs and drawings

- ✔ development rights
- ✔ distribution networks
- ✔ domain names
- ✔ drilling rights
- ✔ easements
- ✔ employment contracts
- ✔ favorable financing
- ✔ favorable leases
- ✔ food flavorings and recipes
- ✔ franchise agreements
- ✔ know-how
- ✔ literary works
- ✔ location value
- ✔ management contracts
- ✔ medical charts and records
- ✔ non-compete covenants
- ✔ options, warrants, grants, rights
- ✔ patent applications
- ✔ permits
- ✔ procedural manuals
- ✔ product designs
- ✔ proprietary computer software
- ✔ proprietary processes
- ✔ proprietary products
- ✔ proprietary technology
- ✔ schematics and diagrams
- ✔ shareholder agreements
- ✔ subscription lists
- ✔ supplier contracts
- ✔ technical documentation
- ✔ trade secrets
- ✔ trained and assembled workforce
- ✔ trademark and trade names
- ✔ training manuals
- ✔ use rights (air, water, land)

Each year that you file taxes you'll want to talk to a CPA or another depreciation-trained professional before you complete the deprecation portion of your tax forms. Depreciation rules can change from year to year—and can even change midyear. Your depreciation figures often end up being end-of-year adjustments made by your bookkeeper or CPA.

Depreciation and amortization regulations can be quite complicated. It's not necessary for an asset to be new for it to qualify for either depreciation or amortization. There are also special rules that allow you to depreciate a higher percentage than is typical or to assume a shorter life than usual for an item. One most notable "special" depreciation rule is the recent Section 179 Hummer Law, which I mentioned earlier. As you recall, this special rule allowed for a first-year write-off of any new vehicle up to $125K.

It can be difficult to understand why intangibles appreciate and why, for instance, you would be allowed to depreciate a building when we all know that real estate generally increases in value.

As an intangible example, let's talk about goodwill. Let's assume you bought someone else's going concern. The purchase also gives you the goodwill with the monetary value attributed to it as an asset on the most frequent financial statements prior to your purchase of the firm. Additionally, let's assume you purchased the client list as part of this business buy. Were you to then kick back in your easy chair, never attending to customer service, those goodwill/client list assets would depreciate in value. As your customers left your firm, the assets would decrease until you had no customers and the goodwill had no value.

So, that's the IRS's take on goodwill amortization. When you buy a business from someone else, the former owner can no longer grow that asset, and so it must depreciate.

> *When you buy a business from someone else, the former owner can no longer grow that asset, and so it must depreciate.*

In general, it's more difficult to understand intangibles than tangibles. It's hard sometimes to wrap your mind around when you have an asset (or not) and how you amortize it. The most common amortizable assets are the costs attributable to research and development and to lease acquisition. If, for example, you are a software developer and you're creating a digital communication tool to compete with Microsoft Outlook, all of the costs of that development can be amortized until you actually sell your first product. If you purchase a property and not only have to pay the purchase price but also have to fork over money for a commission fee to your real estate agents, document fees, and fees paid to your lending institution for points, all of these intangible assets could be amortized.

The details and principles behind the depreciation and amortization rules are voluminous enough to be a book on their own, so the best advice I can give you now is to make sure that you describe each asset, tangible or intangible, to your tax preparer. If you're not sure that it qualifies, tell her or him and let that accounting professional decide.

When it comes to buying or selling a business, how assets are listed—tangible or intangible—is critical. The seller normally wants as many business assets as possible to be declared intangible. The reason is that intangible assets are generally treated as capital gains during the sale, and the rate for capital gains is a low 15 percent. If, for example, you're selling your business for $1.2 million, $200,000 of which is designated as hard (tangible) assets with the rest being the intangible expansive client list you've built up over the years, you'll pay only the current percentage of capital gains tax on that $1 million list. The $200,000 worth of physical assets would be taxed at your ordinary tax rate, which could run as high as 39 percent.

Of course, if you're buying someone else's business, you're going to hope for the opposite situation—more tangible than intangible assets in the company you're purchasing. That's advantageous because intangibles have fifteen- to thirty-year amortization lives. To go back to our example of a business worth $1.2 million, if you're the buyer and that $1 million client list is deeded an intangible asset, amortized over thirty years, your tax deduction will only be $33,333 each year.

On the other hand, if $1 million of the purchase price is for hard assets, you might be able to amortize them over a period as short as three years. Now the expense you can claim for each of the next three years jumps to $333,333.

Whichever way you go, whether you're the buyer or seller, your counterpart must proceed identically. In other words, if you as the buyer call that $1 million of the $1.2 million purchase price for the business a tangible asset, your seller must do so on her or his financial statements as well. In fact, there is an IRS form that you both must file and sign off on that assures you've agreed on asset types for the sale. What I recommend is that at the time of the sale, whether you buy or sell, you make sure that the terms of the contract spell out which part of the purchase price of the business is tangible and which is intangible. This kind of arm's length transaction makes the IRS happy as well, and anything that makes the IRS happy will make your business life easier.

Depreciation has to do with hard (tangible) assets, which fall into one of many classes of depreciation, depending on what asset type they are. Something you bought off the shelf, such as QuickBooks or other business software, would fall into the three-year depreciation category. Business furnishings such as desks, chairs, filing cabinets, and even computers are five-year assets, while heavy equipment such as saws and drills are seven-year category assets.

> *...anything that makes the IRS happy will make your business life easier.*

The IRS has categorized these assets according to how long it estimates each will last. In other words, your new computer will be obsolete, or perhaps even broken, after five years, but that heavy-duty table saw you bought is going to last seven years. If your business is farming, your bull has a shorter asset life than does your cow.

Buildings have much longer lives. Any improvement you make to your company's office or warehouse—putting up shelving or repairing walls, for example—can be depreciated over 15 years. The commercial building itself has a 39-year life. If you purchase residential property as rental income, you can depreciate that for 27.5 years.

Depreciation gets considerably more complicated than that, however. In the case of vehicles, for example, cars, work trucks, and six-wheeled trucks vary in depreciation years. These "lives" are important to know, or have access to, for several reasons. Section 1031 of the IRS code allows you an asset trade without affecting your taxes as long as no money changes hands. But the traded assets must each or all belong to the same depreciation class and have the same monetary value.

To explain: Say that I have an older model Mercedes-Benz car worth $20,000 and you have a new Toyota Corolla worth the same. We can trade with minimal reporting requirements to the IRS. If, however, I wanted to trade my Mercedes for your 2004 Ford F-150 truck worth $20,000, I'd have to report the sale of my car and the purchase of your truck. The IRS would require that I report depreciation recapture and any gain on the sale.

What's important to remember, as you determine the depreciation class for your assets, is that you can't go back and change them the next year to suit your purposes. I've only seen one instance in which the IRS allowed a tax filer to reclassify an asset.

A 1031 can be advantageous. To explain, let's go back to the example of trading two cars. Let's assume we don't qualify for 1031, so I'm selling my car and you're selling your car. I bought my gorgeous baby blue Ferrari twenty years ago, when it was new, for $15,000. A collector car now, it's now worth $100,000. If I were to sell it for $100,000, I'd have to report an $85,000 gain. In a 1031 situation, that gain doesn't disappear. Though deferred, it stays with you as you make any further trades. Once you've purchased your final vehicle or other asset, you must pay the taxes on the gain.

There's a way to get around that to your advantage, however, and since real estate trades are far more prevalent than vehicle trades, let's look at real estate as an example. Let's assume you're thirty years old and about to buy your first rental property. Because it's a residential rental asset, its IRS depreciation is 27.5 years. You pay $20,000 for the property. Now it's five years later, and you want to sell it and buy a bigger rental property. What you do instead is trade it, for $20,000 cash plus your current property. The buyer has a gain to report, because she sold her $40,000 property and only paid $20,000 for yours. You, however, have no gain because you took that $20,000 property and some more cash and bought more property. Now, assume it's another five years later, and you do the same thing with this current property, trading it plus $40,000 for a better piece of rental property, valued at $80,000. At this point you've gained $60,000 in rental property for which you've paid not taxes.

One of the really cool benefits of a 1031 is that you could do this with more than one property if you wished. If you have time on your side, a 1031 could be an excellent strategy in which you could go, for example, from ownership of a $20,000 rental property to ownership of a $200,000 rental property without ever paying any taxes on your gain. As federal tax law stands, there would be no estate tax on your property were you to die. As of 2013, what would normally be taxed at 55 percent would now incur no taxes on gain for your heirs at all.

This is a fabulous tax strategy if you can keep it in place throughout your life. It's also another reason why consulting a tax professional is important.

At its most basic, determining depreciation or amortization is fairly simple math: the purchase price of the item divided by the number of years of "life" of the item according to Uncle Sam equals the depreciation or amortization you can write off for your annual taxes. That calculation is what is known as straight-line depreciation; that is, each year's depreciation is for the same amount.

Double declining depreciation is not something you can easily figure with a pencil and a calculator. If you're going to use this depreciation type, you'll want software that does the calculating for you. With double declining, most of the depreciation is taken early on in the life of the asset. A new car is a very good example of this. We all know that a new car loses 30 percent of its value the minute you drive it off the lot. Double digit declining the depreciation on your new car therefore makes good sense.

Some state depreciation regulations don't agree with the U.S. federal rules, however. Your state might not allow double depreciation, for instance. You'll want to check with your tax preparer.

While you've undoubtedly heard of income tax, sales tax, and self-employment tax, the lesser-known federal alternative minimum tax (AMT) is a schedule you must understand as well. Passed in 1986, this tax legislation originally said that if you and anyone with whom you're filing jointly make more than $156,000 annually, you are extremely wealthy and must pay additional federal tax. The ceiling on this regulation has since moved to $250,000. There is discussion underway about repealing the tax, as two adults raising a family on $250,000 are really not wealthy.

The IRS has a tax schedule specific to each type of tax, whether it's capital gains, interest, dividend, sales, or any other. Depending on the tax code for the current year, one tax type might be taxed at the ordinary rate, while another will be taxed at its own rate. Some taxes, such as the AMT, might not apply to you at all. While it's important for business owners to know what each type of tax means and to whom it's applicable, the tax code is not for neophytes. You'll want a professional preparer.

You'll periodically come across an IRS 179 deduction. The easiest way for the government to stimulate the economy, a 179 is an additional and specific write-off to stimulate your spending in that area. The benefits are two-sided: the U.S. economy gets more money into the marketplace and you get a bargain on the product the government is currently pushing.

In 2009, for example, the IRS created a premium 50 percent depreciation deduction, which means that everything you purchased could be written off up to 50 percent the first year. After the first year, the depreciation schedule is as usual. So, were you to buy a $100,000 piece of equipment, the first-year write-off would be $50,000; years two through five would be $10,000.

There is a downside to depreciation, however. When you sell an item, you must recapture the depreciation. The amount of recapture depends on several factors such as asset type, how long you've owned it, and whether it's a business or personal use item.

Basically the IRS is saying, "You had this asset, you got to use it, and now you've gotten money for the sale of it. Let's look at whether we allowed you too much depreciation based on its real value at the time you sold it." In some cases, recapture could be more than your gain on the sale of the item. In fact, even when you lose money on the sale of the item, you could end up with a depreciation capture. Then, to add insult to injury, you'd have to pay taxes on it.

To prevent this kind of financial setback, you should have a planning session with your CPA before you sell a major asset, such as a business or high-priced vehicle. The planning session strategy would be to prepare a sample tax return, with alternate scenarios to determine which depreciation plan of action is advisable. Scenarios would vary the selling price and the value of intangibles and tangibles (hard assets). The price you get for the asset your business sells is important, but more important still is the real cost of selling it. Seeking professional advice before acting on any sale is crucial to keeping that real cost down.

Let's run through an example, with calculations.

- ✔ You've purchased a new building worth $425,000.

- ✔ Its land value is $80,000 of that total figure.

- ✔ This leaves $320,000 to be split between the building and the furniture and fixtures that were included in the purchase.

- ✔ You split building and furniture and fixtures as follows (due to your cost segregation study that the engineers performed on your building):
  - o   Building: $302,500
  - o   Furniture and fixtures: $42,500

- ✔ You bought the building on June 1, 2013, and began using it on that date.

- ✔ As you can see, you would have $10,821 of depreciation for the year of purchase

Your depreciation would look something like this:

| 12/31/13 | 2013 FEDERAL SUMMARY DEPRECIATION SCHEDULE | | | | | | | | PAGE 1 |

NO.	DESCRIPTION	DATE ACQUIRED	DATE SOLD	COST/ BASIS	BUS. PCT.	CUR 179/ SDA	PRIOR 179/ SDA/ DEPR.	METHOD	LIFE	CURRENT DEPR.
	SCHEDULE E ·									
	BUILDINGS									
1	BUILDING	6/01/13		302,500				S/L MM	39	4,208
	TOTAL BUILDINGS			302,500		0	0			4,208
	FURNITURE AND FIXTURES									
3	F&F	6/01/13		42,500				200DB HY	7	6,073
	TOTAL FURNITURE AND FIXTURE			42,500		0	0			6,073
	LAND									
2	LAND	6/01/13		80,000						0
	TOTAL LAND			80,000		0	0			0
	TOTAL DEPRECIATION			425,000		0	0			10,281
	GRAND TOTAL DEPRECIATION			425,000		0	0			10,281

Notice that the building is a commercial building and therefore is depreciated over 39 years with a straight-line method

Notice that the F&F (Furniture and Fixtures) are double declining balance method, half year (because it was bought in the middle of the year) and 7 years life.

Figure 20: Depreciation Example for Commercial Building

Credits

A credit is more advantageous for your tax bottom line than a deduction, because it lets you write off all that you spent for that item. The U.S. government issues tax credits to prompt residents and business owners to perform actions it deems advantageous. The best and most recent example of such a credit is the first-time homebuyer's tax credit. Realizing that the recession was adversely affecting the U.S. housing market, the federal government set out to encourage people to buy new homes by offering a tax credit equal to 10 percent of the purchase price of the house up to $8,000. The only stipulations were that the buyer had not purchased a home before, that he or she intended it to be a primary residence, and that the transaction be completed by an agreed-upon date.

While this credit was for individuals, many business credits are available as well, such as the credit for hiring disenfranchised youth. The credits change each year, but the IRS website readily shows you what is current. Each credit has its own rules and restrictions.

There are four types of credits: carried back, carried forward, refundable, and nonrefundable.

- ✔ *Carried back:* This type of credit is retroactive, so were you to spend money on a credit item in 2013 that was allowed to be carried back to the 2012 tax return you could request the credit on your 2013 tax form to apply the credit to 2012 taxes. Of course, since those taxes would presumably have been paid already, you could expect a check from the IRS for this 2012 carryback.

- ✔ *Carried forward*: This is a credit that you have earned but cannot take as a credit until filing a tax form for a subsequent year.

- ✔ *Refundable*: This is a credit that, when exceeding the amount you owe the IRS for the same time period, entitles you to a refund for the difference.

- ✔ *Nonrefundable*: This is a credit that, when exceeding the amount you owe the IRS for the same time period, cancels out that time period's debt to the IRS for you but does not entitle you to the difference.

As examples of refundable and nonrefundable, let's say you earned a $1,500 tax credit in 2013 for hiring the disenfranchised, and without that credit you owe the IRS $1,000 in taxes. If this credit is refundable, you will get a check from the IRS for $500. If it's nonrefundable, you won't have to pay the $1,000 you owe, but you won't get any $500 check.

Financing

You have several options for financing your business. While many think first of a bank, that's not your only option—and, in fact, probably shouldn't be your first option. You may have family or friends who would be willing to lend you money, or you could borrow via your own credit cards. If you're willing to give up a little of your profit, you might consider angel investors or standard investors who might want 10 percent of your company and a 5 percent interest rate on the loan, for example. You can also try to raise money through events such as big poker nights or fund-raising balls.

In theory, the Small Business Administration (SBA) should be one choice, but in actuality, it won't consider lending your firm anything until you've been in business for two years. I find that rather ironic since the point of the SBA is to help small businesses—the firms that struggle to survive the first two years.

Keep in mind that if your own funds are the source of the financing for your new business—or some of the source—that is a loan. You and your business are not one and the same. Keep reminding yourself of that. Even if you're working 20-hour days, and it seems like your business is your only life, your business is still a separate entity from you personally. If you pay for something on behalf of your business, your business has made a loan to you, and it needs to repay you. We touched on this earlier—the idea that your business must pay a reasonable interest rate to anyone or anything that loans it money: you, your family, your friends, your bank, and so forth.

You should consider something else, however, and that's the gift tax rule. You or anyone else can give someone else up to $14,000 each year, not as a loan but as a gift. I, Shauna, could accept $14,000 annually from each of my parents, for example. This money does not have to be declared and so is not taxable. My caution, however, is that you don't accept a gift for the absolute maximum. Were you to do so, say from your mother, the IRS would say, "You've accepted $14,000 this one time from your mother. But did she never give you a birthday gift? Did you not get a Christmas or Hanukah present from her? You mean she never took you out to dinner all year long?" To avoid these questions from Uncle Sam, I suggest you accept a gift of $13,500.

Let's assume that your business needs $100,000 to get started and your parents are willing to provide that. The best way for you to receive the money is to accept a $13,500 gifting from each of your parents, and then draw up a loan document for the remaining $73,000. Loan documentation isn't difficult; you can easily find an acceptable template on the Internet. The applicable federal rate (AFR) is what you'd want to claim as the interest rate you repay to your parents. The IRS website will list the current APR by term of loan. A loan that comes due in less than a year is called short-term; in one to five years is called midterm; and in over five years is long-term.

Here's a great money-saving hint, though: Once you have the loan, the lender can forgive up to $14,000 (or, better yet—following my suggestion—$13,500) of the loan each year, per the gift tax rule. He or she can even forgive the interest portion of the loan. So, the smartest thing you can do is to design the loan amount and term so that the payments due each year are less than $13,500 total. In that case, you've ended up with a loan that is in practice a gift but still adheres to the loan document requirements of the IRS.

A large percentage of small business owners start out without family that has money to lend them or financial institutions that are willing to do so. Many of these new business owners use their credit cards to get started. The danger here is overuse of credit cards by those who can't manage their money. It might sound like a good idea to finance your firm with your own cards—who wants to borrow elsewhere if you have your own means, right? But the danger is the interest rate if you don't pay what you must each month and on time, and of course the resulting hit on your credit score, which can have long-term effects on your ability to get a small business loan down the line.

Additionally, credit cards don't typically have permanently fixed rates. Getting into the habit of jumping at credit cards that offer comparatively low interest rates for their introductory periods, and then failing to notice when an introductory time period expires and the rate jumps sky high, can cost you far more than the fixed rate that a financial institution might have offered.

This issue is comparable to the problems many people are having in the United States right now, trying to keep their own homes from being foreclosed on. Many of these folks signed up for an ARM—an adjustable-rate mortgage for which the initial interest rate is very low, but which at some point requires a large balloon payment or later has a massive rate hike that can cause people to default on their loans when they cannot later refinance.

Jumping on a low-interest credit card bandwagon and planning to jump off when the rate climbs is all well and good if you are able to do so. Typically small business owners don't have a good handle on what and how much all the early business expenses will be. They buy equipment or pay fees with their credit cards, assume they can get out from under those bills in thirty or sixty days, and as a result don't worry about the interest rate—or what the interest rate will be after the introductory offer expires. Then an unexpected expense occurs, or a client fails to pay on time, or a "sure" client prospect falls through, or you just plain forget that your business revenue has to pay your own utility bills, too, and you must pay the credit card late, along with its high fee.

For some pointers on this credit card problem, I recommend you read about Dave Ramsey's cash-only programs.[34]

To avoid these problems as much as you can, you must budget and do your pro forma planning, as well as prepare your cash flows, before you even start your business. Included in your budget would be the schedule in which you'll pay off

---

34. See www.daveramsey.com.

credit card bills and the means for doing so, which should only include those cash sources you know you have. Crystal balls don't belong in business budgeting.

Every business owner should have an emergency fund for his or her business. I feel lucky to have had a mentor when I started my business who told me that for every dollar I grossed, ten cents should be put into a savings or money market account and should not be touched. Following his advice has allowed me, in this cyclical business, to have a fail-safe in spite of uncertainties elsewhere.

Having such a fund to fall back on allows entrepreneurs to compete for larger and more lucrative jobs, to make logical rather than desperate decisions about expansion, and to be a little choosier about their clients.

Because I was saving 10 percent of all I brought in, I learned to live off less than I made, which is the first step for anyone in getting out of and staying out of debt. Additionally, when financial times were rough, I had my own bank, my own cushion, which saved me from having to borrow against high-interest credit cards. Yes, as a new business owner you might not be able to spare 10 percent of each month's profits, but surely you can spare something—5 percent, 2 percent. No matter how small the amount you set aside, getting into the habit of saving and of living within your business's means can set your business up to win and can keep you out of debt except for unforeseen disaster.

The need for a budget goes hand in hand with this idea of saving regularly. This is the area in which your business most resembles your personal life and patterns. Running your business without a budget is analogous to shopping at a superstore without a shopping list. You might enter the store with margarine and socks in mind but leave with a purse you didn't need, a bouquet of flowers too pretty to resist, and new DVDs just because they were on sale. You might have budgeted $12 for your shopping and ended up spending $50.

Many new entrepreneurs have similar lack-of-resistance issues for their businesses. The owner is so excited about his or her business, and in walks a sales rep for a sign company, offering attractive new business signs. The owner is talked into believing he or she must have those signs to help the company's marketing, only later realizing those dollars were earmarked for payroll. The fact is, however, that if you don't have a budget, there's really no way to stick to it. And this problem will repeat itself time and again. As a business owner, you must budget, and you must spend accordingly.

Besides budgeting, you have another important business task: pro forma planning. In contrast to budgeting—which starts when you are open for business and have day-to-day operations and money from those that must be managed—your pro forma tasks must be started before your business opens, and even before you make any purchases to start the business. Your pro forma documents and figures are what you'll use to solicit start-up funds from lending institutions. Your pro forma work includes documenting your best guesses of what your market is, how many customers your business might have, the amount of revenue you'll make from each customer, and how often each customer will frequent your store.

If, for instance, you're opening up a retail store that sells toothpaste, you might assume that customers would need to replenish their toothpaste supply every three months. If you're opening up a Curves franchise, while the customers may walk in your door to exercise three times each week, for purposes of pro forma, you'd document a monthly return, as that's how often they'd pay your bill.

So, to contrast budgeting and pro forma planning, the former is about scripting and dictating your actual expenses and working with historical data, while the latter is about assuming what your company's future sales might be and planning as if those assumptions will occur. Pro forma assumptions could include new sales, the purchase of new equipment, and even new hires. A business owner who wants to succeed must budget and do pro forma preparation. Both planning tasks are vital.

Payables

Payables are your bills—the payments that your business owes to other businesses and people for services and products that they provide for you.

Payables can drown your company if you do not watch what the business is spending and where the money is being spent. So always remember to keep your eyes open for deals, coupons, and discounts, especially when you are first starting your business.

Terms

First off, let's talk about terms. Often, as you may choose to do, a business will offer terms to its clients. Common terms you may see are below. The most important thing you need to know about terms is how the terms are going to affect your cash flow and the operations of your business.

***x%/xx* net *xx*:** This set of terms is often something like 2%/10 net 30 or 1%/15 net 45. These terms describe a discount that you will receive if the payment is received within the first number of days: in our first example, you get a 2% discount if payment is received within 10 days, with the balance then due in 30 days. These terms are more commonly used with manufacturing or products businesses, but I have seen them in almost all types of companies.

Due on receipt: This set of terms is basically as it states, that the payment for the item is due on receipt of the item. Typically a business using these terms will give you a seven-day grace period (long enough for a check to arrive by post), so make sure you look for and know the true due date.

Additional terms: Here are some other terms that you may see in common business practice.

- ✔ EOM: Payment is due by end of month.
- ✔ ROG/COD: Payment is due on receipt of goods/cash on delivery.

When to Pay

You can think about your businesses payables in different ways. The two most common are (1) pay as they come in and (2) pay as due. A large part of your decision about when to pay your payables is related to how you, as an owner, view money.

For many owners, especially when starting out, paying bills when they are due seems to be the most common choice—if simply because cash flow tends to be tight. Personally, I believe that if the business cannot afford itself (i.e., never go into debt of any kind beyond maybe an owner's initial contribution to get things started), then it should not be in business. I believe that you should pay all bills as they arrive, and that way you are never robbing Peter to pay Paul if you don't really have the funds to spend.

How to Pay

There are also multiple ways to pay invoices. You can pay them by

- ✔ *Cash*: This is rarely recommended these days.

- ✔ *Credit card on file*: Just remember to pay it off every month!

- ✔ *Check*: I would recommend against this one, if possible—too many ways for identity thieves to snag your checking account information.

- ✔ *Account*: This means that you have an account with the vendor that you settle at some predetermined time (monthly, quarterly, etc.).

Receivables: How to Collect Your Money

Barter is not usually going to be an option when you first start a business, though you shouldn't rule it out for contractors or in cases where a client prospect is also a business whose service you might need.

Now that you are in business, what you next must decide—prior to that first customer walking through your door—is how you're going to get paid by that customer. You have to determine what payment options you'll allow for your customers and how you will make that happen. Once you've done work and you are waiting on payment, this is called a receivable.

Barter is not usually going to be an option when you first start a business, though you shouldn't rule it out for contractors or in cases where a client prospect is also a business whose service you might need. If you decide to take barter, you need to be very careful that you still have enough liquid cash coming in from other sources to pay for your rent, utilities, and staff! Barter is going to be the exception.

So you first need to decide on your common, everyday process for taking payments. This will generally be cash, check, or credit/debit card. Not accepting credit or debit cards could seriously impact your ability to make sales, as customers probably pay this way more often than they pay with cash. Not accepting checks, however, is more common and will likely not impact your ability to close a sale as much as your not offering credit card purchase options. The advantage, too, of accepting credit card and debit card payments, as compared with checks, is that you get paid at the time of the transaction, and you're generally assured you have the money. Checks, on the other hand, go into your company's bank account sometime after that check is deposited into your bank and cleared through the bank of the check writer—and only if the money is there. Bounced checks can be a costly and time-consuming headache.

While new check-processing technology allows your cashier to scan each check and determine if the funds are really in the bank account, it still doesn't put the money in your company's account any earlier than the time-honored end-of-day deposit in the banking process. I'm not suggesting you refuse to take checks as payment. In fact, even were you to do so, you might consider accepting checks from loyal customers who've proven themselves creditworthy. Of course, there are business types—such as plumbers, landscapers, residential air conditioning repair companies, and similar—that would be seriously hampered by not accepting checks as payment. No plumber wants to carry around all the equipment needed to process a credit card payment; and if he or she doesn't have the equipment, that charge is no more secure than a check would be. And no homeowner is going to want to have a few hundred dollars' worth of cash sitting around the house in case the washer goes on the fritz and the repair company won't take a check.

In general, the check and credit card processing will cost you money, but—at least in the case of credit cards—nowhere near what you'd lose in sales if you didn't offer the service. To be able to accept credit card payments, expect to pay three to five percent of the sales transaction to the finance company that processes your credit card payments for you.

Let's say you're a retailer and you have a shirt for sale at $100. A customer wants to buy the shirt with his Visa. If the fee to the credit card processor is five percent, your take on that sale drops from $100 to $95 (not counting all the other costs of goods sold, such as what you paid the manufacturer for the shirt and the wages paid to the salesperson who helped the customer pick out the shirt and the cashier who rang up the sale).

If you're like most Americans you probably have at least one debit card (sponsored by Visa or MasterCard) and one credit card. You probably understand the difference between the two, and the fact that you can use that debit card as either a credit or debit transaction whenever you make an offline payment. (Online payments with debit cards are always run as credits.) In general, credit payments are those allowed by the issuing company without any need for financial backing by the user and with confidence that the user will repay the issuing finance firm at a later time. Debit payments, however, are uses of the funds immediately available in the financial account of the cardholder. In either case, no risk is assumed by the merchant accepting the payment for goods or services provided. It might seem, then, that the merchant might not care whether a customer uses his or her Visa- or MasterCard-sponsored debit card as a debit or credit.

That, however, is not the case. As a business owner, you must be aware that allowing customers to run their debit card as a credit card transaction will cost you more—in other words, you'll make less profit on the transaction—because the bank powering that transaction for you will usually charge you more. To not allow that customer to use the debit card as a credit payment, however, might have that customer walking out the door without a purchase.

There are two reasons customers prefer to run their debit cards as credit. The first is that they do not wish to enter their PIN (personal identification number) in public. But the most important reason is that their bank rewards them for credit charges. Banks offer points as rewards for credit purchases, and these points can be used for entertainment coupons, restaurant and travel discounts, and even gift cards at major retailers. Customers can even apply their points back to their accounts, earning cash that is deposited to their bank accounts. The banks don't generally offer these points for debit card transactions.

I have a friend who banks with Chase. She just converted her accumulated rewards points. She ended up with $100 deposited back to her checking account, $20 worth of AMC movie tickets, and a $25 gift card for dining at Applebee's. Had she run her debit card as a debit transaction when she bought her groceries, filled up at the pump, bought new clothes, and dined out, she'd have lost $145. My friend would never shop where she couldn't pay with her debit card as credit. She'd lose money doing that.

Another consideration about credit payments is the bank on which they're drawn. Not all banks are approved. Wells Fargo, Chase, and Bank of America, for example, are approved banks. A local Midwest bank with only three branches might not be approved. While banks that are not approved won't be turned down by your credit card vendor firm, their use might cause you to incur a greater fee than that of approved banks. Your rate per transaction, depending on the credit card bank, could be $0.49 or 8 percent of the transaction. Yes, the latter could be a small fee, but if you're a furniture store, for example, and your customer is buying a $1,800 living room suite, accepting that credit card drawn on an unapproved bank could leave you with a $144 transaction fee. That's a big cut of your profit. The way some companies deal with credit card charges is to charge the customer a small surcharge, perhaps 4 percent.

There's no perfect answer on the issue of accepting credit card payments. If you went shopping at your local Macy's and were told the store was now adding a surcharge to your purchase when you paid by credit card, you might well walk out the door and drive to the nearest Kohl's where your credit card is the same as cash. These major retailers know this. What some of them do, as an alternative, is to sell at a premium. In other words, that man's shirt we talked about earlier, which was priced at $100, might now have a $105 price tag to offset credit card fees.

The first two years my own CPA firm was in business we did not accept credit cards. Then the recession hit, and it hit the Phoenix area especially hard. People began to rely more and more on their credit cards just to get by. What we found out then was that if we didn't accept credit cards our collections rate would skyrocket, as people either failed to pay or paid with bad checks. I made the determination that it was preferable for our bottom line to take the credit card payments with their 5 percent fee, which would pay us *now*, than to wait six to eight months (and after much collections effort) to get paid or, in the case of bad checks, to sometimes not get paid at all.

My own business's experience with personal checks is that their owners have been more reliable about paying than those who are used to using their plastic to get by. I don't know if this is unique to the accounting industry, but I've been lucky enough to have been paid with checks by people who actually have had the money in the bank to cover the checks. You shouldn't assume your firm will have the same positive experience, however. Checks can definitely be a nightmare.

Should you decide to accept credit card payments at your business, you then have to decide which credit cards you'll take. The four major cards are Visa, MasterCard, Discover, and American Express. Virtually any U.S. firm that accepts credit cards accepts Visa and MasterCard, while Discover is the next most common. American Express, despite its advertising to the contrary, is not "accepted everywhere." The reasons behind the popularity have to do with fees to the merchants accepting them. American Express, while it offers many bonuses to its members, pays for these by charging merchants more than any other credit card provider. Discover offers the next heftiest fee. The lesser fees of Visa and MasterCard are almost identical.

If you're doing business overseas, keep in mind that not all countries take all four credit cards. In Argentina, for example, you can only pay with your Visa.

If you're doing business overseas, keep in mind that not all countries take all four credit cards. In Argentina, for example, you can only pay with your Visa.

We've talked a lot about retailers and merchants and the advantages of being paid right away. In service firms, of course, credit card payment notwithstanding, you won't necessarily get all your money at the time services are rendered. You can try, of course, but if your industry standard is to bill customers—or at least those who've earned credit worthiness through continued on-time payments—you'll have to wait to be paid thirty to ninety days after delivery of the goods or services. If you do not, you risk losing customers to competitors who do offer invoicing.

Many professional service firms have moved to taking a prepaid retainer and then, once that's used up, coming back to the client for another retainer. In my CPA firm, for example, the tax return doesn't get filed until I get paid. It sounds a little like taking a hostage but, unfortunately for many service firms, clients seem to forget the service they've received once they walk out the door with what they need from you.

It's very depressing, actually—and perhaps silly to say in the world of business, but it's kind of hurtful, too. You feel like you've done an excellent job for your customers; they say they're very happy. They also say, "Oh, yeah, I'll send you that check right away." A week goes by and they don't. Now you're in the position of having to call them—to work yet again for your money. In the event enough time elapses that you must turn to a collection firm, you've lost even more money on the transaction.

> *The engagement letter confirms in writing (with signature by all parties) that the product or service will not be delivered completed to the client or customer until payment has been made.*

Collection firms can be quite costly. In fact, I've seen collection fees as high as 50 percent. To avoid this fee and the onus of collection efforts, I've learned to do two things: get paid before handing over the fruits of my service (completed tax forms, for example), and provide engagement letters. The only exception to payment upon delivery is with long-term clients who have continually paid me on time. Those I will invoice.

The engagement letter confirms in writing (with signature by all parties) that the product or service will not be delivered completed to the client or customer until payment has been made. An alternate engagement letter might be that you will deliver the completed product or service, but if you are not paid in full within X number of days, the client will be responsible for any cost of collections including the fees demanded by an outside collection agency.

Sample and template engagement letters are probably available from your industry's trade association. In Arizona, for example, we have the Arizona Board of Accountancy, the State Bar of Arizona, the Arizona Restaurant Association, the Arizona State Board of Cosmetology, and so forth. Other sources of help would be the Small Business Development Association, SCORE, and any labor union to which you belong. You might also get online and do keyword searches on a major search engine. It took me two minutes, searching "sample engagement letters," to find ten sources including downloadable PDFs of engagement letters, some specific to industries, others specific to the laws of a particular state.

When it comes to making decisions on how to accept payments, you're far from alone. There are lots of business people who've had to make these decisions before you and have learned from their mistakes as well as their successes. Find these people and ask them for their help. There's no need to reinvent this wheel.

Collections

Once a customer has not paid you in more than thirty days, unless your terms are longer, I highly recommend that you begin the collections process. This process has many stages, and it is a process that you can outsource to organizations to handle for you. Please remember to be open and honest about your collections process with your clients, otherwise they won't be your clients for long.

Stages in the collections process can include a nice reminder letter, a reminder phone call, a sterner letter, and a more aggressive letter sent certified return receipt, all the way up to small claims court. It is important that you handle the process quickly and without pause, as the longer you wait, the less likely you are to get paid. Many businesses have moved to a cash-up-front or half-cash-up-front policy that limits the amount of receivables they have outstanding.

Pay attention to your collections on a monthly basis; often a simple phone call from the owner will prevent lack of payment from the customer. If you do decide to proceed and use an external agency (many owners don't want this responsibility or the negative feelings that can come with it), make sure that your engagement letters, or contracts with clients, contain a provision by which any fees of collection are at the clients' expense.

Taxes

We have already touched upon taxes earlier, so this is purely a recap.

- ✔ *Income taxes*: The best way to save for them is to put at least 30 percent of your cash into an account at another bank—out of sight, out of mind!

- ✔ *Payroll taxes*: The best way to save for them is to put the payroll amounts and at least 15 percent of the total payroll dollar amount into the payroll account. Don't spend that money on anything besides payroll.

- ✔ *Sales taxes*: The best way to save for them is to save just as you would for income taxes; I recommend that you take the sales tax rate for your city/town/locality and put that money into a separate account. Again, out of sight, out of mind. That way there is no temptation to use that money for anything else, as it is not yours.

Pricing Strategies

How to price your product is one of those very tricky decisions. You need to look at market conditions, the quality of your products, your overhead costs, your selling costs, and about a thousand other factors. Often what a business owner does is pick a price that seems reasonable and then try to manage expenses to make sure the business owner is continuing to make profit. I would recommend, before you go into business, that you prepare the pro forma financial statement based on the pricing strategy that you are picking, to determine whether or not you will make a profit as your best guess estimate. You can, of course, start the business and go from there, but it is a lot more painful to find out that you have the wrong price point after you've already started selling to clients. If you're priced too low to start and later need to raise prices, you may lose clients—but if you're priced too high at the beginning, you may not get the clients in the first place.

Cash Flow, Budgeting, and Forecasting

In your company's budgeting process, there are three distinct elements: determining cash flow and cash reserve, budgeting, and forecasting.

Cash is the lifeblood of your business. Your company's cash flow and cash reserve determine if your business is healthy. Cash reserve is simple to understand. It's the money that is sitting in your financial institution in a readily available account, should you need emergency business funds or want to start a new project. Cash flow, in contrast, is the amount of funds left over (or expected to be left over) in any given time period after you've paid your expenses out of your company earnings. When you go through your company budget and or forecast process, you're almost certainly going to be talking about your cash flow.

Budgeting for your business is much like budgeting for your personal life. You compare your income (your salary or wage) against your outgo (your mortgage, your car payments, your grocery bills, and the cost for your medical insurance, for example). In business, your income is your business's revenue, while your outgo would be things such as your office lease, the wages paid to your staff, purchases of equipment and supplies, and so forth. In either case—personal or business—you look realistically at what money comes in the door and make sure that what goes out is less than what came in. Of course, if you have more outgo than income, you have a problem. I am a firm believer in paying yourself first. This will help you determine what percentage should go into savings before you spend elsewhere. Note, however, that while this is a good objective for your company's future, your new business is not likely to generate enough funds for this in its first two years.

Plenty of software is available to help you budget, some of which is excellent. Arguably the best known and most used is QuickBooks by Intuit. Once you've entered your expenses into the application, it then creates a budget for you, in which you can make modifications. The software will, for example, study your historical budget and notify you that your average monthly overhead cost has been $1,000. You might look at that in surprise, thinking, "Oh, my goodness, I don't want to spend more than $300 a month on this. I need to cut back." In contrast, you might find out via QuickBooks that your assumed $300 monthly overhead expense is considerably higher than actual, in which case you can afford to dine out once a week, or perhaps spend another $200 on a contract worker who can take a little more of the workload from you.

Forecasting, while similar to budgeting in that it's looking into your business's monetary future, makes its determinations through a comparison of specific scenarios to each other. Rather than saying "You'll spend this much on this because you spent this much the last six months" as you do when budgeting, your forecasting will determine that if you do this much of A and this much of B, you'll get results C, but if you instead do an alternate amount of A and an alternate amount of B, you'll get results D—and which would you prefer? It can also be a comparison of "business as usual" with the results of adding a new scenario into the present business mix. As an example of a forecast, you might note: "I'm going to hire an advertising person, and my expectation is that she is going to add $100,000 in revenue"

Of course, the danger of forecasting is that your assumptions could be way off. If, in the above example, you had projected $500,000 additional revenue from this ad rep and she only brought in $100,000, the decisions you made based on the $500,000 assumption would be seriously flawed. You might end up spending money that could jeopardize your company's health.

Excel is an excellent tool for forecasting, primarily because of its ease in altering your figures time and again. The best forecasting process is to start with your present budget, put those figures into an Excel spreadsheet, and then alter it with what you believe to be reasonable future assumptions. You could forecast, for example, that your sales will increase by 7 percent next year. Entering that figure into your spreadsheet will change all columns affected by this increase—total revenue, profit, and so forth. You could then take an additional look at what would happen were you to realize a 10 percent sales increase instead. Again, the new figures would automatically populate in Excel. What Excel can't do for you, of course, is determine if that 7 or 10 percent assumption is reasonable.

Your forecasting will be unreliable if you fail to consider all the expenses involved. Going back to the example of considering a new advertising hire: The new ad rep will cost you not only salary but also probably benefits, mileage reimbursement, perhaps additional utility costs if she or he works unusual hours in your office, a percentage of the revenue of each sale if you offer commission or bonus on top of the salary, and possibly purchase of equipment such as a laptop and a cell phone. You might even reimburse some home office expenses, such as Internet connectivity, and expense-account items such as taking a client or prospect out to dinner.

It's best to get help with your early forecasting from experts. You could turn to someone at SCORE or SBDC or to a trusted business friend or former colleague. It's probably best to build your forecasting spreadsheet, enter your current budget, and then talk over assumptions and ideas with your trusted helper. No matter how astute any of us is on these matters, just having a second brain—especially an experienced one—can help assure that we've entered all factors into our forecasting.

You might consider creating a board of directors or an advisory group. It could be family and friends, former colleagues, perhaps a former instructor. Invite them to the firm or a pleasant location with some privacy, buy them pizza and drinks, and pick their brains about some of the business decisions you're trying to make. This kind of group brainstorming can be especially helpful as the idea of one feeds off that of another. You could end up with a great idea none of you expected before you began your session.

You might consider joining or even starting a Mastermind group. The Mastermind concept was developed in the 1920s by Napoleon Hill, author of *Think and Grow Rich*. In his book, Hill talks about the Rockefellers and other successful captains of industry. Hill's Mastermind format is a group of twelve people from varying industries and one additional person who acts as what he calls the controller—keeping the meeting focused and taking notes for the presenters. These folks' businesses are to be of similar size (generally determined by gross revenue). The meetings are monthly, and each focuses on one group member, who presents her or his issue or obstacle and invites feedback from the others.

Were you to belong to a Mastermind group and trying to do business forecasting, you could present an idea such as the aforementioned new advertising salesperson and have the Mastermind members help you forecast the effects. The Mastermind presentation is to be about your top three issues. In this case your issues might be:

- ✔ Should I hire a new ad rep?
- ✔ How might this new hire affect my business in general?
- ✔ If I decide to hire, should I make her or him a contractor or employee?

The right Mastermind group can be especially helpful when you have the right mix of industries, with members who have expertise in areas with which you're not familiar. Let's assume that you are selling a high-tech software program. You know nothing about human resources or even what to pay a sales rep. Your group might have an employment attorney and/or human resources professional who can advise you on the appropriate wage package and the legal ramifications of hiring. There might be a long-time retailer or service provider with a lot of experience in finding just the right salesperson and knowing the best recruitment sites on which to advertise your opening.

Don't think, because your turn in front of the Mastermind group only comes once every twelve weeks, that the group is not going to be helpful each week. Another person's issues might be ones you need to learn about, and you might be able to help others with their issues. You might also find a client or two among the members. When your turn does come, it's generally a full 8-hour day, so there's plenty of time for sharing and learning.

Amazing Masterminds Group in Arizona actually sets up Mastermind groups for those interested. Founder Dave Sherman, known as the "the networking guy," lives in Phoenix. He's set up two or three local groups that have been active for at least a couple of years. Businesspeople who join Mastermind find they get very involved in the groups and tend to stay for quite some time.

In contrast to forecasting, budgeting is an internal management process. When you budget, you simply look at your financial statement categories with an eye toward where cuts or increases might need to be made. External companies that might become involved in your business—potential collaborators, buyers, or lenders, for example—tend to look more at your forecast. To a bank, you might say, "Here is my budget." But you'd also say, "Here is my forecast spreadsheet that shows what will happen when I commit to making your loan payment and the interest on it. You can readily see my company will still make a profit."

While a loan application is the most common reason for forecasting, other common drivers are the consideration of a new partner, new staff, or the introduction of a retirement plan for yourself and your employees. When considering all the things that affect your forecasted change, don't forget the positive impacts, some of which are slightly intangible. A retirement plan, while costly, might lure employees who turned down your job offer before—employees who could sell more, produce more, be sick less often, motivate other staff, create a happier office atmosphere, and stay with your firm longer than others.

No matter what plans you might be considering in your forecasting, keep in mind that no matter how trained, skilled, or worldly wise you might be, talking to others nearly always offers advantages far greater than you anticipated.

Go Get Started!

So, we have covered quite a bit of information in this book. Everything from deciding if you should start a business to getting it started, finding the right people, getting it opened, and understanding more about your responsibilities and requirements as an owner. Are you ready for the next step? Are you ready to get started?

This book is meant to give you a basic understanding of the main issues and most important ideas that I believe every new business owner should have thought deeply about and, hopefully, worked out before they start their new adventure. I know there are many small details that aren't covered in this book (if I tried to do that, this book would be over a thousand pages long!), so if you have questions, please don't hesitate to e-mail me: Shauna@TaxGoddess.com.

I look forward to hearing about all of your successes in your new ventures! Please keep in contact and let me know how you made your millions!

With all the best wishes for your success, happiness, and joy in whatever it is you do every day:

May you always love your work—and therefore love your life!

Your Tax Goddess,

~ Shauna ~

Financial Ratios

Performance Ratios

Cash Flow to Assets

✔ Formula: [Cash from Operations ÷ Total Assets]

✔ What Does the Ratio Describe?
- o It relates a company's ability to generate cash as compared to its asset size. It reflects the likelihood of a business to have cash to pay bills when necessary.

✔ For Which Industries Is This Ratio Most Useful?
- o All industries, but mainly those that rely on assets to produce income. Example: machine shop

✔ How Should This Ratio Be Used?
- o This ratio should be looked at over a period of time, perhaps once a quarter or once a year. These values should be compared as a trend analysis.

Earnings Per Share {EPS}

✔ Formula: [Net Income Dividends on Preferred Stock ÷ Average Outstanding Shares]

✔ What Does the Ratio Describe?
- o This ratio is the earnings that the company is making for each share of stock that is outstanding.

✔ For Which Industries Is This Ratio Most Useful?
  o Mostly publicly traded companies

✔ How Should This Ratio Be Used?
  o This ratio should be looked at over a period of time, perhaps once a quarter or once a year. These values should be compared as a trend analysis. An increasing EPS value means that the overall trend of the company is good.

Gross Profit Margin {GPM}

✔ Formula: [(Gross Revenue – COGS) ÷ Gross Revenue]

✔ What Does the Ratio Describe?
  o The gross profit margin is not an exact estimate of the company's pricing strategy, but it does give a good indication of the financial health of the product lines being produced. Without an adequate gross profit margin, a company will be unable to pay its operating and other expenses and build for the future.

✔ For Which Industries Is This Ratio Most Useful?
  o This ratio is good for all industries.

✔ How Should This Ratio Be Used?
  o This ratio should be looked at over a period of time, normally monthly and yearly. These values should be compared as a trend analysis. An increasing GPM means that the gap between sales price and production costs is increasing, leaving more money to pay for operating expenses or, alternatively, to go towards your bottom line.

Note: This is the easiest of the ratios to manipulate. Many times, especially for the purchase or sale of a business, the sales price of the business is tied to the GPM. It is imperative that you look into the values making up the gross profit margin to determine if they are valid!

Price / Earnings Ratio {P/E}

✔ Formula: [Market Value per Share ÷ Earnings per Share {EPS}]
  o Sometimes referred to as "the multiple"

✔ What Does the Ratio Describe?
  o Generally a high P/E ratio means that investors are anticipating higher growth in the future. This ratio is a prediction/expectation of a company's performance in the future.

- o The average market P/E ratio is 20–25 times earnings. *However*, a low P/E doesn't necessarily mean that the company is undervalued. It could mean that the company's growth is flat or slow or that the company is in financial trouble.

- o The P/E ratio can use future estimated earnings to get the forward-looking P/E ratio.

- o Companies that are losing money do not have a P/E ratio.

✔ For Which Industries Is This Ratio Most Useful?
- o Normally larger corporations, those that can be valued on the market. Remember, smaller companies can be valued as well, using localized valuations, and so this ratio may still be useful.

✔ How Should This Ratio Be Used?
- o This ratio should be compared to other ratios for companies in the same industry or even to the market in general.

Profit Margin

✔ Formula: [Net Income ÷ Gross Revenue]

✔ What Does the Ratio Describe?
- o This ratio describes, of each gross dollar of revenue generated, how much hits the bottom line (net income).

- o A low profit margin can indicate pricing strategy and/or the impact competition has on margins.

✔ For Which Industries Is This Ratio Most Useful?
- o This ratio is best used for companies that produce a product.

Note: This ratio is not useful for companies losing money, since they have no profit.

✔ How Should This Ratio Be Used?
- o This ratio is often used in conjunction with the GPM. If the GPM is low, but the profit margin is high, there could be heavy competition in the marketplace for the product and its pricing, but the company could be very good at handling its overhead and operations costs to compensate.

Return on Assets / Investments {ROA} or {ROI}

- ✔ Formula: [(Net Income + Interest Expense) ÷ Total Assets]
- ✔ What Does the Ratio Describe?
  - o This ratio describes whether the company is generating a return on the company's assets.

  - o For Which Industries Is This Ratio Most Useful?

  - o An asset-heavy industry (e.g, machine shop) or a financial industry (e.g., stocks, bonds, traders)
- ✔ How Should This Ratio Be Used?
  - o This ratio helps a company decide if it would be helpful to move forward on a new project. If the ROA/ROI is above the cost of borrowing money to fund a new project, then the project should be accepted.

Return on Equity {ROE}

- ✔ Formula: [Net Income ÷ Shareholders Equity]
- ✔ What Does the Ratio Describe?
  - o This ratio indicates what return the owners of a company are making on their investment (as owners).

  - o Note: a 0.18 ROE means that the company is creating $0.18 for every dollar invested by the owners.
- ✔ For Which Industries Is This Ratio Most Useful?
  - o Any industry
- ✔ How Should This Ratio Be Used?
  - o Averaging the ROE over the past 10–15 years can give you a better idea of historical growth.

  - o It's helpful to review ROE if there have been changes in the business, changes in ownership, or changes in strategic vision. These historical ratios can help you look at the bottom line of various changes.

Activity Ratios

Asset Turnover

- ✔ Formula: [Gross Revenue ÷ Total Assets]
- ✔ What Does the Ratio Describe?
  - o It helps describe the amount of sales generated by each dollar of assets.

- o Companies with low profit margins tend to have high asset turnover; those with high profit margins have low asset turnover. It indicates pricing strategy (high volume or high price).

- ✔ For Which Industries Is This Ratio Most Useful?
  - o Asset-heavy industries

  - o This ratio is useful for growth companies to check if, in fact, they are growing revenue in proportion to sales.

- ✔ How Should This Ratio Be Used?
  - o A trend analysis in this number may be useful. This ratio is set as a benchmark or goal.

Collection Ratio

- ✔ Formula: [Accounts Receivable ÷ (Gross Revenue ÷ 365 Days)]

- ✔ What Does the Ratio Describe?
  - o This is the ratio that indicates the average number of days it takes to collect the company's unpaid invoices.

- ✔ For Which Industries Is This Ratio Most Useful?
  - o All industries

  - o This is one of the most important ratios if the company is having cash flow issues.

- ✔ How Should This Ratio Be Used?
  - o Remember that this ratio can be seasonal, so long-term trend analysis should be performed.

Inventory Turnover

- ✔ Formula: [Cost of Goods Sold ÷ Average or Current Period Inventory]
  - o For more accurate inventory turnover figures, the average inventory figure [(beginning inventory + ending inventory) ÷ 2] is used when computing inventory turnover. Average inventory accounts for any seasonality effects on the ratio.

- ✔ What Does the Ratio Describe?
  - o This ratio indicates inventory level.

  - o A low turnover is usually a bad sign because products tend to deteriorate as they sit in a warehouse.

  - o Companies selling perishable items should have very high turnover.

✔ For Which Industries Is This Ratio Most Useful?
  o Inventory heavy, warehouses used

✔ How Should This Ratio Be Used?
  o It should be used when also looking at the growth or fall of gross sales.

  o This could be good or bad, depending on the situation; it could indicate a higher inventory purely because of a higher demand, or it could show that sales are slowing.

Financing Ratios

Debt to Asset Ratio

✔ Formula: [Total Liabilities ÷ Total Assets]

✔ What Does the Ratio Describe?
  o What portion of the company's assets are being financed through debt

✔ For Which Industries Is This Ratio Most Useful?
  o Companies that use heavy machinery

✔ How Should This Ratio Be Used?
  o The lower the percentage, the less of a credit risk is a company; the assets, or money-producing capabilities, of the company are not tied to debt, which, if left unpaid, could be a detriment to the abilities of the company to make money.

  o Companies with higher ratios are placing themselves at risk in an increasing interest rate market or in a market with a lack of liquidity and lending options.

Debt / Equity Ratio

✔ Formula: [Total Liabilities ÷ Shareholders Equity]
  o Sometimes investors use only long-term debt instead of total liabilities for a more stringent test.

✔ What Does the Ratio Describe?
  o Indicates what proportions of equity and debt that the company is using to finance its assets

  o Similar to the debt to asset ratio

✔ For Which Industries Is This Ratio Most Useful?
  o All

✔ How Should This Ratio Be Used?
   o Look for trends. A raise in the rate over time could mean many things. For example: The company is taking on more debt to finance projects, or shares are being bought back because there is an excess of cash flow!

   o A low ratio of 0.26 means that the company is exposing itself to a large amount of equity. This is certainly better than a high ratio of 2 or more, which would expose the company to risks such as interest rate increases and creditor nervousness.

Liquidity Ratios / Warnings

Acid Test

✔ Formula: [(Cash + A/R + ST Investments) ÷ Current Liabilities]
   o A/R = accounts receivable; ST = short term

Note: Inventory is *not* included, and it can be a very large part of assets for some companies!

   o This is a more strenuous test than the working capital ratio.

✔ What Does the Ratio Describe?
   o A test to determine if a firm has enough short-term assets to cover its current debts. Does *not* include the sales of current inventory.

✔ For Which Industries Is This Ratio Most Useful?
   o Any, particularly inventory or product businesses

✔ How Should This Ratio Be Used?
   o Companies with ratios less than 1 should be looked at with extreme care; this means they cannot pay their current debts.

Working Capital

✔ Formula: [Current Assets ÷ Current Liabilities]

✔ What Does the Ratio Describe?
   o If the company has enough assets to cover its immediate liabilities

   o Similar to the acid test. However, this ratio includes inventory.

✔ For Which Industries Is This Ratio Most Useful?
   o Inventory-heavy industries

✔ How Should This Ratio Be Used?
   o Anything below 1 indicates negative W/C (working capital).

- o Anything over 2 means that the company is not investing excess assets.
- o Most believe that a ratio between 1.2 and 2.0 is sufficient.

Interest Coverage

- ✔ Formula: [EBITDA ÷ Interest Expense]
  - o EBITDA = earnings before interest, taxes, depreciation, and amortization
- ✔ What Does the Ratio Describe?
  - o The company's current cash flow
- ✔ For Which Industries Is This Ratio Most Useful?
  - o Any
- ✔ How Should This Ratio Be Used?
  - o Under 1, the company is having problems generating enough cash to pay its expenses.
  - o Ideally you want this ratio to be over 1.5.

Schedule C 2013

SCHEDULE C (Form 1040) Department of the Treasury Internal Revenue Service (99)	**Profit or Loss From Business** (Sole Proprietorship) ▶ **For information on Schedule C and its instructions, go to** *www.irs.gov/schedulec.* ▶ **Attach to Form 1040, 1040NR, or 1041; partnerships generally must file Form 1065.**	OMB No. 1545-0074 20**13** Attachment Sequence No. **09**

Name of proprietor		Social security number (SSN)

A	Principal business or profession, including product or service (see instructions)		B Enter code from instructions ▶			

C	Business name. If no separate business name, leave blank.	D Employer ID number (EIN), (see instr.)

E Business address (including suite or room no.) ▶

City, town or post office, state, and ZIP code

F Accounting method: **(1)** ☐ Cash **(2)** ☐ Accrual **(3)** ☐ Other (specify) ▶

G Did you "materially participate" in the operation of this business during 2013? If "No," see instructions for limit on losses   ☐ Yes   ☐ No

H If you started or acquired this business during 2013, check here . . . . ▶ ☐

I Did you make any payments in 2013 that would require you to file Form(s) 1099? (see instructions) . . . . ☐ Yes   ☐ No

J If "Yes," did you or will you file required Forms 1099? . . . . ☐ Yes   ☐ No

Part I   Income

1	Gross receipts or sales. See instructions for line 1 and check the box if this income was reported to you on Form W-2 and the "Statutory employee" box on that form was checked . . . . ▶ ☐	**1**	
2	Returns and allowances	**2**	
3	Subtract line 2 from line 1	**3**	
4	Cost of goods sold (from line 42)	**4**	
5	**Gross profit.** Subtract line 4 from line 3	**5**	
6	Other income, including federal and state gasoline or fuel tax credit or refund (see instructions)	**6**	
7	**Gross income.** Add lines 5 and 6 . . . . ▶	**7**	

Part II   Expenses   Enter expenses for business use of your home only on line 30.

8	Advertising	**8**		18	Office expense (see instructions)	**18**	
9	Car and truck expenses (see instructions)	**9**		19	Pension and profit-sharing plans .	**19**	
				20	Rent or lease (see instructions):		
10	Commissions and fees . .	**10**		a	Vehicles, machinery, and equipment	**20a**	
11	Contract labor (see instructions)	**11**		b	Other business property . . .	**20b**	
12	Depletion	**12**		21	Repairs and maintenance . . .	**21**	
13	Depreciation and section 179 expense deduction (not included in Part III) (see instructions)	**13**		22	Supplies (not included in Part III) .	**22**	
				23	Taxes and licenses	**23**	
				24	Travel, meals, and entertainment:		
14	Employee benefit programs (other than on line 19) . .	**14**		a	Travel	**24a**	
15	Insurance (other than health)	**15**		b	Deductible meals and entertainment (see instructions) .	**24b**	
16	Interest:			25	Utilities	**25**	
a	Mortgage (paid to banks, etc.)	**16a**		26	Wages (less employment credits) .	**26**	
b	Other	**16b**		27a	Other expenses (from line 48) . .	**27a**	
17	Legal and professional services	**17**		b	Reserved for future use . . .	**27b**	

28	**Total expenses** before expenses for business use of home. Add lines 8 through 27a . . . . . ▶	**28**	
29	Tentative profit or (loss). Subtract line 28 from line 7	**29**	
30	Expenses for business use of your home. Do not report these expenses elsewhere. Attach Form 8829 unless using the simplified method (see instructions). **Simplified method filers only:** enter the total square footage of: (a) your home: _____ and (b) the part of your home used for business: _____ . Use the Simplified Method Worksheet in the instructions to figure the amount to enter on line 30	**30**	
31	**Net profit or (loss).** Subtract line 30 from line 29. • If a profit, enter on both **Form 1040, line 12** (or **Form 1040NR, line 13**) and on **Schedule SE, line 2.** (If you checked the box on line 1, see instructions). Estates and trusts, enter on **Form 1041, line 3.** • If a loss, you **must** go to line 32.	**31**	
32	If you have a loss, check the box that describes your investment in this activity (see instructions). • If you checked 32a, enter the loss on both **Form 1040, line 12,** (or **Form 1040NR, line 13**) and on **Schedule SE, line 2.** (If you checked the box on line 1, see the line 31 instructions). Estates and trusts, enter on **Form 1041, line 3.** • If you checked 32b, you **must** attach **Form 6198.** Your loss may be limited.	32a ☐ All investment is at risk. 32b ☐ Some investment is not at risk.

For Paperwork Reduction Act Notice, see the separate instructions.   Cat. No. 11334P   **Schedule C (Form 1040) 2013**

IRS 20-Factor Test on Employment Status

As an aid to determining whether an individual is an employee under the common law rules, twenty factors or elements have been identified as indicating whether sufficient control is present to establish an employer-employee relationship. The twenty factors have been developed based on an examination of cases and rulings considering whether an individual is an employee. The degree of importance of each factor varies depending on the occupation and the factual context in which the services are performed. The twenty factors are designed only as guides for determining whether an individual is an employee; special scrutiny is required in applying the twenty factors to assure that formalistic aspects of an arrangement designed to achieve a particular status do not obscure the substance of the arrangement (that is, whether the person or persons for whom the services are performed exercise sufficient control over the individual for the individual to be classified as an employee). The twenty factors are described below:

1. **Instructions**. A worker who is required to comply with other persons' instructions about when, where, and how he or she is to work is ordinarily an employee. This control factor is present if the person or persons for whom the services are performed have the RIGHT to require compliance with instructions. See, for example, Rev. Rul. 68-598, 1968-2 C.B. 464, and Rev. Rul. 66-381, 1966-2 C.B. 449.

2. **Training**. Training a worker by requiring an experienced employee to work with the worker, by corresponding with the worker, by requiring the worker to attend meetings, or by using other methods, indicates that the person or

persons for whom the services are performed want the services performed in a particular method or manner. See Rev. Rul. 70-630, 1970-2 C.B. 229.

3. **Integration**. Integration of the worker's services into the business operations generally shows that the worker is subject to direction and control. When the success or continuation of a business depends to an appreciable degree upon the performance of certain services, the workers who perform those services must necessarily be subject to a certain amount of control by the owner of the business. See United States v. Silk, 331 U.S. 704 (1947), 1947-2 C.B. 167.

4. **Services Rendered Personally**. If the services must be rendered personally, presumably the person or persons for whom the services are performed are interested in the methods used to accomplish the work as well as in the results. See Rev. Rul. 55-695, 1955-2 C.B. 410.

5. **Hiring, Supervising, and Paying Assistants**. If the person or persons for whom the services are performed hire, supervise, and pay assistants, that factor generally shows control over the workers on the job. However, if one worker hires, supervises, and pays the other assistants pursuant to a contract under which the worker agrees to provide materials and labor and under which the worker is responsible only for the attainment of a result, this factor indicates an independent contractor status. Compare Rev. Rul. 63-115, 1963-1 C.B. 178, with Rev. Rul. 55-593 1955-2 C.B. 610.

6. **Continuing Relationship**. A continuing relationship between the worker and the person or persons for whom the services are performed indicates that an employer-employee relationship exists. A continuing relationship may exist where work is performed at frequently recurring although irregular intervals. See United States v. Silk.

7. **Set Hours of Work**. The establishment of set hours of work by the person or persons for whom the services are performed is a factor indicating control. See Rev. Rul. 73-591, 1973-2 C.B. 337.

8. **Full Time Required**. If the worker must devote substantially full time to the business of the person or persons for whom the services are performed, such person or persons have control over the amount of time the worker spends working and impliedly restrict the worker from doing other gainful work. An independent contractor on the other hand, is free to work when and for whom he or she chooses. See Rev. Rul. 56-694, 1956-2 C.B. 694.

9. **Doing Work On Employer's Premises**. If the work is performed on the premises of the person or persons for whom the services are performed, that factor suggests control over the worker, especially if the work could be done elsewhere. Rev. Rul. 56-660, 1956-2 C.B. 693. Work done off the premises of the person or persons receiving the services, such as at the office of the worker, indicates some freedom from control. However, this fact by itself does not mean that the worker is not an employee. The importance of this factor depends on the nature of the service involved and the extent to which an employer generally would require that employees perform such services on the employer's premises. Control over the place of work is indicated when the person or persons for whom the services are performed have the right to compel the worker to travel a designated route, to canvass a territory within a certain time, or to work at specific places as required. See Rev. Rul. 56-694.

10. **Order or Sequence Set**. If a worker must perform services in the order or sequence set by the person or persons for whom the services are performed, that factor shows that the worker is not free to follow the worker's own pattern of work but must follow the established routines and schedules of the person or persons for whom the services are performed. Often, because of the nature of an occupation, the person or persons for whom the services are performed do not set the order of the services or set the order infrequently. It is sufficient to show control, however, if such person or persons retain the right to do so. See Rev. Rul. 56-694.

11. **Oral or Written Reports**. A requirement that the worker submit regular or written reports to the person or persons for whom the services are performed indicates a degree of control. See Rev. Rul. 70-309, 1970-1 C.B. 199, and Rev. Rul. 68-248, 1968-1 C.B. 431.

12. **Payment by Hour, Week, Month**. Payment by the hour, week, or month generally points to an employer-employee relationship, provided that this method of payment is not just a convenient way of paying a lump sum agreed upon as the cost of a job. Payment made by the job or on straight commission generally indicates that the worker is an independent contractor. See Rev. Rul. 74-389, 1974-2 C.B. 330.

13. **Payment of Business and/or Traveling Expenses**. If the person or persons for whom the services are performed ordinarily pay the worker's business and/or traveling expenses, the worker is ordinarily an employee. An employer, to be able to control expenses, generally retains the right to regulate and direct the worker's business activities. See Rev. Rul. 55-144, 1955-1 C.B. 483.

14. **Furnishing of Tools and Materials**. The fact that the person or persons for whom the services are performed furnish significant tools, materials, and other equipment tends to show the existence of an employer-employee relationship. See Rev. Rul. 71-524, 1971-2 C.B. 346.

15. **Significant Investment**. If the worker invests in facilities that are used by the worker in performing services and are not typically maintained by employees (such as the maintenance of an office rented at fair value from an unrelated party), that factor tends to indicate that the worker is an independent contractor. On the other hand, lack of investment in facilities indicates dependence on the person or persons for whom the services are performed for such facilities and, accordingly, the existence of an employer-employee relationship. See Rev. Rul. 71-524. Special scrutiny is required with respect to certain types of facilities, such as home offices.

16. **Realization of Profit or Loss**. A worker who can realize a profit or suffer a loss as a result of the worker's services (in addition to the profit or loss ordinarily realized by employees) is generally an independent contractor, but the worker who cannot is an employee. See Rev. Rul. 70-309. For example, if the worker is subject to a real risk of economic loss due to significant investments or a bona fide liability for expenses, such as salary payments to unrelated employees, that factor indicates that the worker is an independent contractor. The risk that a worker will not receive payment for his or her services, however, is common to both independent contractors and employees and thus does not constitute a sufficient economic risk to support treatment as an independent contractor.

17. **Working for More than One Firm at a Time**. If a worker performs more than de minimis services for a multiple of unrelated persons or firms at the same time, that factor generally indicates that the worker is an independent contractor. See Rev. Rul. 70-572, 1970-2 C.B. 221. However, a worker who performs services for more than one person may be an employee of each of the persons, especially where such persons are part of the same service arrangement.

18. **Making Service Available to General Public**. The fact that a worker makes his or her services available to the general public on a regular and consistent basis indicates an independent contractor relationship. See Rev. Rul. 56-660.

19. **Right to Discharge**. The right to discharge a worker is a factor indicating that the worker is an employee and the person possessing the right is an employer.

An employer exercises control through the threat of dismissal, which causes the worker to obey the employer's instructions. An independent contractor, on the other hand, cannot be fired so long as the independent contractor produces a result that meets the contract specifications. Rev. Rul. 75-41, 1975-1 C.B. 323.

20. **Right to Terminate**. If the worker has the right to end his or her relationship with the person for whom the services are performed at any time he or she wishes without incurring liability, that factor indicates an employer-employee relationship. See Rev. Rul. 70-309.

Contributors

Below, in alphabetical order by first name, are the contributors to this book—all very helpful resources to new business owners. If you are looking for help, I recommend that you contact these professionals first. If you need someone you don't see here, please e-mail me: Shauna@TaxGoddess.com.

✔ **Connie Kadansky**

Sales coach, Exceptional Sales Performance
www.linkedin.com/in/salescallreluctance

✔ **Dale Wernette**

Sales management and assessment expert, SHERPA & Associates
www.linkedin.com/in/dalewernette

✔ **Dave Barnhart**

Blogging/social media expert, Business Blogging Pros
www.linkedin.com/in/davebarnhart

✔ **Donald Kupper**

Technology expert, CMIT and EcoPod Gardens
www.linkedin.com/in/donaldkupper

✔ **Fred Kroin**

Business coach, Goal Partners
www.linkedin.com/in/fredkroin1

✔ **Ginny McMinn**

   HR professional, McMinn Business Solutions
   www.linkedin.com/in/ginnymcminn

✔ **Lee Steele**

   Online marketing and strategy, Strategic Insight
   www.linkedin.com/in/leesteele

✔ **Mike Wahl**

   Cartoonist, Off the Wahl Designs
   www.linkedin.com/pub/mike-wahl/31/b54/5a2

✔ **Piyush Parikh**

   Systems expert, Engineer Your Business
   www.linkedin.com/in/piyushparikh

✔ **Susan McCall**

   Associate broker, commercial division director, Susan McCall, PC
   CCIM, CCLS, CLSS, CCSS
   www.linkedin.com/in/susanmccall

✔ **Tina Wahl**

   Head bookkeeper, Tax Goddess Business Enterprises, PC
   www.linkedin.com/pub/tina-wahl/21/612/670

Link for Free Consultation with the Tax Goddess

I know that this can be a scary new world with lots of questions involved; therefore, I want to make sure you know you are not alone.

Since you purchased this book (or were given it as a gift) I am offering a free 30-minute phone call with me, the Tax Goddess, at your leisure. Just call my office, 602-357-3275, or go to our website to get to our scheduling system (www.TaxGoddess.com or www.timetrade.com/book/VP8N6). I am looking forward to meeting every one of you! ☺

~ Shauna ~

List of Acronyms

AFR	applicable federal rate
AMT	alternative minimum tax
A/R	accounts receivable
ARM	adjustable-rate mortgage
BOP	business owner policy
CAM	common area maintenance
CD	certificate of deposit
CEO	chief executive officer
CFO	chief financial officer
COD	cash on delivery
COGS	cost of goods sold
CPA	certified public accountant
DBA	doing business as
DMA	designated market area
E&O	errors and omissions (insurance)
EBITDA	earnings before interest, taxes, depreciation, and amortization
EFTPS	Electronic Federal Tax Payment System
EIN	Employer Identification Number
EOM	end of month
EPS	earnings per share
FHA	Federal Housing Administration
FICA	Federal Insurance Contributions Act
FLP	family limited partnership
FUTA	Federal Unemployment Tax Act
GAAP	generally accepted accounting principles

GP	general partnership
GPM	gross profit margin
HR	human resources
IRA	individual retirement account
IRS	Internal Revenue Service
IT	information technology
LLC	limited liability company
LLP	limited liability partnership
LP	limited partnership
LT	long-term
MBA	master of business administration
MLM	multi-level marketing
OBT	"on-board terrorist" (in an organization)
PC	professional corporation
P/E	price/earnings ratio
PEO	payroll employer organization
PIN	personal identification number
PLC	public limited company
PPC	pay per click
PR	public relations
ROA	return on assets
ROE	return on equity
ROG	receipt of goods
ROI	return on investment(s)
SBA	(U.S.) Small Business Administration
SBDC	Small Business Development Center
SEO	search engine optimization
SEP	Simplified Employee Pension
SCORE	Service Corps of Retired Executives
SIC	Standard Industrial Classification
ST	short-term
SUTA	State Unemployment Tax Act
W/C	working capital

www.ingramcontent.com/pod-product-compliance
Lightning Source LLC
Chambersburg PA
CBHW061350210326
41598CB00035B/5943